W9-BOA-942

Parent Talk

Dr. Kevin Leman
& Randy Carlson

THOMAS NELSON PUBLISHERS
Nashville

To all the hard working, committed parents of toddlers to teens, who have helped make our national "Parent Talk" radio program and seminars a success.

Dr. Kevin Leman and Randy Carlson

Published in Nashville, Tennessee, by Janet Thoma Books, a division of Thomas Nelson, Inc., Publishers, and distributed in Canada by Word Communications, Ltd., Richmond, British Columbia, and in the United Kingdom by Word (UK), Ltd., Milton Keynes, England.

Library of Congress Cataloging-in-Publication Data

Leman, Kevin.
Parent talk / Kevin Leman & Randy Carlson.
p. cm.
ISBN 0-8407-3447-6
1. Parenting—United States. 2. Child rearing—United States. 3. Talk shows—United States. I. Carlson, Randy, 1951- . II. Title.
HQ755.8.L447 1993
649'.1—dc20 93-25513
CIP

Printed in the United States of America

2 3 4 5 6 - 98 97 96 95 94 93

Contents ......

Preface ....

As cohosts of "Parent Talk," we've never been known for playing it safe or doing the usual thing. So, when our publishers approached us on doing a book, we said, "Why not answer questions parents are asking by letting the readers of the book 'tune in' on our 'Parent Talk' program?"

Thomas Nelson bought our idea and the result follows. We've gone through hundreds of conversations with people from all over the country and pulled out some of the best compilations of "Parent Talk" advice (and humor) that we can offer. Please keep in mind that the names of all callers and other details have been changed to protect privacy, but we want to assure you that everything we share is based on a "Parent Talk" program or one of our seminars that we give from time to time in cities throughout the country.

In addition, we have arranged all the material under basic problem areas so you can take your choice: read straight through if you like, or just select topics that are of particular interest to you at this time in your parenting pilgrimage. In particular, if you are a new parent, you may be wondering what lies ahead. To get a good idea, read this book from cover to cover and you will be much better prepared for what happens a few months or years down the line.

Bringing up children is one of the most joyous but also most demanding challenges any person can take on. To succeed you need all the help you can get. We're not saying that our Reality Discipline approach is perfect, but we do know it works for us as we raise our own kids.

Randy and his wife, Donna, have used Reality Discipline successfully with their three children (Evan, fourteen; Andrea, eleven; and D.J. [Derek], eight). Kevin and his wife, Sande, used Reality Discipline to bring up two daughters now in college: Holly, twenty-one, and Krissy, nineteen. Their son, Kevey, fifteen, is a sophomore in high school. In addition, the Lemans are taking a "refresher course" in raising children. In recent years they've been blessed with Hannah, six, and baby Lauren, who will have just turned one when this book is published.

From personal experience, we know Reality Discipline isn't a gimmick; nor is it a complex, involved approach that only trained psychologists and counselors can use successfully. We've seen it work with thousands of parents in every kind of family, and we know it can work for you!

Randy Carlson and Dr. Kevin Leman
Tucson, Arizona, 1993

WOULD YOU LIKE TO KNOW THE SECRET OF BEING A GOOD PARENT?

RANDY: Welcome to "Parent Talk"! No, not the actual radio program that's on six days a week across the country, but the next best thing—this book, which really does contain the secret to being a good parent. Yes, I know that sounds presumptuous, but my distinguished colleague, psychologist and cohost of "Parent Talk" Dr. Kevin Leman, and I believe that Reality Discipline—properly and consistently applied—is the best and most effective way to parent yet devised.

In a given year we respond to thousands of SOS calls from parents who ask just about every kind of question, from fingernail biting to unwanted pregnancies, from bed wetting to when and how to spank. "Parent Talk" is carried by almost one hundred radio stations, and we are reaching well over twenty million listeners each year on a weekly basis. Kevin, parents trust us. . . parents need us . . . parents count on us. . . .

KEVIN: Holy crow! This is too much responsibility for a baby of the family like me. I'm out of here!

RANDY: I should have known better than to have teamed up with somebody who was nicknamed "Cub" when he was only eleven days old. I know you're just kidding, Kevin, as you often do on the show, but we're trying to be serious here for a minute. Besides, I'm a baby of my family,* too, and I'm willing to stick around and explain Reality Discipline to our readers. I'm sure you agree that it's the very heart and soul of "Parent Talk" . . .

KEVIN: You bet your sweet bippy it is. No matter what the question, whether it's the Ankle Biter Battalion or the hormone group, Reality Discipline is the key to the problem.

RANDY: That's a pretty strong statement. Do you think we can back it up?

KEVIN: We back it up every day on the air, don't we? And we've seen Reality Discipline work with clients we've counseled for a combined total of thirty-four years. Reality Discipline is the tool parents need to help their little buzzards shape up. . . .

RANDY: Little buzzards! Kevin, shouldn't we let moms especially know what you mean by "little buzzards"?

KEVIN: Not to worry, Mom. Down here in Tucson we affectionately call kids "little buzzards," and we also talk a lot about "pulling the rug out and letting those little buzzards tumble."

RANDY: That might sound like punishment to a lot of folks . . .

KEVIN: We never tell parents to punish. We tell them to discipline, train, and teach their kids, but that doesn't mean that there

* As Adlerian counselors, Randy and Kevin make strong use of the science of birth order, which is discussed in more detail in Chapter Seven.

might not be some kind of "pain" or consequence involved. That's how the kids learn what the real world is like and how it works. Reality Discipline gives the child a chance to make his own decisions and then live with the result of his mistakes and his failures or his good choices and his successes.

RANDY: You know, Kevin, when we tell people they can give children choices, some moms and dads might think that sounds permissive . . .

KEVIN: Not on your autographed copy of Dr. Spock! The last thing you can call Reality Discipline would be "permissive." But the best thing about it is that it is not authoritarian. Reality Discipline helps parents—in Christian churchgoing families, in particular—avoid making some big mistakes. Authoritarian parents often tend to think that they own their children; that they are judge and jury of every little thing that happens; that their children can't fail; and—here's the favorite—"Look, Kid, I'm the boss and what I say goes!"

Because "Parent Talk" reaches a large number of families who use Christian principles in raising their kids, we'd like to emphasize Ephesians 6:3–4; in fact, you could say it's our motto. The Apostle Paul tells us that children have the responsibility to obey and respect their parents, but parents have the responsibility not to frustrate or abuse their kids and, instead, they should bring them up with firm but loving guidance and training.

RANDY: You know, Kevin, Ephesians 6:4 is a perfect description of Reality Discipline, and what I hear you saying is that, in the final analysis, parents really are "the boss."

KEVIN: We always say that parents are in healthy authority over their kids. In other words, I never let my kids use me or manipulate me, but at the same time I don't come down on them with "It's my way or the highway!" That can work with some kids for a while—maybe while they grow up, but later in life it can come back to haunt everybody.

RANDY: Okay, at "Parent Talk" we're not permissive, nor are we authoritarian. We hit a happy medium—maybe the best way to describe it is authoritative. A child doesn't care what you know about parenting; what he wants to know is, "Do you care about *me?" That's really the essence of Reality Discipline. By holding kids accountable, or, as you say, Kevin, "pulling the rug out," parents use a combination of love and limits, which helps children feel safe and secure as they grow and develop during their maturing years.*

KEVIN: We always like to say, "Love and discipline go hand in hand." Pulling the rug out means the parent goes into action and just doesn't do a lot of talking. Kids can smell it in a minute if you just talk and don't really mean it. And after you pull the rug, you stick to your guns and hold your children accountable for their actions. That's how they learn from any experience.

RANDY: That sounds pretty noble, Dr. Leman, but I have a letter here from a mother who is talking about Reality Discipline and pulling the rug out, and her daughter, well, let me put it this way, her daughter doesn't like you, Kevin.

KEVIN: What? You are going to read that letter on the air?

RANDY: Why not? This mom talks about her eleven-year-old daughter who is very strong-willed. Her daughter says, and I quote, "I hate Reality Discipline and Kevin Leman. I wish you would have never read his stupid books!"

KEVIN: Stupid books? I would love to talk to that kid.

RANDY: Do you want to call her?

KEVIN: Sure, do you have her number?

RANDY: Yes, I even have her name—Lynsey. Let's give Lynsey a call here. . . . Hello, Lynsey? This is Randy Carlson, from "Parent Talk." I've got a letter from your mom and she says you are her very strong-willed, firstborn daughter and that you screamed at her one day and said you hated Reality Discipline and Dr. Kevin Leman, and you wished your mom had never read his stupid books or listened to him on his stupid radio program. What don't you like about Reality Discipline, Lynsey?

LYNSEY: I don't know. I just don't like it.

RANDY: Well, what does your mom do that you don't like?

LYNSEY: She takes away my privileges, like my dance classes, and stuff.

RANDY: Do you mean that if you do something you're not supposed to do you can't go to dance class?

LYNSEY: Yeah.

RANDY: You think that is not fair? You think that is Dr. Leman's fault . . .

KEVIN: Lynsey, guess who this is.

LYNSEY: Uh, oh!

KEVIN: You hate Reality Discipline and my stupid books? True?

LYNSEY: Yes!

KEVIN: Lynsey, what do you do that makes your mom use Reality Discipline?

LYNSEY: Sometimes I talk back to her.

KEVIN: Randy, did you hear that? Lynsey, what would you like her to do when you talk back? Say, "Oh, thank you, Sweetheart, for talking back to Mommy"?

LYNSEY: No.

KEVIN: Then what would you expect her to do?

LYNSEY: Just send me to my room.

RANDY: Lynsey, when you grow up and become a mom and you have a little Lynsey of your own and she does something like talk back, what do you think you'll do?

LYNSEY: I'll send her to her room.

KEVIN: That's very interesting! What about allowances? Do you get an allowance?

LYNSEY: Yes.

KEVIN: Do you get the same allowance as your sister?

LYNSEY: Yes.

KEVIN: Do you think that is fair when you both get the same allowance?

LYNSEY: No, not really.

KEVIN: What would you do if I told you that Randy and I are going to talk to your mother and tell her that you need a raise? Would you like Dr. Leman's stupid books then?

LYNSEY: No.

KEVIN: You are a tough little buzzard! Is your mom there? We'd love to talk with her.

MOM: Hello, this is Lynsey's mom, Gloria.

RANDY: Gloria, what do you think about what Lynsey just had to say?

GLORIA: I just laughed.

KEVIN: We are supposed to tell you that we think she needs a raise.

GLORIA: Well, she can get a raise. All she has to do is some of Elizabeth's chores for the week and she can get Elizabeth's share of the money. Each girl can get more money if she decides to do the chores her sister doesn't want to do.

RANDY: Tell me, Gloria, did you pick up Reality Discipline by reading Kevin's book, *Making Children Mind Without Losing Yours*?

GLORIA: Yes, and I heard both of you at a seminar too.

KEVIN: You know, I coined the term *Reality Discipline* when I wrote *Making Children Mind.* Tell us, Gloria, what were you doing before you used Reality Discipline?

GLORIA: Crying a lot. It would all build up. I'm a pleaser and I like to make my kids happy, but sometimes they would just get so out of hand I would end up screaming at them, and that is not the way to handle things.

RANDY: So what are you doing different now?

GLORIA: I just pull the rug out and let the little buzzards tumble!

KEVIN: I think I've heard that somewhere before.

RANDY: You think Reality Discipline is working in your family? Is it a positive tool?

GLORIA: Oh, yes, indeed, otherwise why do you think Lynsey would scream at me that she hates Dr. Leman?

KEVIN: That reminds me. I had a kid in my office the other day who started crying, and I said, "What's wrong?" And he said, through his tears, "I don't like all those new ideas you are giving to my mother."

RANDY: What did you say?

KEVIN: You know . . . good old sensitive me . . . I just laughed.

□ ○ △ □ ○ △

RANDY: We didn't have time on the air to go down the line with Gloria and talk about how she applies all the Reality Discipline principles that we've been mentioning, but it sounds as if she's holding Lynsey accountable, and she's learning that no one can always have things her own way. When you don't cooperate with life and meet your responsibilities, life does not cooperate with you and the piper must be paid.

KEVIN: Even though Lynsey doesn't like me or my books too much right now, I'm glad to see that her mom is sticking to her guns. That's one of the big keys to making Reality Discipline work.

RANDY: Kevin, I think we're ready now to talk with other parents and try to help them with questions they've been asking. Any special place you want to begin?

KEVIN: Well, Randy, my heart always goes out to the moms of the really young kids—the ones I call the Ankle Biter Battalion. I think a lot of moms know what I mean when I say, tongue in cheek, "We have met the enemy and they are small." But there are ways to "conquer the enemy" with firmness and love—in other words, Reality Discipline. So, let's get to it!

□ ○ △ □ ○ △

USING REALITY DISCIPLINE MEANS . . .

1. Being in healthy authority over your children.
2. Holding your children accountable for their actions.
3. Combining love and limits on a consistent basis.
4. Dealing with every child as the unique individual he or she is.
5. Being tough but always fair.
6. Using action instead of words.
7. Sticking to your guns and following through with enforcing consequences.
8. Following the biblical instruction not to exasperate your children and make them angry and resentful, but to bring them up with loving discipline and godly advice (see Eph. 6:4, *The Living Bible*).

CHAPTER 1

■●▲■●▲

DOES "PULLING THE RUG" EVER INCLUDE SPANKING?

RANDY: To spank or not to spank. That's a major question when we talk to parents about the reality of disciplining their children. It's a very controversial word and first of all maybe we need to define it.

Just what is "spanking"?

KEVIN: Spanking is an action-oriented discipline to be used with children who are openly defiant. They look you in the eye and say, "Hey, I am going to do what I want to do."

I hope some people call in and defend the decision never to lay a hand on Little Buford. And then I'd like others to call and give testimony as to how effective spanking can be when it's done correctly. I think there are many myths about spanking that need to be laid to rest, like, for example, if you spank your child you will damage his or her psyche for life. I would like someone to point out a "psyche" for me. I have been looking for one in my children and haven't found it yet. I find dirty clothes on the floor. I find other things that haven't been picked up, but I haven't located the psyche.

RANDY: I have heard you say, Kevin, that you could count on your hand the number of times you have spanked your children over the last twenty-one years.

KEVIN: Well, maybe I would need two hands. Remember, we've had a couple of "late blessings" in life with Hannah and Lauren. But I'm doing the same with Hannah right now at age six as I did with the three older ones. When the time comes and we go eyeball to eyeball and she just plain defies me, I lovingly lay a swat on her little popo and, guess what? Hannah doesn't die. Neither did Holly, nor Krissy, nor Kevey.

RANDY: As I predicted, spanking always lights up our "Parent Talk" board, and here's our first question:

When is a child old enough to be spanked and how should it be done?

CLAUDIA: I have a nine month old and I have been swatting him on the hand every once in a while for misbehaving. Is this okay?

KEVIN: Why do you swat him?

CLAUDIA: He plays with the stereo, and I don't want him to get into the habit, so I say no, and then I give him a little swat on the hand. He is catching on, but I am wondering if this is too young.

KEVIN: I'm on record, Claudia, as saying, first, nine months is too young to swat a child. I think age two is about as early as I would ever like to start with a swat on the child's popo or bumbum. Second, I don't recommend swatting a child on the hands or the backs of the legs. Nor do I believe it is ever right to slap a child in the face.

And, when applying a swat to a child's bottom, which is the best and most natural place to administer this kind of discipline, I don't like using objects like paddles or spoons. I think the same loving hand that helps a child up when he falls is the same loving hand that should administer the swat. The idea behind the swat on the tail is to get the child's attention and to let him know that Mom or Dad is very displeased with what just happened.

RANDY: I think it helps to be even more definitive. When we talk about a swat, no way are we talking about leaving marks on children. It gets back to the purpose of spanking, which is direction, discipline, teaching—redirecting the child.

KEVIN: It is part of the guiding process. Scripture tells us to train up our children and guide them. Parents who emphasize "spare the rod and spoil the child" often misunderstand the spirit of God's law and overdo it. I always like to remind parents that the shepherds used the rod, for the most part, to guide their sheep, not whack them over the head.

I recall a woman at one of our seminars who talked about the picture of Jesus with a little lamb over his shoulders. Her incredible rationale for spanking her own children was that shepherds in Bible times would break the legs of lambs that strayed, then put them in splints and carry them on their shoulders until they healed. That way, the little lambs learned to stay near the shepherd, and not stray again from the right path.

The lady was right about what shepherds did to sheep back then, but it left me wondering how far she'd go when spanking one of her own little lambs. It makes me shudder to even intimate that "discipline" means beating the living daylights out of a kid, but there are some parents who think that way. That's why we always talk about disciplining children in love. If you love the child, you will discipline the child, but you won't abuse the child. Discipline and love go hand in hand.

RANDY: Another thing to remember is that some children will respond more favorably to spanking than others. I can count on one hand the number of times I was spanked as a child, while my oldest brother, Warren, was spanked regularly. My parents tell me that spanking was very effective with me, but it had little effect on Warren. With some kids you can spank and spank, and it just becomes a power struggle. But if you're going to spank at all, Claudia, it shouldn't be done any younger than eighteen to twenty-four months. Kevin leans to twenty-four months, but I would go down to maybe eighteen.

Why isn't a light swat useful for disciplining a child under eighteen months?

CLAUDIA: I don't swat my nine month old very hard, and it seems to get his attention. Besides, how am I going to get him to stop playing with the stereo?

KEVIN: Don't you think, Claudia, that you could take your nine month old by the shoulders, look him squarely in the eye and say no!? That will accomplish as much as hitting. Some people say it's okay to start swats at nine months, but I don't agree. Randy says start at eighteen months, but I'm for waiting until the child is right around two years old. If you get into the habit of hitting, even with so-called light smacks on the hands, your little nine month old will likely be clobbering other kids when he gets to be eighteen months. And then you'll be asking, "Where did *that* come from?"

At twenty-four months (and some kids may be ready at eighteen months) you can explain that the swat is for disobeying and then you can give the child a big love to reassure him.

What is the best way to discipline a child under two years?

CLAUDIA: Okay, I see your point, but if I can't give my nine month old a light swat, how do I keep him away from the stereo? It's too big to move out of his way.

KEVIN: Then just remove him from the scene. It's the best single thing you can do.

CLAUDIA: But what happens if he just crawls right back and does the same thing again?

KEVIN: There is not a little "ankle biter" who doesn't, in fact, crawl with great speed and accuracy back to whatever he wants. You could pick him up and remove him again, and if he crawls back one more time, I would invite you to use a brand new discovery called a "playpen." It has soft but firm walls that say, "Okay, you sit here for a while." For a nine month old, a playpen is a very good form of discipline because discipline should start very early. Spanking, however, should not start that early.

Won't using a playpen as a form of discipline give the child a negative feeling about playpens?

CLAUDIA: If I use a playpen to keep my child away from the stereo, what happens when I try to take the playpen along to someone's house so my child can nap in it?

KEVIN: To be honest, I could care less if a nine month old or even a fifteen month old has a negative feeling toward playpens. If the child doesn't catch on to what the parent wants when the parent says no! and removes him from the scene, then the parent needs a way to make the child accountable, even at that young age, and a playpen is perfect.

As for the child being negative on playpens and not wanting to sleep in one, that seldom happens. When it's nap time and the child is sleepy, the playpen will be fine. And if the child isn't sleepy, you're going to have just as much trouble whether you put him in a playpen or in a crib. [For more on bedtime battles, see Chapter Four.]

□ ○ △ □ ○ △

How badly does a child have to behave before he deserves to be spanked?

NANCY: I have a two year old and I'm wondering when it's proper discipline to spank him. What does he have to do to earn a swat? I don't want to be swatting him for things that don't matter that much.

KEVIN: It isn't that they "earn a swat" as much as they now understand what the swat means. I think a swat on the bottom is particularly useful when a two year old is disobeying and doing something that can cause him harm. For example, he picks up a fork and wants to see if it will go in that little hole in the wall—that is, the electrical outlet. Or the child keeps running toward the street when he's been told time and again not to.

NANCY: So it's when they're going to hurt themselves rather than when they are destroying something?

KEVIN: If a two year old is willfully and repeatedly attacking the stereo with his toy hammer or pulling on the dials, it may well be time for a swat on the tush. But particularly if the two year old is running toward the street or doing something that puts him in danger and is gleefully defying you, that's another good reason for a swat. And while there may be tears, I think the key is that you always pick the child up, hold the child, stroke the child, and reassure the child that Mommy or Daddy loves him very much. That is the most important part of discipline.

□ ○ △ □ ○ △

Is the best way to handle a temper tantrum to just let the child get it out of her system by herself, or are there times when a spanking might help?

SALLY: When my daughter was two and a half or three, I'd tell her no and she'd stomp her feet, turn in circles, lie down and kick and scream. Things like that. I'd ask her two or three times to stop and if she persisted, I would spank her.

KEVIN: Sometimes a swat on the tail brings things to a head. I would agree with you there. But let me just counter that I still think the first option is not to pay attention to a power tantrum. My first recommendation is to walk away or pick the child up and put him in his room, close the door, and let him continue his tantrum with no audience—no reinforcement. That's what counts.

RANDY: At the same time, Kevin, I think a spanking is appropriate if you give direction to a child and the child basically looks you in the eye and says, "No way!" and then drops to the floor and throws a tantrum. There are times with my own children when a spanking is appropriate because it breaks the cycle. Kids do get in a temper tantrum cycle.

KEVIN: I agree. They sort of cross a threshold and they get so far into that tantrum that you can't reason with them. To put it bluntly, there are times when kids are sort of "asking for it." When you meet their challenge and give them a swat, it helps them get it all out of their system and then they can go on with life and so can you. Sally, what was the effect when you would give your two and a half year old a swat if she persisted with a temper tantrum?

SALLY: It usually quieted her right down. As you say, the swat is what helped her "get it out of her system."

RANDY: I think the principle to remember is that if you have a child whose purpose is to behave in a very powerful way in order to control you, then you have to take proper steps.

KEVIN: And those proper steps always mean removing your sails from the child's wind.

RANDY: Ah so, venerable Dr. Leman uses ancient philosophical wisdom. Would you care to explain how moms are to "remove their sails from the child's wind"?

KEVIN: Any time a child acts in a powerful way, he is huffing and puffing and wants to blow you around. If you get overly involved with his huffing and puffing—if you argue with him or fly into a rage and spank him in anger, or allow him to keep your attention completely riveted on him—you have "hoisted your sails into his wind," so to speak. If you refuse to argue, if you refuse to tell him more than once, if you refuse to engage in a running battle with him, you do, in fact, take your sails out of his wind. The idea is to disengage from the child's power. The child gains power as you play his game and flex your muscles and "open your sails." And when you open your sails, it just allows his wind to catch you and drive you farther up the parental wall.

RANDY: That's why we suggest first trying to pick the child up and move him to another place where he can have a tantrum without an audience. In other cases, a good swat may be necessary, but the point is, at all times you are in healthy authority over your child. The child is just not getting his or her own way. There are times when a young child defies you, he may well need a spanking, but the two things you should never do are: (1) completely ignore the child or (2) get so involved in your child's temper tantrum that your sails are in his wind—that is, he is controlling you instead of you controlling him.

□ ○ △ □ ○ △

When does spanking turn into abuse?

DONALD: When I was a child, my father whipped me with anything and everything. I am talking belt buckles, anything he could get his hands on. Was this abuse?

RANDY: Yes, you *are* talking abuse. What has that done to you, Donald?

DONALD: Well, my dad told me, "My father did it to me, and I'll do it to you." I've heard that sometimes it takes the third generation to break the cycle, and I tried to do that when I had my own family. I was married at eighteen, and I found myself being tempted to abuse my own son physically when I tried to correct him. I'm glad I was smart enough to break the cycle of abuse because my son grew up to be 6′1″ and two hundred pounds and now he could "abuse" me if he wanted to! But, seriously, I am thankful I did not teach him to abuse *his* future son.

When should you stop using spanking as a form of discipline?

KEVIN: We have talked about eighteen to twenty-four months as the time to start spanking, but, Randy, what about the other end of the scale? When does the effectiveness of spanking start to diminish?

RANDY: We have found that when a child turns twelve or thirteen, the effectiveness of a spanking starts to diminish a great deal. In fact, if a parent is spanking a child at ages twelve, thirteen, or fourteen, it's probably a sign that the relationship has deteriorated badly. Kids will either just laugh at you, or you can make them more angry.

KEVIN: Good point, counselor. Donald, are you still there? A minute ago, Randy asked you an important question that you didn't get to answer fully. He wanted to know how the abuse that you got by way of belt buckles and so forth influenced your life. What have you struggled with as an adult? I'm thinking particularly of anger.

DONALD: For several years, I had hard feelings toward my father. We live approximately four blocks apart, but I see him maybe once a year.

KEVIN: Donald, I have another question. At any time when your dad was beating on you, did you feel he was loving you?

DONALD: No, he never told me that he loved me.

KEVIN: Well, you see, letting the child know you love him or her is the whole key to what we are trying to do with discipline. As a parent, you don't spank a child for your good; it is for the child's good. And if you're too angry, too upset—whatever—and can't tell the child afterward, "I love you," you shouldn't be using that kind of discipline at all.

□ ○ △ □ ○ △

What are the dangers in starting to spank a child too early?

LORAINE: I probably spank my children too much and I'm trying to correct that, but I'm also afraid that I started spanking them too early—well before they were even eighteen months. What should I look for as a result of that?

KEVIN: I think, basically, there are two big dangers. First, you run the risk of extinguishing the child's spirit. Breaking the child's will is how you teach him to be responsible and accountable, but breaking his spirit shatters his self-image and leaves him with low self-esteem. Second, you run the risk of raising a child who's going to be too powerful and he'll learn to use power just as it was used on him. What you are teaching the child is that Mommy or Daddy is bigger and more powerful, and that is really what's important in life—being powerful.

And one more thing—spanking too early or spanking abusively as Donald's father spanked him can cause anger and resentment that lasts for years, sometimes for life. When we asked Donald about how being beaten had affected him, he told us he lives four blocks from his dad and sees him only once a year.

I'm sure you remember, Randy, the time we had the privilege of appearing on a talk show with Josh McDowell, who speaks everywhere as a representative of Campus Crusade for Christ, particularly to high school and college kids, and Grace Ketterman, the author who is a child psychiatrist and specialist in child development. One thing Josh said on that show that I'll never forget, because it's such great advice for all parents, is this: *Rules without relationships lead to rebellion.*

I'm confident that Josh, and Grace, would agree that spanking done by a parent who does not seek to build a loving relationship with his child will eventually lead to rebellion by that child. What we want to keep bringing home to parents is that whatever you do to discipline them, your kids need to know that you love them.

CHAPTER 2

■●▲■●▲

WHAT'S THE BEST WAY TO USE REALITY DISCIPLINE WITH TODDLERS?

RANDY: Okay, Kevin, as daddy of five children—count 'em, five! —what has been your greatest frustration as a disciplinarian?

KEVIN: Remembering the children's names??? Seriously, I have to go back to our powerful little firstborn, Holly, who had a mind of her own and then some. She was tough.

RANDY: And undoubtedly there were times when she whined, when she was stubborn, or when she, perish the thought, had a temper tantrum. Kids can drive their parents straight up the wall or to the cuckoo's nest by using these three major weapons. So in this chapter we want to focus on some basics for disciplining children when they whine, when they set their feet and won't cooperate, and, above all, when they resort to that most dreaded of all scenes, especially in the supermarket checkout line, the temper tantrum.

KEVIN: First of all, I want to say that we have solved all of our disciplinary problems in the Leman family. My wife and I are so old now we go to bed about ten after eight, and we just say, "Children, the house is yours, your folks are going to bed."

RANDY: So you just leave the older ones to take care of the two young ones, eh? I'm not sure that would work at our house, although it sounds tempting.

KEVIN: Just fantasizing a little, Randy. There are nights, however, when we wish we could do just that. Anyway, here comes our first question. . . .

How do I handle a two year old who has such violent temper tantrums he may hurt himself?

AUDREY: Our two-year-old son is usually affectionate, but when he gets angry he hits his head against furniture or on the floor. My husband and I ask each other, "What do we have here? And what can we do about this?"

KEVIN: Some people might think you have a stupid kid on your hands. Any kid who is running around hitting his head on the floor could be suspected of being sort of stupid, don't you think, Randy?

RANDY: Not stupid, Kevin, just very powerful.

AUDREY: Actually, he's extremely bright. It's just that he gets so angry. . . .

KEVIN: Of course, he isn't stupid! But seriously, Audrey, it sounds as if you have a powerful little buzzard on your hands at the age of two and there are a couple of things you need to remember: First, two year olds lack the language development necessary to express how they feel. When they pull their hair or hit their heads on the floor in frustration, there is also a purpose for their behavior—to show you how powerful they are and that they can pull your chain.

Second, when you see a powerful child, you know that somewhere in the family there is a powerful adult. So with this kind of child, you don't want to use extremely powerful methods of control because it is usually going to backfire on you. Little kids operate with very simple logic. They think, Okay, if you've got the right to be powerful with me, I've got the right to be powerful with you.

RANDY: It sounds to me, Audrey, as if you are feeling almost overwhelmed by your two year old. When a child acts this way, you need to ask yourself some important questions, like, "How do I feel about this behavior?" and "How am I responding to what my child is doing?" At "Parent Talk" we often mention the three goals of misbehavior which are, one, attention-getting behavior; two, powerful behavior; and three, revengeful behavior.

As a general rule, if you, the parent, are feeling annoyed, the child's behavior is usually for the purpose of getting attention. If you are feeling angry, then the child's purpose usually centers around expressing power and gaining power. And if you are feeling hurt and discouraged, the purpose of the child's behavior would be revenge. Children who behave with purposes of revenge have serious emotional problems. You can find a lot of these people in your local state prison. Most of us parents are responding to either attention-getting or powerful behavior in our children. So when your two year old is having a tantrum, it's my guess you are feeling more than annoyed—probably irritated and angry—and this is why we seem so sure that your little boy is a powerful character.

AUDREY: It's true—his behavior does make me angry, and sometimes I am a bit frightened because I think he'll hurt himself. What exactly do I do when he's having one of these tantrums?

KEVIN: Obviously, in this case words aren't going to do much good. When a two year old is banging his head on the floor, it is very appropriate to pick him up, put him in his room, or if he's still sleeping in a crib, put him in his crib and leave the room. The point is, the two year old has to go to a "time out" area where he can be safe until he calms down. Because your boy is usually affectionate, after he calms down would be a good time to cuddle and rock him as you talk quietly to him and let him know that everything is okay. Remember not to make a mountain out of a molehill. Realize that this is the way your little guy is and it won't do a lot of good to get angry or panicky when he has one of these tantrums. Parents often fan the fires that cause temper tantrum behavior because they are being too powerful with their kids.

How can a parent be too powerful with a child?

AUDREY: What did you mean when you talk about a parent being too powerful with the child?

KEVIN: One of the primary ways a parent can be too powerful is to use spanking as the primary means of controlling a child's behavior. If that's the case with you or your husband, my suggestion is to back off and, instead of spanking the child, put him in a safe place and give him time to calm down. Also, it will help to back off on any other powerful behaviors you may be using with your child, such as making every decision for him, criticizing or correcting him at every turn, or comparing him to older children and saying things like, "Why don't you act like your big brother?" Remember, powerful behavior from a parent will always breed powerful behavior in a child.

□ ○ △ □ ○ △

How can I make my eighteen month old stop his continual fussing and whining?

DONNA: My little boy seems to fuss and whine about every little thing. If we say no, he can't do something, he'll fuss. We've been teaching him to say Please, but when he wants some juice he doesn't say Please, he just goes over to the refrigerator and stands there and whines. He acts as if the whole world is coming to an end because he can't have his juice.

RANDY: Looking at it from a developmental standpoint, Donna, it's asking a lot of an eighteen month old to remember to say Please when he wants some juice. Eighteen month olds struggle with being able to put their thoughts into words. Naturally, they get frustrated when they aren't able to express what they want to say. You may be able to get him to say Please when you're holding something out to him, but it's probably asking too much of the boy right now to associate going over to the refrigerator and saying Please because he's thirsty and wants a drink. That's why he just grunts or whines to get a response from you.

Instead of seeing this as an irritating imposition, view it as a wonderful teachable moment. Your child wants something. If you're busy at that moment, you might say, "Just a minute, Honey." Ignore his whining until you are able to come over and open the refrigerator door. At that point, to help him with language development, say, "Can you say 'Please'?' If he says Please, fine. If he continues to whine, get him his juice anyway. He's thirsty and he needs a drink.

You could have a bottle of juice or a sipper cup with the unspillable top handy inside the door so he could just reach in and take it, or you might want to hand him his juice, hold him, and talk to him some more about saying Please. Once he has his juice, put him down and go about your business.

DONNA: But what if he continues to whine and fuss after he has his juice, which is often the case?

KEVIN: One other simple alternative here, Donna, is that most small children don't mind having their drinks at room temperature. You could keep a bottle or sipper cup of juice handy somewhere in the room where he can simply go over and get it when he wants it. I think the key here is not to make a big deal out of your child's whining. Faithful listeners to "Parent Talk" know that Randy and I underscore that the child's personality develops in the first few years of life. How you handle these situations is really going to help determine the kind of personality your son develops. So I wouldn't get upset or excited if he continues whining after he gets his juice. I would just walk away and not pay much attention. That way there is no reinforcement for whining.

DONNA: So we should just ignore him? Right now, we're always telling him to stop fussing because it drives us crazy.

KEVIN: Trying to reason with an eighteen month old just doesn't work. The only thing he will understand or respect is action. When you plead with him to "Stop fussing!" it just reinforces his attempts to control you.

RANDY: But there is a big difference between ignoring a child and acting as if you're not paying attention. We aren't saying to completely ignore him. Act as though you don't hear him and see what happens. If he doesn't get a response, he may stop. Other times you will have to take action and put him in his playpen or in his room for a "time out" session.

KEVIN: I'd just like to add, Donna, that your little boy is fussing because there is a payoff. My guess is that you are like a lot of moms. I call you "mother hover" because when you have that little firstborn you tend to sort of hover over him to be sure he doesn't get into this or that. Mother hovers sort of "overmarshal" their children. I suggest that you just back off and don't respond so actively and directly when your child whines and fusses. The more reinforcement he gets from that kind of behavior, the more he's going to do it.

RANDY: What we're trying to emphasize is not to give the child reinforcement for his whining. Yes, you have to satisfy his needs because that's basic. Yes, you can use these teachable moments for language development, but don't reinforce whining and fussing. Another good idea is that when the child isn't whining or fussing, hold and love and play with the child—give him positive reinforcement for acting happy and secure.

Remember, Donna, as you are programmed yourself, you program your children. The more easygoing you are, the more you can take things in stride, the more the same will be true of your child. Meet his needs without fanfare and deal with his unnecessary whining without fanfare as well. Whining is a part of life and it will pass, particularly as your child develops his language skills. For most kids, some whining is a part of life—just part of growing up—so take it as it comes.

□ ○ △ □ ○ △

Doesn't putting a two year old in his room to kick and scream just reinforce his temper tantrum behavior?

SHARON: My two year old is usually a sweet, happy little guy, but when he's told he can't do something, he can throw a big time fit, kicking, screaming, whatever. And we do what you say—we pick him up and put him in his room. But then he'll lie there and kick and scream for half an hour to forty-five minutes. Somebody just told me I'm reinforcing his temper tantrum. What do you think?

RANDY: I don't think so. Kids have a way of letting their emotions get out of hand. Sometimes they are throwing a tantrum and they don't even know why. When our kids were younger and having tantrums, and I'd sense that this was what was happening, I'd go in and pick up Andrea or Evan and just hold them. I wouldn't say anything. I wasn't there to correct them and I wasn't there to reinforce that what they were doing was wonderful. I just held the child and stroked his or her head. And after I held them awhile, they would settle down and would go to sleep. I think that when a parent really struggles between letting a child continue to throw a tantrum and wanting to pick up the child, in my book, it's okay at least at times to go in and hold the child and, after he settles down, walk away without making a big deal out of it.

KEVIN: I agree that at times that can work nicely if a child is willing to be held. Sometimes the child might still be so angry he will stiffen up and fight anyone who tries to touch him. It just depends on the child.

SHARON: Well, I must say that once my boy finishes his tantrum he comes out and he's happy as a lark.

RANDY: I think you can see, Sharon, that you have two options: If your little guy wants to scream for half an hour and he comes out happy afterward, that's fine. But I also think that if there are parents listening who have a real problem with letting a temper tantrum go on and on, then going in and holding the child close without saying anything is okay too. The point is, however, you have to be careful not to reinforce the child's negative behavior and his power trip. You still have to be in control.

□ ○ △ □ ○ △

Our three year old has developed real behavior problems since her little brother was born. What's wrong?

WANDA: Our oldest child was a delight for the first three years. We had few problems, "the terrible two's" included. But when the new baby came, she began whining and crying about everything. It's getting serious. Do you have any ideas?

KEVIN: What have you done to get her to stop?

WANDA: I've tried spanking her. I've tried taking things away from her. I've tried sending her to her room for five-minute time-outs, but she just cries, whines, and screams all the louder. I've tried just about everything, and it's only getting worse. I don't know what to do with her.

KEVIN: Anytime a child is using attention-getting behavior, you have to look for the cause. What's the child's purpose? In this case, the purpose is obvious: You have a new baby in the house. In a three year old's eyes, a new baby is The Thing! Your three year old now has competition, so your three year old is out to gain your attention.

WANDA: Okay . . . what about taking things away from her that mean a lot to her? Would that make her stop?

KEVIN: No, why do that?

WANDA: Well, I want to get her to understand that if she whines she will be deprived of things.

KEVIN: So you think taking something away is going to make her understand that she isn't supposed to whine and cry? Wanda, this is a typical mistake by a lot of parents. The kid is whining and crying, and we say, "All right, I know what we should do, let's take her blankey away, or her little teddy bear, or whatever." But when you do that, the child says, "Oh, I see, we're at war, are we?" And then the kid goes into her arsenal of tricks and before long it *is* war and you can't remember what started the fight. It can get really crazy.

RANDY: When a child loses her position as top banana in the family, of course she's going to react. For moms in your situation, it's easy to tell the child, "Be quiet . . . don't touch the baby . . . I can't play now . . . I have to feed baby . . . you're bugging me." All of this constantly makes your little girl feel that the "baby is more important than I am" and naturally she is going to whine for attention!

Think of special things that you can do with your little girl, particularly things that are associated with the baby. You can have her help you bathe, change, and hold the baby. Also, you should plan something special every day to do just with your three year old while the baby is sleeping.

KEVIN: You know, Randy, McDonald's ran a television commercial a few years ago that showed all the relatives and other people coming over to see the new baby. While they *oooh'ed* and *ahhh'd* over new baby, older brother was totally ignored and feeling really sad. His dad noticed and understood, and said, in effect, "Johnny, would you like to go to McDonald's for a hamburger?" Of course, the little boy was delighted and they took off to have a great time where he was made to feel special! That commercial says it all about how an older child can feel displaced by a new baby and what to do about it.

□ ○ △ □ ○ △

How do you handle a toddler who wakes up from a nap cranky and just wants to fuss and cry?

LORI: I have a three year old who wakes up from her naps in just a horrible mood. She doesn't want anything to do with me, so I'm wondering what I should do. Insist that she allow me to hold her or just ignore her? It's getting to the point where I don't want to put her down for her nap anymore.

KEVIN: A lot of kids are like that. It's part of their constitution. They just wake up real hard. My experience has been that with these kids you just leave them alone. When they come out of their room crying and fussing, little blankey tucked under their arms, don't run over and try to hold them or whatever because chances are they'll try to reject you at that point. You've got to sort of let them "come to."

LORI: Come to think of it, her father takes a long time to wake up. So you're saying I should just wait her out?

KEVIN: Yes, just put yourself in your child's place. Have you ever decided to take a nap, but you know you have to get up and be someplace in about an hour? So you set the alarm and it goes off and it jars you awake and you tell yourself, "I should never have taken a nap, I feel so groggy." I think that's how some little kids may feel inside when they wake up from a nap cranky. And then, when Mom pounces on them and says, "Here, sit on Mommy's lap," no wonder the child resists.

RANDY: So, we're saying, Lori, to just back off and not run to the rescue. If her crankiness is a physical thing, then she isn't crying to get back at you or get your attention. It simply is the way she is. The point is, you need to look at the purpose of your child's behavior. If it's to get your attention or be powerful, then you may need to deal with it in some action-oriented way. If it's your child's natural reaction to wake up feeling groggy and tired and wanting to be left alone, then respect that and leave the child alone and let her get her crankiness out of her system. After a while, she will probably come to you to be held (as most little ones do after waking up from a nap), but wait for her timing. If she has another agenda and wants to get your attention and control you, you'll soon know that and then you'll have to take other measures.

□ ○ △ □ ○ △

How do I handle a three year old who quotes Scripture in his defense when being disciplined?

RITA: We have a very bright three-year-old boy who has a unique way of defying us when we discipline him. He quotes the Bible or phrases he's picked up at church, such as, "No weapon formed against me shall prosper," or "I have no more pain in Jesus' Name."

KEVIN: Do not provoke a powerful little buzzard to wrath! This kid isn't building a rocket in his bedroom right now, is he?

RITA: It's hard not to laugh when he does this, but at the same time he knows that he can get to us this way.

RANDY: What do you do when he defies you by quoting Scripture?

RITA: Usually we have to walk away and go into the other room to laugh and regain our composure. Then we come back and try to deal with it. Sometimes we have to resort to spanking him for talking back like this. We have certain rules for which he gets a spanking.

KEVIN: Would you like to share those rules with us?

RITA: Well, Rule #1 is talking back to us. Another rule is no lying. He loves to tell us his one-year-old brother did this or did that. And the third rule is never going into the street. Those are the three things that he can get spanked for.

RANDY: Your three year old is obviously pretty bright. Is he learning Scripture in your home?

RITA: Yes, and at church.

RANDY: If he is quoting Scripture as a way of "defending himself," this could be a wonderful opportunity. After you have administered whatever discipline he needs, you can sit down and talk to him about what the Scripture he is quoting really means.

KEVIN: Also, Randy, after the kid goes ahead and quotes Scripture, wouldn't it be a good idea to just say, "You did that really well. You learned that in Sunday school, didn't you? But, my, your room is messy. Let's clean it up and make it look nice. God would like that, don't you think?" Then guide the child in cleaning up his room (or in doing whatever you've asked him to do).

If he continues to talk back and be absolutely defiant, then he may need a swat. But my first response to his quoting Scripture wouldn't be a swat "because he's talking back." Quoting Scripture is his rather unique way of telling you he doesn't want to do something, which isn't exactly unusual for little children. By the way, since your little guy is so bright, it might be fun sometime to counter his Bible quoting by saying, with a big smile, "Honey, I've got a new verse for you to work on: 'Children, obey your parents in everything, for this pleases the Lord.' "

It seems to me, Rita, that you should just try to take your little boy's novel way of rebelling in stride. In any situation where a child tries to divert, sidestep, or change the focus of getting something accomplished, the parent should never be sidetracked. Always be sure there is follow-through. Don't argue, debate, or get caught up in a power struggle. You can acknowledge your child's feelings or thoughts, but you want to stay on course and get him to cooperate.

□ ○ △ □ ○ △

What can I do with a child who dawdles and won't get dressed?

RANDY: We have two parents on the line—a mom and a dad—with different problems concerning children who won't get dressed. Holly, you go first. . . .

HOLLY: My son is almost four and I want to know more about how to sidestep power struggles with him. I'm trying to get him to learn to dress himself, but he always just throws a major fit. He won't try to put on any clothes himself, and he won't let me help him, particularly with his shoes and socks. I try to control my anger, because I know that doesn't do any good, but I'm just having real problems.

KEVIN: You just said you try to control your anger, but don't always succeed. Is that right?

HOLLY: Right, and my four year old likes to make me angry. He knows how to pull my chain.

KEVIN: Of course, because that's one of the ways he gets you to pay attention to him. At a recent seminar that Randy and I did, we outlined the three goals of misbehavior in children: (1) to get attention; (2) to gain power; (3) to get revenge. Randy made the statement that when a child goes from attention-getting to being powerful, it is probably because he is getting more and more discouraged. It's quite possible that your strong-willed little four year old is not getting enough positive attention for the things he does right in life.

Putting on shoes and socks is difficult for a four year old to learn, particularly if the shoes and socks are a little tight and if the shoes have laces that need tying. So you need to do two things: When he refuses to try to put on his shoes and socks or let you help him, then you have to handle his power tantrum. Refuse to raise your sails into his wind. Let him know he can't play inside or outside until he is fully dressed. Then, put him in his room. This way he learns there is no payoff for having tantrums and refusing to get all his clothes on.

At the same time, you need to find ways for him to succeed and encourage him when he does. For example, maybe he can handle getting his T-shirt over his head. If he does cooperate in getting dressed, encourage him and let him know you are very happy to see that he's trying hard.

□ ○ △ □ ○ △

DON: I also am having a power struggle with our five-year-old son over getting dressed, putting on his shoes, and so on. He is one of four children and our only boy. He is a slow starter in the mornings. This is particularly a problem because I have an early morning exercise class three days a week. This gym offers child care, and I like to take him along to give my wife a break from having the usual "four kids in the morning hassle." But he keeps making me late because he dawdles at getting dressed.

RANDY: And how does that make you feel, Don?

DON: Well, I'm getting irritated because it's obvious that he's not suffering any consequences; I am, because he's making me late. He doesn't care if we go or not, so there is no incentive to get ready.

KEVIN: You can't expect a powerful child to be too considerate of your needs; he's only interested in his. I suggest that you simply pick him up under one arm in whatever state of dress or undress he's in, grab the rest of his clothes, and put him in that cold car seat. Then belt him in with that cold seat belt and tell him, "Sorry, kid, but I can't be late and we're going whether you're dressed or not."

DON: He won't like that. He'll scream bloody murder.

KEVIN: Exactly. Even five year olds have a budding sense of modesty and know they shouldn't run around in public in their skivvies. He probably will start pleading with his mom, "Mom, Mom, I can't go out like *this*!" You just be gentle, kind, and firm, but say, "Sorry, Son, I can't be late and we're going, whether you're dressed or not."

DON: I guess it is worth a try. . . .

RANDY: Suppose you try it. What is the worst thing that could happen?

DON: I could arrive at the gym with a child who is practically naked.

KEVIN: But remember, you can take his clothes with you in a plastic bag or something. We've done this with our kids when they wouldn't get dressed and were late for school. It really works rather beautifully. Just throw the clothes in the backseat with the child and by the time you hit the first stoplight, he is dressed.

DON: I will try it. I will definitely try it.

RANDY: These days, of course, you have the seat belt issue, so you probably just can't throw him in the backseat with his clothes to get dressed while the car is moving. But you can strap him in with the cold seat belt on that cold seat, as Kevin puts it, and when you get to the gym, just take him in to the child-care facility, hand him to the attendant and say to your son, "It's time for you to get dressed, I have to exercise." But before you leave the room, take the attendant aside and explain your situation. Maybe he or she can invoke a little more Reality Discipline by telling him that, because he didn't come dressed, he will miss the first game, or the first treat, or whatever the group is doing at the moment.

KEVIN: You said it all, a few seconds ago, Don, when you observed that you were the one who was facing the consequences of your child's behavior. What you need to do is get the ball back into his little court and let him face the consequences of not cooperating and getting dressed. That's how he stays accountable and learns to be responsible. That is the bottom line.

□ ○ △ □ ○ △

What is the best way to discipline a five year old for stealing something from the store?

CONNIE: We have twin boys who just turned five. When only one of us takes them along to the store, we usually put them into the shopping cart so they won't get into mischief. If both of us take them, we let them walk along beside us, "like big boys." The other night my husband took the boys shopping alone and didn't put them in the cart. While he was getting some things, they found one of those serve-yourself cookie containers. One twin took a bite out of a cookie and then put it back in. His brother, Mark, took the cookie back out and said, "Daddy, David took a bite out of this cookie." So my husband put them both in the cart and went on with his shopping, but he kept telling David, "I don't know what is going to happen to you. We are going to have to talk to the manager and he might make you stay here and work to pay for the cookie."

KEVIN: This scenario sounds like it's heading for disaster. What happened?

CONNIE: They got in the checkout line and my husband asked for the manager. My husband explained that David had taken the cookie, and then asked the manager, "Would you talk to him about this, please?" So the manager took David aside and his brother kind of tagged along to hear what was happening. A minute or so later, Mark started crying and screaming and ran back to his dad all upset. He kept sobbing, "I want David to come home with us."

RANDY: And what is the question you have for us?

CONNIE: My question is, "Who is right, my husband or me?" I feel that the boys were a bit too young for a store manager to be correcting them. I feel it is our place to do that kind of disciplining right now. My husband thought taking him to the store manager was a great idea because that way he learned a real lesson. I told him I would call "Parent Talk" to see what you thought.

KEVIN: In one sense your husband was using Reality Discipline, trying to make your son accountable for what he had done, but at age five I would have to agree with you. The parent should handle this kind of situation.

CONNIE: That's what I thought. Telling a five year old, "I don't know what the manager is going to do with you," can conjure up all kinds of ideas in his little mind.

RANDY: At that age, what you create with that kind of threat is separation anxiety. What might have worked better is to have Dad go over with his two boys and talk with the manager, all of them together. But when the manager took David aside alone, that created an inordinate amount of anxiety, not only for him, but for his brother, who apparently was the one who got even more upset.

CONNIE: When they came home, my husband said to David, "Tell Mommy what you did." David said, "I stealed a cookie." Then his brother said, "David is a thief!"

KEVIN: Poor David. He uses questionable grammar, and he's a shoplifter—all at the age of five. I think we've got to lighten up on the poor little guy.

CONNIE: It was terrible. They both thought the police were going to take them all away.

RANDY: Tell your husband we're glad that he tried to use Reality Discipline, but it would have been better to hold David accountable in some other way. For example, the next night at dinner Dad could say, "Sorry, David, but do you remember the treat you took last night at the store? That was wrong, and tonight you will have to go without dessert."

Or, another approach would be to make it a point for everyone to go shopping together at the same store in a few days while the event is still fresh in David's memory. He knows that when Mom and Dad are shopping together, both boys get to walk along with them, but this time David has to ride in the cart because he took a cookie from that container right over there. I'd only do these things once, and I wouldn't continue to make an issue of it. David should get the message.

CONNIE: Would a spanking ever be in order for something like this?

RANDY: Only if David showed no remorse whatsoever for stealing the cookie, and he would get defiant and mouthy when you tried to correct him. But in this case, he probably felt badly enough and spanking won't help. What you're trying to do is teach David to be accountable for his actions, and I think the other methods we've suggested open up more possibilities for that.

□ ○ △ □ ○ △

How can I get my child to apologize when she hurts or offends a playmate?

SYLVIA: Our daughter just turned three and she has hit a stubborn streak where she refuses to apologize when she does something wrong. Not long ago she kicked somebody, and over the next two days she totally refused to say, "I'm sorry," even though she: (1) had to sit in the time-out chair for two hours; (2) got some swats on the behind; (3) lost all her toy privileges. Nothing did any good. In the end, I helped her bake cookies and write a little note saying she wanted to be friends with the child she had kicked. Then my husband looked at me and said, "Did we win or did we lose?"

KEVIN: I would say you lost, even though baking cookies is a nice pastime for Mom and her daughter. The problem is, she was getting you totally involved and keeping your attention with her powerful behavior.

SYLVIA: Well, we had run clean out of ideas. We were trying to do what you say—get her to accept the consequences for her actions and be accountable for kicking our neighbor's three year old. The girls play together all the time, but the other day our daughter was in a bad mood and she kicked her friend. We talked to her about hurting other people and her daddy and I both said that we would hold her hand and go with her to help her apologize. We took her over there, but all she did was stand there and not say a word. When I gave her a choice between saying she was sorry and getting spanked, she just laid herself down right over my knee.

KEVIN: She's a powerful little kid. This reminds me of an example I like to talk about concerning when a child gets a gift but doesn't say, "Thank you." All the child does is open the package so she can enjoy the gift. I always tell parents not to hover over the child and say, "Now what do you say to Mrs. Johnson, Sweetheart?" Wait until Mrs. Johnson leaves, then take the child aside and say, "What just happened is wrong. When someone gives you a gift, you should say, 'Thank you.' " Then take the toy from the child and tell her that she can't play with it until such time as she is willing to say "Thank you" to Mrs. Johnson.

RANDY: In a way, Sylvia, this is more between you and your child than it is between your child and her playmate. Right now, your three year old knows that you really want her to say she's sorry and that you're trying just about everything to get her to do it. You definitely have your sail in her wind. What you need to do is back off and set up a situation where there is a strong motivation for her to go and say she's sorry. For example, tell her she can't play with the friend she offended, or any friend for that matter, until she takes care of apologizing for her bad behavior. Then stick to your guns and wait her out.

□ ○ △ □ ○ △

Are "educational toys" a good idea for a one year old?

DIANA: I have a wonderful little fourteen-month-old baby who started playing with educational toys as early as ten months. They're the kind of toy that has pieces in circles, squares, triangles, and what have you, and she has to fit them into the correct hole. At first she seemed to have fun, but lately she's starting to get very frustrated and angry, especially when she doesn't get the right piece in the right hole. And it isn't a whiney kind of frustration. She sounds like it's an "I'm going to tear my hair out" kind of thing.

KEVIN: She shouldn't have those kind of toys to begin with. My advice is to get rid of them.

DIANA: Really? Why do you say that?

KEVIN: What purpose do they serve?

DIANA: I guess it's for eye-hand coordination, that kind of thing.

KEVIN: Just get the kid some blocks—some good, old-fashioned wooden blocks. Diana, the simpler you can make your little girl's childhood, particularly her infancy, the better off she'll be. Here you are with a fourteen month old who is already showing the first signs of perfectionism, and perfectionism is slow suicide. It's especially tough when you start at the age of fourteen months.

RANDY: The difference between plain old wooden blocks and the kind where you have to "fill in the right hole" is that the blocks permit the child to create whatever she wants. It reminds me of our son, D. J. He loves to create things, and one day he came home from first grade and said, "You know, Dad, I wish the teacher wouldn't give us papers with things to fill in. I'd rather that the papers were just blank, and then I could draw in anything I wanted." I think what you're seeing at the tender age of fourteen months is a little girl who is terribly frustrated by having to follow all these predetermined patterns.

DIANA: Okay, suppose I get her some simpler blocks. What if she still gets frustrated and starts screaming and she's mad at her blocks because she builds them and they fall over?

KEVIN: That's always a judgment call for you. There might be times when you need to get down and pitch in and help her a little bit. Show her how to stack the blocks in a simple way so they won't fall down. But basically, do as little as possible for her. Let her have fun with the blocks, or give her some other simple toy to play with instead. My only point is that you want your child to have a childhood. Don't start giving her educational toys until she is almost three, and then be sure that they are the simple kind that she can play with and not be frustrated.

□ ○ △ □ ○ △

Why does my child bite other children and how can I make her stop?

KATIE: My daughter is fifteen-and-a-half months old and she is always biting her fifteen-month-old cousin who's with us four days a week because I baby-sit him. She has bitten him severely on the face and on the fingers. She just goes after him and I don't know how to correct it.

RANDY: What have you tried when she bites?

KATIE: I take her aside and say, "No!" and then I spank her with my spanking spoon. Then I put her in her room until she is through crying. Is this the right thing to do?

RANDY: Well, not really. We need to touch on a couple of things. First, you have to understand that children this age are going through the "oral stage of development." That is, the mouth gives the child a great deal of pleasure and sensitivity and power. Biting is a very normal thing for a fifteen and a half month old to do. Now as to what you can do about it, to spank her is not appropriate. Instead, pick her up, look directly at her and say very firmly No! and then remove her to another room for a time-out.

KATIE: No spanking, not even for biting him in the face? Just pick her up and say No! and put her in the other room?

RANDY: Exactly. And, remember, this little problem has come to pass, not to stay. When your daughter gets to be five, for example, it is highly unlikely she will still be biting. In fact, she will probably quit biting somewhere between two and three. This is a stage she is going through. You let her know very firmly that it is not appropriate to bite and then remove her from the situation. Put her in her room or in her playpen with her toys. This achieves two things: One, it gives her something productive that gets her mind off of biting; two, it gives her little cousin protection from further harm.

KEVIN: Randy said it straight, Katie. He gave you great advice. And I'm sure your little girl's cousin will rise up to call you "Blessed" as soon as he can talk. But let me ask you a quick question. Given a choice, would you prefer to spank your daughter or not?

KATIE: No, I would not prefer to spank her. It's very hard for me, but biting seems to be an especially serious offense.

KEVIN: That's good. Let me tell you two quick things about spanking. First, never hit with a spoon, only your open hand. Second, fifteen months is too young to spank. We recommend eighteen to twenty-four months. I'm on the high end at twenty-four and Randy thinks it's okay to do it at eighteen, but when you start swatting a child who is very young, you simply set yourself up to have a powerful child. (For more on spanking, see Chapter One.)

□ ○ △ □ ○ △

How do I correct a two year old who has picked up a blasphemous phrase and loves to repeat it?

DARLA: We took our two-year-old son along when we were visiting some friends recently. They have an older boy, and they had rented the video *Home Alone.* We all sat there watching it and several times the phrase, "Oh, my God," was used. Later, on the way home, our two year old said, "Oh, my God," and now he says it all the time.

RANDY: How did you react when he began saying this?

DARLA: At first we thought it best just to ignore it, and that he'd forget about it. But he hasn't forgotten. It's been going on for three months, and we're not sure what to do at this point.

RANDY: It's always good not to overreact and reinforce a child for behavior that is not acceptable. But if it's lasted three months and he is still saying it, then you need to think about how you can explain to a two year old that you don't use God's Name like that in your home.

KEVIN: At this point, I think you must look him right in the eye, get his focused attention, and then say very firmly, "We do not say that in this house!" He will understand that. Just by your facial expression he will know that he said something that isn't acceptable.

DARLA: We tried that and it didn't work.

KEVIN: It isn't a matter of just saying it once, or even a few times. You can't say you've tried something and it didn't work until you have really tried it. You have to take time to train the young child. When does he normally use this phrase?

DARLA: He is our only child, and sometimes the three of us will be driving down the road and he will just start saying it, maybe as many as four or five or six times in a row.

KEVIN: You're sort of caught between a rock and a hard place. When he started saying this, you ignored it, and it became a habit for him. Then when you reacted to it, maybe you overreacted a bit and it got reinforced. Now it's something he's doing to get attention.

RANDY: I'd like to go back to the question of whether it's right or wrong to ignore something like this when it first starts. My personal philosophy is that you don't ignore things, hoping they'll just go away. There may be a few exceptions, but ordinarily you need to act when the child is behaving inappropriately. Keep telling him "No, that isn't something we say in our home," but don't overreact and make a big deal out of it. Spanking him could easily backfire and only reinforce the behavior. You'll get farther by withdrawing privileges or depriving him of certain things he wants or likes. For example, if he ever says it at the kitchen table, you might just tell him, "No, we don't say that, and now you are excused from dinner." Or, if he says it while you're driving along together, you can say, "Well, we were going to stop for ice cream, but now that you've said that we can't and we're going straight home." And, one more idea, if he has a little friend over and says it, the friend has to go straight home. Find a consequence that he can understand at the tender age of two, and that's how he will learn to be accountable.

CHAPTER 3

■●▲■●▲

HOW TO MAKE GOD A REAL FRIEND TO YOUR KIDS

RANDY: Making God real for kids . . . not an awesome ogre who's ready to pounce, but a loving heavenly Father Who cares for us and wants us to live in the right way. A lot of parents would like to know how to do it better, and some want to know how to get started.

KEVIN: One of my favorite stories comes from my sister, Sally, who's going to be our special phone guest today. She told me about a little five-year-old girl who was riding home from church in the backseat of the car. Her mom asked her, "What did you learn in Sunday school, Honey?" And the little kid replied, "Jesus and God, Jesus and God, that's all they ever talk about is Jesus and God."

RANDY: Kevin's big sister, Sally, is joining us to talk about how to make God real to your children. She's a preschool educator and a specialist in child development whose book *Making God Real to Your Children*[1] has been featured in *Focus on the Family* magazine. Sally, we're looking forward to talking about really basic stuff on what parents can do to help their kids know God as their heavenly Father and their friend too. Welcome to "Parent Talk." What inspired you to write your books on making God real for little kids?

SALLY: I have worked with preschool children for many years. I've also raised three of my own, and now we have grandchildren too. I think the books began when I was asked to do a seminar on the spiritual nurture of the children in the home, or something like that. It just kind of developed from there.

KEVIN: There is an important truth in that brief story I've just shared about the little girl who said, "Jesus and God—that's all they ever talk about is Jesus and God." Parents have a great opportunity to go way beyond just taking their kids to church, as important as that is. They can show children in such a natural way how God affects their decisions, and the way they live their lives. Kids are a lot like clay. With care and patience, you can form clay into a lovely piece of pottery, but it takes a lot of loving, tender care.

SALLY: I think we always need to try for balance. We've all heard that it isn't what you say or what you tell others, it's how you live your life. And that's so true, especially with little kids. But we also have a verbal mandate from God to teach and tell our children about Him—Who He is and how much He loves them and how wonderfully He has provided for them.

RANDY: In our family, we have approached the whole area of teaching our children about God by using teachable moments that come up through the day. While you're talking, while you're out for a walk, while you're going to the store. The opportunities pop up to talk about how God is the Creator of all this and how much He loves us. And Donna and I have discovered that not only does this make God real for our kids, but it reminds us not to lose sight of the basics and forget the simple but profound fact that everything we see around us reminds us of God's love and care.

SALLY: What you've just said, Randy, is at the heart of what I try to do in my books, especially the newest one which Kevin helped me title: *Mommy Appleseed: Planting Seeds of Faith in the Heart of Your Child.*[2] There are so many things parents can enjoy with their children to bring God into daily life in a natural way without sermonizing or lecturing. For example, gardening is a project that can open up all kinds of opportunities to delight in God's provisions for us. Even a preschooler can enjoy working with Mom or Dad as he helps dig, plant, water, and weed. He can observe how God makes the plants grow, and later he can enjoy the fruits of his labor as he helps Mommy cook dinner for the family, using vegetables that they have raised together. Thank-you prayers just flow for tasty treats God has given us when we helped grow them ourselves. And chances are, if the child is involved in raising the food, he is going to be a little more excited about eating it too. Another simple thing you can do is have the child help you pick a bouquet of flowers that he can take to Sunday school to decorate his classroom, or perhaps you can take them to visit a person who is confined to his or her home. But what you want to tell the child is "When we share with others, Jesus is pleased."

RANDY: Those are great ideas for making God real in the garden, but what are some others areas you cover in *Mommy Appleseed*?

SALLY: The book has twenty-eight activities in all. One of my favorites is sidewalk painting. All you need is some clear water and a few adult-sized paint brushes, anywhere from one-half-inch to one-inch wide, and your child is ready for a wonderful time decorating the driveway or sidewalk. I've had kids stay busy for hours, creating their works of art, which, of course, disappear in a few minutes in the hot sun. As you look at what they're doing, you can ask, "What's happening to your 'paint'? Where did it all go? How did Jesus make it disappear?" Then you can talk about how God gives us the sun and it dries up the water so it goes right back up into the clouds. And then when the clouds get full of water, they shower down the rain and everything gets a drink.

KEVIN: Sally has just given you a taste of actual things she does with kids, Randy. She's director of a preschool back in Jamestown, New York. It's fascinating to watch a three year old walk into the room and then see this woman in her fifties drop to her knees and get eyeball to eyeball with that kid and start to communicate. As you know, Sally's the firstborn in our family—eight years older than I am, and the class of the Leman clan. I am always amazed at how orderly she is in her thinking and the way she does things. For years I've talked about the clear vinyl runners that run throughout her house to keep her carpets impeccable, and I have it on good authority from one of her grown daughters that she ties her big brown garbage bags with a ribbon before she puts them out for the trash man.

SALLY: Actually, Kevin, they are clear trash bags and I do the ribbon in a yellow bow.

RANDY: Did she always correct you when you were kids?

KEVIN: Big sister constantly corrected The Cub, and, of course, he usually needed it. Sally was my second mom and she did a great job.

RANDY: I have been in seminars with Kevin all over the country, Sally, and he really does talk about his big sister with the clear vinyl runners leading throughout her house.

SALLY: I finally got so sick of hearing about that clear vinyl runner that I wrapped it up and gave it to Kevin as a present—with a pretty bow on it, of course.

RANDY: What does a mom do, Sally, when she has a kid like Kevin Leman, whom she's trying to teach about God, and he's just wriggling around and being the baby of the family?

SALLY: First, you must have patience because God is not finished with us yet. Children do grow up, believe it or not, and Kevin is proof positive that it can happen. Moms needs to remember that God is right with them through everything they have to face every day. It's amazing; He gives you the wisdom to handle your child if you just ask Him specifically, and not just in general.

□ ○ △ □ ○ △

What can I do or what can I use to make God real to my children on a daily basis?

ADRIENNE: Hi, Sally, I want you to know that I tie my trash bags with a bow also. We have two little girls—Pamela turned six yesterday and Patty was four last October. Every evening my husband and I try to have a quiet time with the kids. We read from the Bible storybook; then we share what we did throughout the day. And we also pray. We're trying to teach the kids that the Lord is always with them, every moment of the day. He is not somebody who has to be "officially" approached—"Oh-my-let's-go-before-God!" But I'm still looking for more ways to make God real for my kids.

SALLY: Well, I think you're already doing a great job by reading to the girls from Christian books and praying with them. Little sentence prayers about simple things the children think about are best. As for other things you can do, you might occasionally read a story to your girls and then act out the story to apply the message to their lives. And if you read a story about being kind just before going to bed, try to do something nice for someone the very next morning as you remind them, "Remember our story last night before bed? Let's be kind to Mrs. Jones next door today, shall we?" Also, one of the best tools you can invest in is a little tape recorder children can have right by their beds so they can play Scripture tapes and Bible stories. And, oh, yes, if you have a VCR, don't forget the wonderful videos that are available now. Some have biblical settings and others are contemporary stories in which the main characters depend on God to get them out of all kinds of difficulties.

RANDY: Sally, should quiet time with the children emphasize entertainment?

SALLY: Well, we should certainly make it fun for them, but our primary goal shouldn't be entertainment. Kids are constantly entertained anyway, so what we need are tools and techniques to have them settle down and have some quiet moments with God. A tape recorder is a great tool for quieting them down because it has a calming effect. And sometimes, if the child is acting up, you can use it as a means of Reality Discipline—just remove the tape recorder for a night or two to let the child know that misbehavior results in losing something he or she really enjoys.

□ ○ △ □ ○ △

How can you help your child confess having a bad attitude without just preaching and lecturing?

DANA: We've got two children, a compliant firstborn boy, age five, and his little sister, age three. Surprisingly enough, our second born is the strong-willed one, and she can really try your patience. Her brother is much more open to praying and talking about God, but sometimes she has a real problem with her attitude. What we've learned to do is say, "Okay, Melissa, let's cup our hands and say, 'Father, here is my yucky attitude and I give it to You, Lord.' " And then she just 'throws it up' and lays it at His feet.

KEVIN: Now that's what I call making God real! I may try that the next time I get a crummy meal up there in the friendly skies and it puts me in a bad mood!

DANA: Well, it's definitely for adults too. Last Christmas we were putting up the tree and it just kept falling over. It wasn't too long before my husband decided he wasn't having a good time, and he let everyone know it. Finally, Melissa said, "Daddy, you need to pray and ask Jesus to help you have a good attitude because you don't have a good attitude right now. C'mon, Daddy, let's pray." My husband just melted. It was one of the highlights of our Christmas holiday. God was there.

SALLY: That's such a neat story, Dana, and what it demonstrates is that kids usually believe what we tell them and take what we say very literally. The other night I was talking to my little grandson, Ben, and I said, "You know, Honey, one day you might want to ask Jesus into your heart." And he said, "Oh, Grandma, I want to do it right now." And so we had a little prayer and Ben did just that—he asked Jesus to come into his heart. He was lying on his bed and he just yelled across the hall to his sister, "Katie, just ask Jesus to come into your heart!" The next night we were talking about Jesus being in our hearts and he said, "Is Jesus in Grandpa's heart?" and I said, "Yes." And he said, "Is Jesus in Uncle Tom's heart?" and I said, "Yes." Then he said, "Is Jesus in your heart?" and I said, "Yes, Ben, He is." And then he said, "Grandma, is there lots of Jesuses?"

RANDY: Indeed, there is always more than enough of Jesus to go around. Kids are so ready to have Him be part of their lives. We've got another call, Kevin, but first I want to know how it feels to have a sister who is a grandma.

KEVIN: Old, but what is worse is to be out with your baby daughter and have people come up to you and assume that *you* are the Grandpa. *That* makes you feel like Methuselah!

□ ○ △ □ ○ △

Besides saying grace at meals, how can I teach my child to be thankful?

GRACE: I've always been big on thanking God throughout the day for my husband, my children, my house, my strength. I exercise three times a week and even while I'm working out I thank God that my body can function as well as it does. And when I pray with my four-year-old daughter she hears me thank Him for things like that. But because she's only four, I still tend to do most of the leading in prayer time and I basically pray for her when she goes to bed. Sometimes I wonder if anything's getting through.

KEVIN: Talk to any pastor about his congregation and he will probably tell you he wonders the same thing.

GRACE: Somebody just talked about trimming the Christmas tree, and that reminded me of last Christmas Day when we had finished opening our presents. Misty was playing with her new toys, and I said, "This is such a special day. I think we should pray. Misty, do you want to pray?" And Misty said, "Yep, I just want to thank Jesus for all of the things we got for Christmas today." That was the best present I got for Christmas, because it showed me something *is* getting through, and I was so very thankful for that.

SALLY: I think it is really wonderful when children "catch" you having devotional time with the Lord. It's important for them to see you with your Bible open on your lap. They need to come upon you when you're praying. Perhaps you can invite them to sit by you. Maybe they'll participate in the prayer and maybe they won't, but that's okay, because they have seen you talking to God. They sense your dependence on Him and your thankfulness to Him. That's how God becomes very real to them.

□ ○ △ □ ○ △

How can I help my child to trust in God's care when she is afraid at night?

LUCY: I was visiting my five-year-old granddaughter for a few days and every night she had these horrible fears of the dark. She wanted to sleep with her grandpa and me. I checked with my daughter and her husband to see if it was okay for her to come in bed with us for a few nights.* Then I told her. "I'm going to ask God to help you go to sleep at night, because night and the dark are made for rest, and daytime and sunshine are made for play and all the things that we like to do."

KEVIN: Unless, of course, you are a raccoon.

LUCY: The third night we were there, we were having our prayer time and Tammy reminded me, "You forgot to ask God to help me to sleep." So we prayed again and I asked God to help her to sleep that night and to get her rest. We spent five nights there and every night she fell asleep better than she had before. By the end of the week, my husband, who had always been on the other side of the bed listening to us pray, said, "You know, I believe that it really helped for you to ask God to help Tammy go to sleep at night and rest."

SALLY: That's a wonderful little story, Lucy, and it reminds me that it helps to mention to children that everyone is afraid sometimes, even Grandma and Grandpa and Mommy and Daddy. One of the best little books I've ever found to read to a child who may be a bit fearful is called *Here and There and Everywhere: Jesus Is with Me.* Reading it to a young child will help reassure him of God's nearness.

RANDY: I like Lucy's story also because it gives parents a very simple but powerful solution to a common problem. Many chil-

* For more on dealing with bedtime problems, see Chapter 5.

dren are afraid at night because it's dark and the dark is full of scary things. But I'm also hearing something else here. Grandparents can play an important part in the spiritual development and understanding of their grandchildren.

SALLY: Indeed they can. Kids are so used to hearing Mommy and Daddy, and when another loving voice belonging to Grandma or Grandpa breaks in to help in a specific situation, such as being afraid of the dark, it really makes a big difference. I really believe grandparents are God's safety net for so many families. So often I've seen situations where parents aren't willing to take their children to church and Grandma and Grandpa are the Christians in the family who step in to play that role. Eventually, however, because of their quiet and steady witness, the parents start attending church again themselves.

□ ○ △ □ ○ △

How can I help my child deal with nightmares?

NINA: I'm calling to add to what the grandmother just said about helping kids get to sleep at night. Ever since I was a child I've struggled with nightmares and a very wise counselor asked me if I ever prayed and asked God about it. It was as if as he were saying, "They're just nightmares."

Now I have a family of my own with two children, four and two. The four year old has trouble with bad nightmares, too, and I've been telling him that he doesn't have to be afraid because "Jesus lives in your heart." Now when we're turning things off at night and getting ready to go to bed ourselves, we can hear him wake up, but instead of running to us, he'll be talking to Jesus. As early as four years old, he's in there saying, "Jesus lives in my heart. Jesus is powerful." He is using what we have armed him with to defeat the bad dreams and the darkness.

□ ○ △ □ ○ △

Thunderstorms really scare my children. How can I explain that God makes the thunder, but it isn't going to hurt them?

GLENNA: I'm calling to share an idea that might help other parents keep their child calm during thunderstorms. I love them and my kids do too. Where I grew up, we had a lot of thunderstorms, and when we knew one was coming my parents would make popcorn. Then we'd shut off all the lights and just sit there and watch it. It was like a big show. The lightning would flash, and then we'd wait to hear the boom of thunder. It was great.

RANDY: And do you do the same thing now with your own children?

GLENNA: Right. I started when they were very young. I say, "Oh, there's the thunder and lightning. Let's make some popcorn and have a big party." Then we line up the chairs by our big window, turn the lights off, and watch.

RANDY: You're making a good point, Glenna, because parents can transmit fears to their children in ways they don't even realize. Recently we had a thunderstorm and D. J., our youngest child, was playing out in the backyard. The tendency when you see the first bolt of lightning is to run out, grab your kid, and say something like, "Quick, if you don't get inside and it hits that tree standing next to you, you are dead meat." But, instead, we try to say, "Look, lightning is something beautiful but it is also very powerful, and when it gets closer we need to get into the house because sometimes it will strike the trees and it might hurt us." We don't want to transfer fear to D. J., only healthy respect for something that has great power. That's what I hear you doing, and it's a sensible approach, Glenna.

GLENNA: We have tried to tell our kids that lightning is like fire. It can be beautiful but it can also hurt you if you are careless. We teach our kids that God created every flash of lightning and every sound of thunder as completely different. They sit there munching popcorn and cheering God on!

□ ○ △ □ ○ △

How can I make God real to our children when I'm the only Christian in the family?

VIRGINIA: I need some encouragement. I'm a Christian but my husband and his parents who live with us are not. We have two children, a little boy, seven, and his sister is four. Billy really looks up to his dad and his grandpa and I'm trying to keep God alive for him and his sister when their male role models are not believers. I just feel so alone because I don't have any support from the people he is around so much. It's especially hard with Billy because he is not as receptive to God as he was when he was younger.

RANDY: Sally, you probably have dealt with a lot of moms or dads who have to make God real on their own without any support from their spouse.

SALLY: I know it sounds simplistic, Virginia, but God wants you to be faithful. It's your responsibility to get your children to Sunday school and church. As much as possible, make Sunday a fun day and try to apply throughout the week what your children learn in Sunday school. I truly believe God will honor your commitment and someday your kids will realize what God desires for them. And as they begin to understand who God is in their lives, your children will probably start praying for their daddy and their grandparents because they don't know Jesus.

RANDY: Are you able to have Christian music in your home—on the radio or by playing recordings?

VIRGINIA: Yes, but I have to be careful not to overdo it.

SALLY: Take your children along to your local Christian bookstore, and allow them to choose a tape from the tremendous selection of Bible songs and Christian music for kids that is available. Then, as your children learn the music, they will also be hiding God's Word in their hearts. I gave my little granddaughter three new Bible song tapes recently, and within a couple of weeks she had memorized every song. And another benefit is that hearing those tapes will be an encouragement to you too. God is faithful, just don't give up.

□ ○ △ □ ○ △

What if my child doesn't want to pray and he makes noises or is naughty during prayer time?

ROBERTA: We have a five year old and a three year old. Our five year old is a strong-willed child and whether it's mealtime or bedtime, he doesn't want to pray. He will say, "You pray, Mommy." This morning he wanted me to pray for a long time so his oatmeal would cool off.

KEVIN: Wilfred Brimley would be proud of that kid—he wants to do the right thing.

ROBERTA: We never try to force Christopher to pray. We're sure that he will grow into wanting to do it when he's ready. But sometimes when my husband and I pray, he makes noises and is naughty. I'm not sure how to handle that.

KEVIN: This is a great opportunity to use Reality Discipline to show your kids that your relationship to God is very real. When Christopher makes noises during prayer time, you or your husband simply pick the child up and remove him gently and quietly from the scene. Take him to his room and give him a little time out for a few minutes, just to dramatize in an action-oriented way that being noisy and naughty during prayer is not something we do in our house, because we respect God very much.

RANDY: You're totally correct in not trying to force Christopher to pray, Roberta. One thing you might suggest to him is "thinking prayers." Teach him that as he sees things that he's thankful for, he can just think to himself: *Thank You, God, for the clothes I wear. Thank You, God, for the sunny day . . . for the pretty flowers . . . for Mommy and Daddy.* Help him understand that praying can be done without talking out loud.

SALLY: And I like what you said about Christopher growing into wanting to pray aloud. Let him know that he may not want to pray aloud right now, but he probably will someday—and that's fine with you and with God.

KEVIN: That's a great point, Sally. Giving a kid permission to be himself is always a healthy approach.

RANDY: Thanks, Sally, for joining us to share so many great ideas for making God real to our kids. Do you have any final thoughts?

SALLY: First, I hope parents with busy schedules won't get discouraged and think they don't have time to use ideas like those we've talked about. Everything we've discussed is things you can do as part of a daily routine. Second, I want to caution parents that we're not suggesting that they bombard their kids with God all day long either. Instead, look for those teachable moments. I am convinced that if parents will pray for guidance, the Holy Spirit will make those moments happen.

CHAPTER 4

■●▲■●▲

YES, I HAVE TODDLERS, BUT WHEN DO I FIND TIME FOR ME?

RANDY: Ah, yes, the frustrations of being a parent of the toddler or, even more frustrating, two or three toddlers at once. Donna and I still remember when we were on a trip with our two older children. Evan was four and a half and Andrea was about eighteen months. We both got the flu and wound up in a motel, so sick we could barely move, while the kids bounded around the room with limitless energy. I rolled over and said to Donna, "This is your responsibility." She just looked back and said, "Forget it. Just give them away. Give them to anybody. Get them out of my face." But there was nobody to give them to, so we had to tough it out.

KEVIN: At times like that, my best option has always been trying to find someone who will take my kids on a short-term lease. Failing that, the next best choice is to box them up and ship them home Parcel Post.

RANDY: We all know you're kidding, Kevin, at least we *hope* you're kidding. But it's true for parents of toddlers—particularly the moms—there are no time-outs. The clock is always running, and so are they . . .

As a mother of toddlers, how do I find any time for myself?

LORAINE: I have three children, five, three and a half, and eighteen months. I quit my part-time job just before our third child arrived, but I am still busy every minute. I am beginning to resent having no time for myself. Do you have any ideas?

KEVIN: You could have a nervous breakdown . . .

LORAINE: I've come close more than once. Ironically, my worst frustrations occur on Sunday morning—the so-called day of rest. My husband is an elder and he has to leave for church early. So, I wind up feeling like a single parent. As each child came along, I would wake up thirty minutes earlier to get everyone dressed and to church on time. Eventually, I was getting up ninety minutes earlier than I ever did when I only had to get myself ready for church.

RANDY: What was it like getting everyone transported?

LORAINE: I would sometimes feel like such an incompetent, struggling up the sidewalk from the parking lot with two of my kids grabbing my skirt while I'm trying to balance the baby, my Bible, and the diaper bag. I must confess, I would usually arrive in anything but an attitude of worship. Having toddlers pushes you to spiritual and emotional limits that you wouldn't normally find in a relationship with an adult. But, as I said, I am reaching the end of my tether. What can I do?

KEVIN: First, you mentioned that you quit your part-time job. That's good. It's better to get along on one paycheck than have Mom working. But you say that the three kids are consuming you, and you have no time at all for yourself. That's bad. What you must do is figure out some ways to make time for yourself.

LORAINE: But my family needs me; there is always something to be done . . . always somebody who needs this or that.

KEVIN: It sounds to me, Loraine, as if you are a classic pleaser, which is so true of many moms. You want to make life smooth for everyone else. You put everyone else first and yourself last. Am I right?

LORAINE: I'm afraid you are, but what can I do? I can't send the kids back and, as one of you said, there are no time-outs. I'm stuck!

KEVIN: No, you aren't. Your first step is to start putting yourself first—at least a little bit. Find something you really like to do, anything from a class you've wanted to take, to joining the garden club. Schedule something just for yourself, two or three times a week if possible, and then figure out a way to have the children cared for while you do your thing. If it's during the day, hire a sitter, or perhaps you can trade with a neighbor. Let her sit for you while you do your things, and then you can sit for her while she goes out. The point is, you need that time away from your kids. Taking that time will not be selfish; it will be one of the wisest things you can do.

RANDY: Why not get your husband involved? Maybe there is something you can schedule in the evenings. Sit down with your husband and tell him how serious the situation is. Then, leave him alone with the kids. They'll all survive for a few hours, and he'll learn something about what it's like to be in the toddler trenches.

KEVIN: I talked with one mom who decided that she'd do her grocery shopping at night. It was impossible to try to take the three kids along during the day anyway, so she got them all to bed and left her husband in charge while she went out at 10:00 P.M. to go shopping. It was a great time for her to relax. And she met a lot of other tired looking young moms who were pushing their carts up and down the aisle with smiles on their faces. Her only problem was that she found herself spending too much time at the magazine counter because it was so tempting to thumb through all the major women's magazines and read articles about the "outside world" of adults and adult concerns.

I told her it was okay to sneak a look at magazines at the supermarket, but why not just keep a magazine or newspaper handy to read while you're having a cup of coffee, eating lunch, waiting for a doctor's appointment, sitting at the park while the children play, or stirring something on the stove for dinner? A few minutes here and there of adult reading can briefly take a mother out of her children's world and give her a lift to get through the next hour or two of ankle-biter attacks.

RANDY: Another thing you might look into, Loraine, is finding a "Mom's Day Out" program, which is often offered at church. If your church doesn't do it, perhaps you can find one nearby that does. The plan is simple. You bring your kids to the church nursery or preschool area and qualified people care for your children for a reasonable fee while you spend the morning or most of the day shopping or doing what you like.

Also, keep your eye on the church schedule, and the next time there's a women's retreat, be sure you sign up and arrange for your husband or maybe the children's grandparents to take care of the kids for the weekend. It's amazing what thirty-six to forty-eight hours of strictly adult conversation can do to lift your spirits. The only problem is, you probably won't get much sleep the whole weekend because you'll be up all night talking!

KEVIN: Those are just a few ideas, Loraine, for how you can find time for yourself. But I want to reemphasize that your real problem isn't *finding* time for yourself, it's *taking* time. Until you decide that you're worth it and that you've got to put yourself first now and then to simply recharge your batteries, you'll continue to run down and burn out.

□ ○ △ □ ○ △

How can I give my toddlers adequate one-on-one attention when they all want me at once?

ANITA: I have a son who is three and a half, my daughter just turned two on Tuesday, and I also have a seven-month-old boy. Obviously, the baby gets more time alone with me than anyone because I nurse him, and he just needs more care, in general. The two older ones get less of me, but if I do get a minute to spend time with one, the other one wants attention, too.

KEVIN: Kids are like piranha, they seem to smell it when Mom is paying attention to something or someone else and they attack.

RANDY: Donna often said that our kids would wait until she got on the telephone, and then they'd attack. Do you find that happening, too, Anita?

ANITA: Most definitely. The only good thing about that is that they make me keep my telephone calls short—*very* short.

KEVIN: We had a mom call the other day who had a different idea of how to spend one-on-one time with her kids, even when they were all together. Apparently they do a lot of wrestling—just having fun rolling around on the rug. And while they're playing their little games, this mom would focus on one child for awhile, and just talk to her as they roughhoused, or hugged, or whatever. The other two would be there, but her focus would be on one child only, if only for a minute or two. That made that child feel important and special. Then she could switch to another child.

RANDY: I remember that call and I admired that mom for her ingenuity, but I still think that you should try to figure out some ways, Anita, to get child care for two of the children while you do something special with one child—if only for an hour or so.

You can also try putting your two year old down for her nap an hour or half an hour before the three and a half year old, and then take that extra time with the older child. Then, the two year old will probably wake up first from her nap, and there will be some time to spend with her.

You can do the same thing at bedtime. Have your husband play or read with one child, while you play or read with the other one, after you've put the baby to bed. If you schedule this even a couple of times a week it would be special for your older kids.

KEVIN: Something else that ties in with the wrestling idea is to have two different toys for your older children to play with: a set of blocks for the little one, and maybe some Legos for the older one. Sit on the floor between the two kids, and help them as they need it. Talk with the children separately to encourage them with their building and "figuring out" accomplishments.

Do you have any tips to help me get away from my toddlers to have quiet time?

ANITA: You've given me some great ideas, but I have one other problem. One of my biggest frustrations is trying to get a quiet time every morning. I feel to be a good parent, I need God's perspective for the day. But getting the kids to leave me alone long enough to read my Bible and pray for even a few minutes is really hard.

RANDY: We hear the same complaint from many moms. When kids arrive, the word "quiet" doesn't seem to work into their lives much at all.

ANITA: It can be maddening, but it can also be funny at times. The other morning I was trying to have my quiet time and out of the corner of my eye I saw Timmy, my three year old, come into the room. I decided to pretend I was praying so I closed my eyes and naively hoped he'd go away. In a few seconds, I sensed he was right in front of my face, but I kept my eyes shut and continued to act as if I were praying. Then he gently started to rub my legs and I thought, *Oh, no Lord, you know I love my son, but I would like to spend a few moments with you.* I was just starting to feel really guilty about not picking him up to cuddle him or something when he said, "Oh, oh, Mommy, it's time to shave!" That blew my quiet time completely.

RANDY: Perhaps the best way to look at that one is to believe that God wanted you to concentrate on Timmy at that moment.

KEVIN: Toddlers really know how to keep us humble and reminded of what's most important—them! But quiet time with the Lord is important, too, and I think you can adapt some of the ideas we've already shared with how to get one-on-one time with your kids. If you're lucky, you should be able to get all three of them down for a nap in the afternoon, and maybe you can grab a few minutes then. Or, maybe you can put the baby to bed after dinner and you can have your husband do something with the two older children--give them both baths, or whatever. Then you can take a few moments to read the Bible and share with the Lord about your day.

ANITA: I suppose those are possibilities. I really like to have my quiet time in the morning, though.

RANDY: I understand that. So do I. It seems to me, Anita, that your best bet would be to just get up a little earlier and have your quiet time before the children are awake. I know that some days that may not work, but you just have to be patient and grab your quiet moments when you can. One other thought, the Bible says we should pray without ceasing, and you can pray briefly to the

Lord at different times as you go through your day with the children. It's not quite the same as quiet time, but it can give you a real lift.

□ ○ △ □ ○ △

What can husbands do to help their wives with the kids?

WALTER: We also have two toddlers at our house, four-and-a-half and two-and-a-half, as well as a baby who is six months old. I guess I'm calling on behalf of fathers of small children everywhere to see if you have any suggestions for how we dads might really move in and help our wives with the children. I mean something besides simply baby-sitting now and then while they sneak to the grocery store in the middle of the night.

KEVIN: Walter, are you for real, or are you a plant hired by some moms who listen regularly to "Parent Talk"?

WALTER: I'm no plant, and I really would like some ideas on how to get my wife to take more time off—she's a pleaser deluxe. And I'm sure there are other dads out there who would like to get more involved, too.

RANDY: Walter, you have just caused a major traffic jam on the "Parent Talk" control board. We're going to get these moms on as quickly as we can, so here we go . . .

TRUDIE: My husband came home from work last Friday after I had had a very hard week with our two little ones—and I work part-time, too. He said to me, "Honey, how would you like the day off tomorrow?" And so he took the kids away for the *entire* Saturday. I spent the day planting rose bushes. It was just me, all alone in my backyard, down in the dirt, on a nice warm sunny day. It was so peaceful, even the neighbor's dogs were quiet for a change. The whole day was a time of spiritual refreshment—just having those extended hours alone. It helped me reflect on myself and my family, and how blessed I am in so many ways.

□ ○ △ □ ○ △

PAT: A couple of years ago after the birth of our third child–we now have three all under the age of six—my husband started making breakfast every morning so I could have a quiet time. That was really a gift to me because it gave me some precious minutes for prayer and spiritual input.

□ ○ △ □ ○ △

EVELYN: I think it's the hardest thing in the world to have toddlers. We have four kids in all and three are in the toddler stage. It's easy to start feeling that you're alone in the midst of it. My husband doesn't do anything major, but all the little things he does and says make all the difference in the world.

KEVIN: What are these "little things" that he does and says?

EVELYN: I'll get up in the morning and be thinking, *I wonder what today will be like.* There on the kitchen counter I will find a wonderful note that he wrote before leaving for work, telling me what a wonderful wife and mother I am. And sometimes he'll call me during the day just to check in and see how it's going.

KEVIN: Verbal support is great. Most husbands need to do more of it, but does your man actually help you with the physical work?

EVELYN: Oh, yes, his specialty is giving baths and reading to the kids before bed. We work as a team every night to get the kids down and asleep. But just knowing that he really cares about what I'm going through is what keeps me going day in and day out. I know I've got him behind me and I'm not alone in this. I always tell him, "Honey, I can handle anything as long as you support me."

□ ○ △ □ ○ △

VICKY: Our kids love to run errands with Daddy. Usually he'll take one of our three children on a special errand—to the store, or on a trip to the dumpsters, or whatever. On the way back they'll stop for a soda or an ice cream cone, and it's a big deal. He usually does this with a different child each week on his day off. Just having him take one child away when you're used to having three coming at you makes a tremendous difference. And, sometimes he'll even take two along, and that's just about heaven! I usually get two or three hours to do something that I never have time to do otherwise.

RANDY: Well, there you go, Walter. I hope you and other dads out there were taking notes. It's not hard to see that the very bottom line with most of these ideas is "taking time." Raising kids is a very time-consuming task. And what so many dads of the '90s are discovering is that it's a much easier task when parents do it together.

□ ○ △ □ ○ △

With two small children, how do my husband and I find any time for ourselves?

PAMELA: We have two kids, three and a half and six months old. Do you have any practical tips for parents of more than one small child on finding time for each other in their marriage?

RANDY: Get out your date book—the same one in which you schedule birthdays, anniversaries, weddings, holidays, etc.—and just block out time for yourselves. With all you have going, it is so easy to shove your marriage off into a corner. You're not going to *find* time for each other, you will have to *make* it. Sit down with your husband and your date book or calendar for the next month and find at least one afternoon or evening, or even one hour, where you can get together on a date. Get it down in the date book and have it planned in advance. Then don't let anything except a real emergency prevent you from keeping that date.

KEVIN: National statistics show that the typical marriage lasts seven years and produces 1.9 children. One of the reasons marriages don't last is that couples get caught in the tyranny of the urgent and forget what is really important. I know your little ankle biters are the most precious things in the world to you, but I am saying without apology that your marriage is even more important than they are.

The tyranny of the urgent won't let you believe that, of course, because, after all, you have to take care of this, you have to take care of that, and you wind up not taking time to protect and strengthen your marriage.

RANDY: One thing you might think about is being sure you get the kids to bed early, and then taking some time to sit down and talk, just wind down, and share the day. You could start with something that simple, enjoying a few moments of adult conversation and intimacy.

PAMELA: It has been a real shocker having these kids. We were married about six years before we had our first, and we were used to having all kinds of time together. Now we spend all our time raising children.

KEVIN: Chinchillas are much easier to raise. Tell me, have you ever kidnapped your husband from work?

PAMELA: No, I haven't tried that. How does it work?

KEVIN: Find a baby-sitter, a care giver you can trust with your little ones. Then figure out all the other details, pick your husband up after work, and take him away overnight. You probably have some favorite places in mind where you went those first six years before the ankle biter earthquake hit. You can spend a few extra bucks on this, or you can go the budget route. The amount of money isn't as important as doing something fun together. Whatever you do, it's an investment of your time. It will take time to arrange all this, but it's the kind of thing that will say to your husband, "I really love you and I care about our marriage. I want us to be first."

Because so many moms are pleaser types, they wind up running all day and part of the night to "do it all and have it all." Many of them wind up in my office in a state that I call "bonkers." Kids are important, but, as I said to one of our callers, parents are even more important. If parents don't take care of themselves and their marriage, they won't be able to give proper guidance and care to their children. So that one word, Randy, is simple. I like to put it this way: *Prioritize your priorities.*

CHAPTER 5

■●▲■●▲

HOW TO WIN THOSE BATTLES AT BEDTIME

RANDY: Ah, Kevin, darkness has fallen softly on the Tucson desert. Little baby Lauren was lullabied into dream land several hours ago and now you and Sande are just dropping off yourselves. Suddenly her shrill cry pierces the night!

KEVIN: Whose . . . Sande's?

RANDY: No, no, Lauren's, of course, and "Parent Talk" listeners everywhere want to know, what will happen next?

KEVIN: As you well know, Randy, the only words a wife wants to hear from her husband when wee baby wakes in the middle of the night are, "I'll get up."

RANDY: And does Sande hear those words?

KEVIN: Since we've had Lauren, very seldom.

RANDY: Very seldom? Why?

KEVIN: Because Lauren seldom wakes up. She is a very good sleeper—goes to sleep around 7:00 P.M. and wakes up about 7:00 the next morning. She's a twelve-hour sleeper, which is our kind of kid—what we call "non-returnable."

RANDY: Touché, Dr. Leman. Obviously, I'm wrong about shrill cries in the night at your house, but that doesn't mean it doesn't happen in a lot of homes across the land. Today we're going to talk about getting the kids to bed, keeping the kids in bed, and hoping that eventually they fall asleep and stay that way. It all adds up to bedtime battles, not only with little ones, but with three year olds, five year olds, and even eight to ten year olds. Some kids just don't want to go to bed, period. Others start off in their own beds but wind up in Mom and Dad's bed very quickly for any number of reasons. Bedtime can truly be a battleground in many homes.

KEVIN: Remind me a little later, Randy, to talk about milk cartons. Just make a mental note, "Kevin wants to talk about milk cartons." They have something to do with bedtime battles.

RANDY: Will do, but right now I want to share some conversations our producer had with some youngsters to get their perspective on bedtime. This is how it went with a five year old:

> Kay: Allison, tell me about bedtime. Do you like to have to go to bed at night?

Allison: No, I don't.

Kay: Why not?

Allison: Because I just don't like it.

Kay: Just what don't you like about it?

Allison: What I don't like about it is that I have to go to sleep, and I can't go to sleep right when I get to bed. I like to watch TV and stay up. I wish we didn't hardly have nighttime. That's what I wish.

Kay: If you could be a mommy or a daddy, what would you tell your kids about having to go to bed?

Allison: I would say, "We're not going to go to sleep—ever!"

RANDY: Well, there you have the child's perspective. Some parents have children who say, "I am not going to sleep—*ever*!" That brings us to our first question, the most obvious and frequent question we get about bedtime battles . . .

How do I get my child to go to bed and stay asleep?

BRENDA: Our three year old is just like Allison. He's an only child and we have great difficulty getting him to stay in bed and go to sleep. We have tried everything . . .

RANDY: What have you tried?

BRENDA: I have tried . . .

KEVIN: . . . chloroform? Sorry, just thinking out loud.

BRENDA: This has been going on since he was two and we took him out of his crib and put him in a bed. I have tried what Dr. Dobson recommends—as soon as his foot hits the floor, one of us gets up and puts him right back in his bed. We have done this for up to two hours with no success. We have spanked him. We have put a gate up to try to keep him in his room, but he climbed over it and came downstairs.

KEVIN: Sounds like the kid may be a future pole vaulter.

BRENDA: He just looks at us and says, "I don't want to go to sleep," or, "I am not tired," or "I want something to drink," or "I am scared."

KEVIN: Sounds as if he's covering all the bases.

BRENDA: When he says he's scared, we ask him, "Are you really scared?" And then he starts smiling and laughing. I could see that this battle was turning into a power struggle, particularly between him and me because we are both very strong-willed. I decided to cut out his afternoon nap so he'd be really sleepy when it was time to go to bed. That worked for a few days, but after that he became a disaster in the late afternoon.

KEVIN: Three year olds need naps. And so do moms of three year olds.

BRENDA: Right, but now I seldom get him to take a nap. If he does take one, it takes me an hour and a half to get him to lie down.

RANDY: To get Mom involved for an hour and a half as he gets ready for a nap is a lot of fun for a child. So what can Mom do? How can she get him ready for bed or for that nap during the day? Can she win that battle that she knows is almost certain to come? Kevin, what are some techniques she can use?

KEVIN: Well, Randy, with naps or with going to bed at night, I think the techniques are a great deal the same. Again, I'm very biased about three-year-old children needing naps. When a kid moves into his fourth year, maybe you can convince me that he can get by without a nap once in a while, but most kids three and four years of age need naps. The secret is to do things as quickly and as efficiently as possible. I like having a tape recorder in the room. There are so many tapes with good wholesome music, or stories that kids can listen to, which help them wind down and get sleepy. So, when you put them in bed for nap time or bedtime, have some routine that includes playing music or a story.

BRENDA: What happens when he starts telling me he needs a drink, or that he's just not tired?

KEVIN: When your child starts in with that kind of stuff, he's just being powerful with you. Don't get sucked into his games. Remove your sails from his wind. Tell him, "Honey, just close your eyes and listen to your story (or your music) and you'll be asleep in no time." Then quietly tiptoe out of the room and leave him alone.

BRENDA: But what if he gets out of bed and follows me?

KEVIN: Obedience should be taught early in life. It's important for your child to learn that when you tell him something, you really mean it. If you put the child to bed and he gets up and follows you out of the room, he makes sure that he sees your displeasure. Put him back into his bed, and this time, don't do as much gentle tucking in or giving lots of kisses. Be sure the second tuck-in is not as much fun as the first one, so the child can easily see the difference. And then, point your finger at him, if you wish, and firmly tell him that he is to stay in bed. Then leave. If the child persists on willfully defying you by getting out of bed again, it's time for a swat. Then give him a love, put him back in bed, and tell him firmly to stay there. If he still won't stay in bed, resort to holding the door shut for as long as necessary to discourage him. It might mean that he'll wind up curled on his blankey on the other side of the door, fast asleep. That's okay. The point is not to start habits that kids will just continue. If you make up your mind early that you're going to stop this behavior now, you can do it if you stick to your guns and persist for a few nights.

□ ○ △ □ ○ △

What if our child wants to come into bed with us at night?

LINDA: Our three year old sometimes tries to come into bed with us because he says he's "scared." Is he pulling our chain, or is it ever okay to let your child come into bed with you?

RANDY: A child's nighttime fears can be very real. We've already heard our producer interview Allison, age five. Now let's listen in as she talks with Adam, age four, and he tells us why he wants to get in Mom's bed.

> KAY: Adam, what happens in the middle of the night when you can't get to sleep?
>
> ADAM: I come in my mom's bed.
>
> KAY: You do? You come into Mom's bed and what do you do?
>
> ADAM: Nothing. I just lay there.
>
> KAY: What is scary about going to sleep sometimes?
>
> ADAM: Dreams.
>
> KAY: Dreams? Dreams are scary. Tell me about some of your scary dreams.

ADAM: Some are about ghosts.

KAY: Some are about ghosts? What do you do when you have a scary dream?

ADAM: I go in my mom's bed.

KAY: How does that help?

ADAM: It helps the dream go away.

RANDY: And it does. It surely does.

KEVIN: The little Adams of this world always know where to go for comfort—to Mommy's and Daddy's bed. And that reminds me, Randy, I wanted to talk about milk cartons. Can you tell me why?

RANDY: You may be thinking of a milk carton sitting on the breakfast table and on the back is a picture of a missing child.

KEVIN: That's it, Randy. Children see these milk cartons and many of them know what the pictures mean. Or maybe their older brothers or sisters tell them what they mean. A lot of little kids have real fears about someone smashing their windows at night and stealing them away.

RANDY: Do you have any memories of when you were a kid and had fears like that?

KEVIN: Just the other day I talked with Sande about an early childhood memory that I hadn't thought about in years. I was about five and my parents were out for the evening and the baby sitter had put me to bed. I remember lying in bed and just pleading, "Mommy and Daddy, please come home." I just had a terrible feeling of separation from my parents.

RANDY: And in that case they weren't even there for you to run to for comfort. You know some kids want to be comforted so badly they will manipulate their parents. They'll use any kind of excuse to get into your room, get into your bed, and take control. It's hard for many parents to know how to deal with that.

KEVIN: Sometimes you wake up with the kid breathing on you. You just feel this presence and it can be startling when the room is pitch black. Then you realize it is your kid and he tells you he is sick. And guess what? *He really is!*—all over everything!

RANDY: One of our kids did that once. Over the years, I've tried to forget which one, because I had murderous thoughts at the time.

KEVIN: As I recall, it happened to us at least twice, but being sick isn't the usual reason kids want to come in bed with you. First of all, I would point out that getting in bed with Mom and Dad is not even a misdemeanor in most states. Secondly, in a king-sized bed there is plenty of room for Mom, Dad, and a four year old. If the four year old *occasionally* sneaks into your bed, I would let it go and not make a big thing out of it.

RANDY: I agree, because that's probably just a passing phase, but what if a child is in the habit of getting into bed with Mom and Dad almost every night and it continues?

KEVIN: That is not healthy. Then you may have to lock your door and stick to your guns when your little guy starts to wail and holler. There will be a few hectic nights, but after a while the child will learn that it is much more comfortable to remain in his bed than to lie on the floor in front of your door.

□ ○ △ □ ○ △

What if two young children have to sleep together in the same room, and the older one wants to come in with Mom and Dad?

GLORIA: We've tried to use Reality Discipline with our son, age four, to keep him from coming in bed with us, but when he starts wailing outside our locked door, he wakes up his baby sister, who is only ten months. What can we do?

KEVIN: Can the ten month old stay in your room?

GLORIA: We had her in our room for a while, but our four year old still came in through the night. So we took the ten month old out of our room and put her in with her brother, which we much prefer. I don't really want to put her back in our room if I can help it.

KEVIN: With a two-bedroom house you definitely have a problem, but I still think you have to lock the door on your four year old.

GLORIA: But what if he is truly scared?

KEVIN: Most parents, especially moms, can tell when a child is really scared or when he's being manipulative. That's a judgment call on your part, but your best bet is to keep the door locked and let him wail for a few nights. That should be all that it will take to get the message across that he has to sleep in his own bed.

RANDY: Another key is that you could break the cycle by bringing the ten month old back into your room for a week as a way of saying to the four year old, "Until you are willing to stay in your own bed through the night, we are bringing your little sister in with us and we are going to lock the door." I know there are moms out there saying that sounds cruel, but remember your goal —to hold your child responsible for his own sleeping habits.

KEVIN: Randy, you just gave some wonderful advice. Reality Discipline is never cruel, but sometimes it's difficult to administer. It's my guess that the four year old will get the point after only a few nights, and I hope Gloria will give this plan a shot.

GLORIA: Thanks, for a week I'll try it.

□ ○ △ □ ○ △

If your child is scared and wants to lie on the floor next to your bed, is this okay?

VALERIE: In the last few weeks, our three-and-a-half-year-old daughter has started saying she's afraid to sleep in her own bed. We let her know that we didn't want her to get in bed with us, so she began slipping into the room and lying on the pillow shams that we toss over on the floor at night. She crawls up on the pillow shams with her little blanket and sleeps there.

RANDY: I think almost any parent who ever had a three and a half year old can identify with this. All of our kids at one time or another have slept on the floor, at the end of our bed, or on the floor in their brother or sister's room. After our kids would fall asleep, we would usually pick them up and take them back to their room. We have decided that the less we make of it, the better off we all will be. If your little girl is genuinely fearful, let her come in for a couple of nights. You can let her go to sleep on the floor in a sleeping bag, or on something like your pillow shams.

KEVIN: What is fun for kids is to have a sleeping bag right next to your bed. When they get scared with a bad dream or something like that, they can come in, pull out the sleeping bag, and curl up on the floor next to your bed. But I really would encourage you not to get your three and a half year old in the habit of climbing in bed with you. And, be sure your child understands that the sleeping bag is strictly for "emergencies" when she has a bad dream and is truly scared. She can't come in and use the sleeping bag anytime she wants.

RANDY: Valerie, the key is that this is a phase that your daughter is going through, and it should stop after a few days or weeks. If she's always saying she's scared, you need to talk to her about her fears. Our kids told us they were scared and we found that just leaving a light on in the hall stopped some of their problems. If you leave a night light on in their rooms, that might also take care of it. Do they want the door open? Do they want the door closed? I think finding out what it is that's bothering them and trying to adjust the environment for them is a good approach.

□ ○ △ □ ○ △

How can I get a totally defiant three year old to stay down for his nap or to stay in bed at night?

REBECCA: My three-year-old son is a powerful little guy who just doesn't want to go to bed. He is a night owl, and this has got to be biological. He prefers to go to bed at 11:00, but I put him down at 8:00, at least somewhere between 8:00 and 9:00. I have had nights when he will go to bed at 8:30 and lie awake until 10:00 or 10:30 at night. He gets up around 8:00 in the morning. We try to be as consistent with him as we can.

RANDY: Take us through your nap or bedtime routine. What do you do?

REBECCA: We have a very firm routine. It is usually lots of fun. Sometime there's a short video, under thirty minutes, or we'll read him a story because he always needs his story. We have a nap time or bedtime prayer, which he always reminds us to do if we forget. Then we put him to bed.

RANDY: And with all of that he still won't lie down and try to go to sleep?

REBECCA: He's a very intelligent child—he began talking at about a year and now he is getting really mouthy. Yesterday at nap time and last night at bedtime he sat up in bed, crossed his arms, and said, "I am not going to lie down." Today he sat on the couch and said, "I am not going to get off this couch and you won't come over here and carry me to bed."

KEVIN: With a three year old, Rebecca, you need action, not words. You don't explain things to him, you just pick him up and put him in his bed. This could mean that he'll forego his story time—maybe even his prayer.

REBECCA: That's what happened today. He didn't get his story, but he did get his prayer, and I had to actually put him in there screaming and shut his door.

KEVIN: That is all right—that won't kill him.

RANDY: Rebecca, I think you need to look at yourself and ask the question, "How involved do I want to be in the nap time and bedtime of my child?" You understand that bedtime and nap time are important, so the real question is what strategy you can develop to get your child into bed and then stay out of his way and don't get overly involved in his life.

KEVIN: I just want to add that the words we choose to use with three year olds are really important. When a child says, "I am not going to go to sleep," you can say, "Honey, you don't have to go to sleep but you are going to stay in this room and in this bed."

RANDY: I recall one mom who told her child he didn't have to take a nap but that it was just "rest time." He was a big boy and, "Big boys rest, they do not nap."

REBECCA: I tell him that all the time. I say, "I have put you down at 1:30 and you will get up at 3:30. What you do between now and then is up to you."

RANDY: That's good. Your job isn't to force your son to take a nap. You can't force anyone to go to sleep. But you can set the boundaries, and you're doing that. This is a difficult time—a phase that will pass. But you're building a foundation that tells the child he isn't going to win. If you let him win at three and a half, you are going to lose, but when he's thirteen, you will really lose. So stay out of the power struggle. Keep your sails out of his wind, and you'll be okay.

Oh yes, Rebecca, there is one more thing. When our children started arriving, my own mom and dad used to tell me, "Bedtime with those little ones will pass very quickly, so enjoy it." During some of the bedtime battles, I doubted those words, but now I can see that they are very true.

KEVIN: That's one of the biggest blessings in having a couple of bonus babies after you think you've raised your family. I'm glad God gave us little Hannah. Otherwise, I would have missed having her just take my hand, look up at me, and say, "Tired now."

CHAPTER 6

■●▲■●▲

CAN THERE BE JOY IN POTTY TRAINING?

RANDY: Because we like spontaneity on "Parent Talk," I never let Kevin Leman know what my lead question will be. So, Dr. Leman, is it better to potty train your children in the summertime or the wintertime?

KEVIN: I haven't the foggiest idea!

RANDY: Summertime! Can you imagine the kids all bundled up with all of their winter clothes on and suddenly there is an accident and they have to take them all off? It's easier in the summertime—less clothes. I'm a dad and even I know this.

KEVIN: Hannah, our fourth born, never even had a potty chair—did you know that?

RANDY: How did you do that?

KEVIN: I don't know. We were tired by then. We just pointed her toward the bathroom and said, "Hey, kid, go find the potty yourself!"

RANDY: "Parent Talk" is practical, and nothing is more practical than potty training. We decided that a lot of young moms could profit from the wisdom of those who have been through it, so at practically no expense, we have brought in two mothers who have, within the last year, been through the joys of potty training with their oldest children. Andrea and Susie are with us in the studio and I want to ask Susie how it went for her.

SUSIE: Well, it all started when someone recommended "the book" on how to potty train your child in practically no time at all. I got a copy, read it through, and tried to put it into practice.

RANDY: What did this book tell you to do?

SUSIE: I got all these salty treats and all these drinks that were supposed to fill the child's bladder—I went the whole route.

RANDY: And what happened?

SUSIE: After three days, she had never used the potty, and on the third night she woke up screaming, "Mommy, Mommy, potty chair!" It didn't work. My reaction was, "This is it! Forget it! Put it away!"

RANDY: What was your experience, Andrea?

ANDREA: Well, I decided to do the same thing with the same book. We didn't last anywhere near three days before we had to, if you'll pardon the expression, "Flush the whole idea." In fact, we lasted about four to five hours. My poor little Bobby had his tummy so bloated with snacks and drinks that he was just crying in pain. I told him, "Honey, I'm so sorry I did this to you."

KEVIN: I bet I know the book you used. It's full of bad ideas. Randy, have you gone potty today?

RANDY: Have I gone *what!?* Our listeners will have to excuse my colleague. Sometimes it's hard to tell where he's headed.

KEVIN: C'mon, lighten up. I've got a point to make. I just want to know if you've gone potty today.

RANDY: As a matter of fact, I have.

KEVIN: Did Donna give you one of those nice, round, tasty M&M's for doing it?

RANDY: I will not answer on the grounds that I might dignify the question.

KEVIN: Well, to make my point, the obvious answer is no, adults don't get rewarded for performing a natural function and neither should children. But when a supposed expert says you can potty train your kid in practically no time by telling him, "Here, go potty, and I'll give you a treat," the mother is going to be tempted to take the easy route to get the job done and forget something very important about potty training called *readiness.*

My general advice is to buy the little plastic K-Mart potty. Put it on the floor of the bathroom and don't say a word. Let your child discover it. In other words, go slow and easy. To schedule it —as if it's going to be done today—is really sort of funny, and sad at the same time.

What is the best age to potty train my child?

RANDY: From the standpoint of readiness, the usual age for potty training is the mid-two's. Children are generally not prepared until they're right around two and a half because they just aren't able to control that function in their body before that time. There are some moms listening, Kevin, who attempted to potty train their children much earlier and found that they had dismal success because their kids just weren't ready.

SUSIE: Right. Melissa looked as if she was ready. She was showing all the signs, but the first time we tried it, we quickly discovered she wasn't ready at all.

RANDY: I noticed you said "we," Susie, which means your husband was involved too. Kevin, what do you think? Is it unusual for a dad to get involved in potty training the kids? Where are the dads in all of this?

KEVIN: Oh, the dads are usually as far away as they can be. In my case, I was ordered out of the house when Sande wanted to potty train our firstborn. On the other hand, my brother trained his little son how to go potty outside. They live out in a very wooded area, and they have a few farm animals as pets and all that. So my brother—who is also a psychologist, by the way—taught his son how to go potty outside. Well, that was great until the boy's mother took him to the mall and lost sight of him for a moment or two. When she turned around, there he was, watering the potted plants! I think I see our board lighting up. Somebody wants to join our potty training discussion . . .

Is summer really a better time than winter for potty training?

RUTH: About the summer or winter question—I prefer to potty train my kids in the winter because where we are it gets so cold the kids don't go outside very much. In the summer, they get so excited about playing, or whatever, that they don't want to come back in to go potty and so they go—well, you know what they do. So it was easier for me to potty train in the winter.

RANDY: How long did it take you to train your children?

RUTH: About two weeks.

RANDY: Now did you just set a date and say, "This is the day I'm going to start potty training"?

RUTH: Yes, kind of, because my schedule was crazy at the time and I needed to block out two weeks where I could stay home and devote my time to potty training my child. It's very difficult if you have to be running in and out.

KEVIN: Did you tell your husband this was going to be your project or was he part of it as well?

RUTH: Oh, I tried to get him involved, but he wasn't a whole lot of help except teaching our son how to go potty outside.

KEVIN: Whoops . . . sorry I brought it up.

RANDY: Going outside seems to be a real male bonding thing, Kevin.

KEVIN: I guess it is. Little boys are different from little girls.

RANDY: Ruth, thanks for your call, even if you did shoot me down after I thought I had all the answers on summer versus winter. It just shows that on some things, there are no right answers, only answers that work for parents. So we'll give in on that one . . .

□ ○ △ □ ○ △

What's the best way to make the break and take my child completely out of diapers?

BETTY: I've gotten our two and a half year old to use the potty pretty regularly during the day, but I'm a little afraid of trusting him through the night, so he still wears diapers. How can I get him totally trained and into "big boy" pants?

ANDREA: You know, with our little guy, I just decided to take it as it came, and when I felt he was at the point where he had really mastered it, I said, "Bobby, this is the day that you will not wear diapers anymore." He said, "Okay, Mommy." I had given up bribing him with treats, and instead I really used a lot of praise as his reward. I made a big issue out of what a big boy he was and how proud I was. So that day he started wearing his underwear, and then that night I still wasn't sure he was ready to be out of a diaper, but he said, "Mommy, I don't want to wear a diaper, I'm a big boy." And from that first night, he wore "big boy" pants and he's done beautifully.

RANDY: You mean he has never had an accident?

ANDREA: Oh, he's had an occasional problem, but that's to be expected. My point is, I waited until I knew Bobby was really ready because I had taken a lot of time with him, and I didn't insist that he learn to be potty trained in just a few days, or even in two weeks. If you're a little nervous, Betty, about putting your two and a half year old directly into "big boy" underwear, you could use training pants for a while. In fact, these days you can even find "training diapers" for sale. They're similar to diapers, only the child can take them off and pull them back up himself like training pants or underwear.

KEVIN: It's amazing how simple things can be sometimes. Sometimes a kid is really toilet trained, but at night he insists on having his diaper or his Pamper. I've often advised moms to tell their kids, "Honey, we don't have any more Pampers." And it almost always works in just one night, and that's it. What have you done when you felt your child was ready to be out of diapers at night?

SUSIE: We finally got wise to having Melissa insist on wearing a diaper at night. We pretty much did what you advised. We just told her, "Sorry, Honey, we've run out of diapers—no more diapers." And she accepted it pretty well. Once in a while she'd have an accident, but kids are smart. They know that when the diapers are gone, they're gone, and they're going to have to start using control.

□ ○ △ □ ○ △

How do I get my child to use the potty without constantly reminding her?

SHERI: We potty trained our two and a half year old daughter this past summer. It took a couple of months and then we thought we had arrived. Lately, she has stopped telling us when she has got to go, and we see her dancing up and down and we know it's time for her to get to the potty, but we're always having to tell her. How can we get her to realize it's her responsibility to get herself to the bathroom?

ANDREA: When you started training her, did you tell her that she was to tell you when she had to go, and then would you take her? Or did you teach her from the beginning that it was her responsibility to go and take care of it herself? How did you start out with her?

SHERI: I'm not sure I remember, but at the very beginning I think we told her to tell us when she had to go and then we would take her.

ANDREA: I just wonder if that might not be part of it. We went through that very kind of relapse with our little Benjamin, and then we finally decided to focus on the fact that he should be responsible for himself. We even trained him to take his little potty and dump it into the big potty and flush it. He had to do everything himself and be completely independent from us.

SHERI: When we got to the point where our daughter would dump it herself, I just stood there with my fingers crossed, hoping that she wouldn't spill it all over the bathroom.

ANDREA: I know how you feel . . . we have carpet in our bathroom!

RANDY: I was just wondering . . . how long did it take to potty train Kevin Leman?

KEVIN: A day. No problem. Mom just said, "Cubby, be toilet trained," and I was.

□ ○ △ □ ○ △

Do I need some special tips for potty training twins?

CANDY: I have three kids, a two and a half year old and two seven-month-old twin boys. My oldest child is fully potty trained, but I'm a little concerned about my twins. When it's time to train them, am I going to have extra problems with having two of them at the same time—what should I do?

KEVIN: You need two potties.

RANDY: When brilliant insights are needed, "Parent Talk" always comes through.

CANDY: I think I'm getting the message—just do what I did with my older boy, right?

KEVIN: Right, but seriously, two potties aren't necessarily a bad idea, particularly if each twin is ready for training about the same time. You might get different colors or label the two potties with decals so each child could have his own potty. The key is to take potty training in stride and make it fun and a game instead of a project and a problem.

Can a mother get too emotionally involved in her child's potty training?

CANDY: It's funny—I had been working with my two year old—just having the potty sitting out for several months, and he would go when he would go. Then my mother bought me that book you mentioned earlier and after reading it I thought I was doing it all wrong. I thought I was letting my kid be slow and retarded, and that he needed speeding up. By the third day of using the book, I was crying, and I told my mother, "Why did you buy that book for me? It doesn't work."

SUSIE: I know how you felt. After my first day of using that book, I was crying so much my little girl—the one I was trying to train—brought her blanket to comfort *me*. Now, who was the parent and who was the child that night?

RANDY: I think we're onto an important point here. Some parents can get into potty training and they have so much invested in getting their child potty trained quickly that they take it too personally if it just doesn't happen.

SUSIE: I took it way too personally. My pride was way up to here. By the second night, my husband was holding me in his arms and I was just sobbing, "Lord, forgive me for this. I'm really getting on this big pride trip." When I calmed down and was able to let my child learn to use the potty at her own speed, she did a lot better and so did I.

□ ○ △ □ ○ △

How do I handle my mother when she says, "Haven't you toilet trained that child yet?"

MAXINE: My child turned two recently and I'm getting a lot of pressure from my mother who assures me she potty trained me and my brother by age two. If I learned that fast, maybe my daughter could too. What do you think?

KEVIN: We often hear from young moms who are pressured into toilet training their kids early because of things that other people say—particularly the grandparents. One of the things we definitely know about toilet training is that when the kid is ready, he is ready, and not before. Don't be intimidated by your mother or anybody else.

RANDY: It's never good to bring any kind of competitive spirit to toilet training. I've even heard of parents buying potty chairs with little targets painted on the bottom, or floating little targets in the big toilets where little boys can try to "sink" them. I've heard stories about how some kids, in striving for a high score, will train themselves in two days. Occasionally, some of this behavioral psychology really works, but turning potty training into competition isn't a good idea as a rule.

ANDREA: I agree. Competition is one thing you can easily get sucked into as a new mom. You're sort of insecure about getting your child potty trained and you get competitive, especially when you hear about other people who have trained their child at twelve and fourteen months. Those kinds of kids are rare, or their parents have a different idea of what "being trained" really means. I think you just have to read your child's signals, and if the child isn't responding, stop right away. Don't push it for three days as I did and wind up with your child having nightmares.

□ ○ △ □ ○ △

If my child isn't potty trained by the time he's four, is something wrong?

FRANCES: My little boy turned four this past Christmas, and we still do not have him potty trained. We have him wear training pants, but he never tells us when he needs to go potty and he continues to have accidents.

RANDY: Is this your oldest child?

FRANCES: He is our only child.

RANDY: Have you had him checked for any medical problems?

FRANCES: We've seen an MD and a child development specialist. We were also referred to a lady who works with children who have "low sensitivity." She told us it didn't look as if there was anything she would be able to do.

RANDY: The statistics tell us that 20 percent of all children don't get potty trained until they are five years old. So, I don't think, Frances, this is something to overreact about. I know all this doesn't fit into your schedule, and it doesn't seem to fit what you've been told should happen by a certain age—usually two and a half or three—but if your son has been checked medically and there is nothing wrong, I'd try to just relax and accept it. If you don't, it could very easily become a power struggle and you will lose in the long run.

FRANCES: What we've done is put him back in diapers, but we've left his potty chair out, and he knows how to use it just in case he wants to start on his own. Every once in a while I test him, but he says, "Oh, no, I haven't gone at all this morning." It's noon and I can see his diaper is soaking, but I try not to make an issue of it and I just say, "Right, okay."

KEVIN: My only suggestion would be to stop asking him if he has to go potty. Put the responsibility for it clearly on his side of the court. Also, school will be starting for him soon, and his friends will make sure that he uses the potty. Kids have a way of doing that.

RANDY: Oh, the joys of potty training—that's the title of our show today, but sometimes it isn't too joyous when it seems to take forever. It's interesting how there's a whole vocabulary connected with this business of going potty, and, of course, there are some words we really can't use on the air . . .

KEVIN: Picture the scene: Two moms of toddlers are out to lunch and one of them says, "Excuse me, Helen, but I have to go potty." When you spend enough time with the little ankle biters, you start using their language!

□ ○ △ □ ○ △

When potty training really "gets serious," do I practically have to put my life on hold?

HEATHER: My little girl turned two a few months ago, and she's been using the potty chair off and on, but not consistently. What I want to know is, when do I get serious about it? Do I have to stay home for two weeks and not go anywhere else when we get "serious"?

RANDY: I'd like to ask our in-studio experts, Andrea and Susie, what they did. Tell me, did you just bite the bullet and stay home for a while?

SUSIE: When I "got serious," as Heather puts it, I stayed home with Melissa a couple of days, but I stayed real laid back about it. When she had to go, she went. Then after a couple of days, I started going out to the store with her, and if she had an accident, I didn't make a big deal out of it and get all upset. I would just take her wet pants off and put on some dry ones. I think my big salvation was not getting into a big stew over the accidents—not getting all worked up when we had a "failure."

ANDREA: When I "got serious" with Bobby, it sounds like he was pretty much where your child is right now. I think the thing holding me back was that it just seemed like such an insurmountable hill to climb. But I think it's like the Nike ad—you just have to decide to go ahead and *do it.* One thing that really helped me was that when we went out shopping, or whatever, he wasn't wearing a diaper, but I put plastic pants over his underwear in case he had an accident. It saved a lot of embarrassment and mess that way, and I still didn't feel bound to the house.

□ ○ △ □ ○ △

If M&M's are taboo, what's the best way to show my approval while my child is learning to go potty?

TERRY: Although my daughter isn't fully trained, there are times when she says, "Oh, Mom, I have to go," and then she'll go into the bathroom and go. And when she does, I just say, "Oh, great, good job, Honey; let's wash our hands." But I don't make a big deal out of it and give her treats, or anything like that.

KEVIN: Terry, let me encourage you. You said something that everyone needs to hear. On "Parent Talk," we often draw a definite distinction between praise and encouragement. Many parents mean well, but they will praise their child by saying, "My, you're a *good* boy because you did this, or a *good* girl because you did that." You should never associate "being good" with what children are supposed to learn and be responsible for themselves. It is much better to encourage a child by focusing on what the child has accomplished. Going potty is a very natural procedure. The bells and sirens do not have to go off to signal this event. You know, sometimes little Buford goes and, for lack of a better term, he does a "big potty," and Mom goes over, looks in the potty and exclaims, "Oh, would you look at *that*! Ralph, come here quickly!"

Ralph puts down his sports page, goes over, looks in the potty and showers his son with praise: "Oh, hey, that's *really* neat. What a *good boy* you are, Buford!"

Ralph and his wife are a ridiculous hypothetical example, but some parents go through exactly this kind of routine and all that's needed is a quiet bit of encouragement from time to time by one parent or the other. You mentioned that when your daughter uses the potty, you tell her, "Great!" and "Good job!" Those are encouraging words and, in my book, they are much different from praise. You're on the right track. You hang in there. Things are going to go well.

RANDY: Maybe the best way to sum it all up, Terry, is to take potty training in stride. I got through it. So did my wife—and all our kids made it through too. In fact, I know of very few children who go off to college without being potty trained. The important thing is the attitude a parent takes toward potty training, that it's matter-of-fact, a natural process, a part of life, but it doesn't have to be accomplished in some set time. I wonder how many adults even know at what age they were potty trained or by what method. A relaxed attitude is more important than looking for instant success with a certain method. Toilet training is a *process*, and if you keep that in mind eventually you—and your child—will succeed.

CHAPTER 7

■●▲■●▲

COURAGE! BED WETTING ALMOST ALWAYS STOPS BEFORE THEY LEAVE FOR COLLEGE

RANDY: Wetting the bed or wetting your pants—either one can be a pretty devastating experience for a kid. Kevin, have you ever had it happen to you?

KEVIN: I've never wet the bed, but I did almost pee in my pants one night when I missed the last flight out of LaGuardia to Buffalo.

RANDY: Well, as we know, bed wetting is no small problem in many homes. Statistics bear out that twice as many boys have problems with bed wetting as girls: at age five, 7 percent of the boys and 3 percent of the girls; at age ten, 3 percent of the boys and 2 percent of the girls; and at age eighteen, 1 percent of the boys wet the bed, while bed wetting is almost nonexistent among girls.

What are the causes of bed wetting?

KEVIN: The truth is, nobody knows the exact cause or causes. We do know that statistics show that bed wetting often runs in the family. Seventy-five percent of the kids who wet the bed have a close biological relative who bed wets or has in the past. But it's a big mystery as to why. All we can come up with are "predisposing factors." For example, sometimes slower muscle or neurological development can make bladder control more difficult for some kids. In other cases, some kids just have too small a bladder to hold a whole night's quantity of urine. Another factor may be delayed or lax potty training.

But maybe the biggest one of all is psychological stress. For example, a child may be hospitalized between the ages of two and four and this can cause bed wetting later. Sometimes when a child enters school he starts wetting the bed. Another common cause of stress is when a new baby brother or sister arrives to take the attention off the firstborn.

RANDY: One of the things we hear from many parents is that kids who wet the bed are often deep sleepers. Parents can't even wake them up through the night to go to the bathroom because they're just too far gone into dreamland.

KEVIN: That's another thing—dreams. Sometimes a kid may wet the bed during his rapid eye movement (REM) stage of sleep because he's dreaming he's going to the bathroom and that's exactly what happens—in his bed! But, Randy, I'm wondering if, in some cases, the child isn't subconsciously depending on his parents instead of assuming personal responsibility for controlling his bladder?

You see, I'm from the old school, and I believe parents should keep the responsibility squarely on the shoulders of the child as much as possible. I don't mean ridicule him or pressure him, but simply leave it with him. It's his problem. He's the one who has to learn—and he *will* learn. As the statistics point out, ninety-nine out of a hundred stop by the time they are old enough to get married. Children do learn to control their bladders.

RANDY: But in the meantime, bed wetting can be a real hassle, and our producer is already signaling that we have several people who need help with this problem. . . .

□ ○ △ □ ○ △

My child is a deep sleeper and wets the bed regularly. Should we see a doctor?

JANE: Our youngest child is five and he's the only one who's ever had a bed wetting problem. Our other four children never had a problem at all. At first we thought maybe it was just because he hadn't gotten into the habit of getting up in the middle of the night to go to the bathroom. I've been trying to get him up around 2:00 or 3:00, but I've discovered that you cannot wake him up. He's in such a deep sleep, he's practically unconscious. When I finally do get him aroused, he just cries because he doesn't know where he is or what he is doing. Should I have a doctor check him out?

KEVIN: You know, it's interesting. The AMA's *Family Medical Guide* states that a common belief, which claims that children who wet the bed sleep more deeply and generally pass more urine than other children, is a "medical myth." Yet, by some strange coincidence, we continue to hear from a lot of parents who have deep sleepers who wet the bed. For your own peace of mind, the next time you take your son to the pediatrician, mention your concern and see what he or she says. Then you can take it from there.

RANDY: One thing you could try is to get him to take a nap in the afternoon, so he might not sleep so soundly through the night. Of course, five year olds are usually not too enthused about taking naps, so don't make a big issue out of it. Just try to get him to rest, and if he drops off, great. But the key is not to overreact. One of the things you don't want to implant in your child's mind is, "Oh, dear, my child has this major problem. We better do something quickly!" Many families have kids who are struggling with this problem, and each family has to develop its own strategy for dealing with it. The first rule is don't make a big deal out of it.

□ ○ △ □ ○ △

How effective are drugs in stopping a child's bed wetting?

ELEANOR: My youngest son is eight and is still struggling with wetting the bed. It got to the point where he said, "Mom, let's go see the doctor to find out why I'm wetting the bed." We took him to the doctor and had him tested for any physical reasons he might wet the bed, but they were all ruled out. And while the doctor didn't suggest having him tested psychologically, he did prescribe medication called Tofranil and that cut his bed wetting way down.

RANDY: According to one of the official manuals we use, Eleanor, organic causes of bed wetting might be diabetes, seizures, or urinary tract infections. Obviously your doctor ruled all those out, but he still prescribed the Tofranil?

ELEANOR: That's right. Tofranil is an antidepressant, and for some reason it works 80 percent of the time.

RANDY: Tell me again how effective the Tofranil has been.

ELEANOR: It has helped immensely. Now Bobby wets the bed only once about every two weeks. He takes two of the pills a day, one after school and one before bed. The thing I don't like about it, though, is that there are always side effects from taking this kind of stuff. And the doctor also admits that once he stops taking the drug, he will immediately go back to wetting the bed. So drugs don't seem to be the final answer.

RANDY: We are not medical doctors, but it's my guess that ideally your boy should learn to stop bed wetting without drugs. You should check with your doctor to see if it's okay to cycle him off the drug occasionally to see if he does go back to wetting the bed. Let your doctor know you don't want to have your son use drugs any longer than necessary.

ELEANOR: Thanks. That's what we'll try to do.

□ ○ △ □ ○ △

Can a child control his bed wetting if he really wants to?

MONA: We took our nine year old boy to the doctor concerning his bed wetting, and he told us nothing was physically wrong. And he also didn't suggest any drugs. He just sent us home and told us to do the best we could. It's frustrating because there are no road maps.

RANDY: We know that one in every ten kids at your son's age has this problem, even if it's on an occasional basis. We understand how embarrassing this must be, especially for him.

MONA: We try not to let him have anything to drink after dinner, and to make sure he goes to the bathroom just before bedtime, but he still wets the bed. It is all so very frustrating and terribly embarrassing for him. He wants to stay overnight at a friend's house, but he's afraid to go because they would find out that he wets the bed. I'm afraid he just doesn't have any control over it.

RANDY: You may remember the movie made for television by Michael Landon several years ago. I believe it was his own story of what it was like to experience the ridicule and humiliation of being a bed wetter. His mother would hang his sheets out the window from the second story to dry, and he would run all the way home from school ahead of the other kids to pull them in before they could see that he had "wet the bed again." So, it's not too hard to imagine the devastating humiliation that wetting the bed can cause for a nine year old, not to mention kids who are ten or twelve.

MONA: Yes, and if they have a brother or sister who lets it slip that their brother wets the bed, it can really be bad. When my boy found out that they had let his friends know he wets the bed, he was totally devastated. He just ran up to his room and cried. He said, "Oh, Mom, I'm so embarrassed—all these people *know.*" I told him, "It's okay—after all, none of us is perfect."

KEVIN: I believe you said that you feel your son just doesn't have any control or he would stop wetting the bed, to avoid the humiliation, if for no other reason.

MONA: That's right—I really believe he can't control it.

KEVIN: I can understand why you might feel that way, but I'd like to make an observation. Once we say that a person has no control over something, we let him off the hook.

MONA: Well, to be truthful, the doctor never actually told my son that he doesn't have any control.

KEVIN: That makes my point. As you look at the behavior in children, parents are always a key. If your boy believes that you feel it isn't his responsibility because you think he has no control, he'll continue wetting the bed. There shouldn't be a lot of lectures or ridicule. Just keep giving him quiet encouragement. Let him know that you know he can stop—that no one can do it for him, it is up to him.

MONA: Well, we don't tease or ridicule him in any way. I don't know what kind of signals I might be sending him, but I admit that I'm not convinced that he can really control it. With all of the torment and humiliation he goes through, I just can't imagine that he'd bed wet on purpose. It's just too humiliating for him. The only explanation I've come up with is his deep sleep patterns.

KEVIN: As I mentioned earlier, the medical experts tell us that there is no scientific correlation between deep sleep patterns and bed wetting, although I think a lot of moms find that hard to believe. I'm not trying to say he "bed wets on purpose." But no matter what the antecedent condition is, you still have to work on the premise that there is no way you can control your son's bladder. He's going to have to find a way to deal with it sometime, and the more you keep the responsibility on him, the better.

So, I would always work on keeping him accountable. It doesn't mean that you don't sympathize and say, "I know that's embarrassing, Honey, but listen, you just go up and clean up the mess and come down to breakfast. You'll have a good day in spite of this." You take it in stride but you still let him know it's his problem, not yours. Yes, it affects you as a parent, but you should always try to keep it on his shoulders as best you can.

□ ○ △ □ ○ △

Can "The Pad and the Bell" really help deep sleepers stop wetting the bed?

ROBERTA: I have a success story that might encourage other parents. The second of our six children was a bed wetter. He also had polio at about fifteen months. We had trouble getting him toilet trained, and he kept wetting the bed at night because he was such a heavy sleeper. We read in the paper about the Pad and the Bell and, even though we were short of money at the time, we decided to go ahead and buy one, and it was the greatest investment we ever made. It took about thirty days and he was fine.

RANDY: That's great to hear, Roberta. The Pad and the Bell is one of the treatments of choice recommended by many doctors and research shows that it works about 60 percent of the time. Different kinds of units are available, and they run off of nine volt batteries. In one case, an actual pad goes into the underwear of the child, and they have a girl's and a boy's model. A sensor wire leads from the pad inserted into the underwear into a box that buzzes when the pad gets wet. In another case, the child sleeps on a pad that attaches to his underwear and the sensor wire leads to a wristwatch type of buzzer. Which type did you use?

ROBERTA: Ours was simply a pad that attached to his underwear. I guess the theory is that when the pad gets wet, the bell goes off, and when the child hears the bell, there is an automatic reflex action that tightens the muscle that controls his bladder. Our son was between four and five when we used it with him.

RANDY: The Pad and the Bell is a simple behavior modification technique, and, while we at "Parent Talk" aren't big fans of behavior modification, there are exceptions where it can prove useful, and I believe this is one of them. The price of the Pad and Bell units runs somewhere between $50 and $60.

ROBERTA: As I recall, that's just about what we paid. It certainly worked for us and it could be a good alternative to using drugs.

□ ○ △ □ ○ △

Why does my child wet the bed at home, but nowhere else, for example, at friends' or at his grandparents'?

LOIS: I have four children, three older boys and then a younger daughter. My middle boy is a bed wetter and he's ten now. He wets the bed six nights out of seven at home, but when he stays with friends or his grandparents, he is much better and seldom wets at all.

RANDY: Why do you think that is?

LOIS: My theory is that when he's sleeping somewhere else, he doesn't sleep as heavily as he does at home. When he's at someone else's house, he worries about wetting the bed, and doesn't want to do it because it will be so embarrassing. One summer he went an entire week at my mom's without wetting the bed and we thought we were home free. But when he came home he went right back to it—generally every night.

RANDY: How do you respond each morning to his bed wetting? Who cleans it up? What's the routine?

LOIS: He gets out of bed and goes directly to the shower. Then he strips the sheets off the bed and puts them in the laundry basket and he's off to school. So far, we haven't made any big deal out of him doing his own laundry. My biggest concern right now is next year he'll be in fifth grade and they go to camp for a week. If he's still wetting then, I don't know what we'll do.

RANDY: Have you ever sat down with your son and asked him why he thinks he wets the bed, or has he ever asked you why he wets the bed?

LOIS: Not really. He's heard us talk to doctors about it, and we all feel strongly that it's connected to his sleep pattern. We've watched what he drinks before bed, and we try getting him up at night, but he's still usually wet by morning and he will never remember that anyone has gotten him up, or anything like that.

RANDY: According to the AMA's *Family Medical Guide*, cutting down on drinks before bedtime really doesn't help prevent bed wetting. They claim that the amount of liquid a child drinks has no effect on the problem.

LOIS: Well, our experience bears that out. We've controlled his liquid before bed and it hasn't done any good at all.

KEVIN: Maybe the experts want to claim that the amount of liquid a child drinks has no effect on whether or not he wets the bed, but I'd still cut way down on water in the evenings and absolutely no caffeinated drinks like chocolate milk and sodas before bed. Common sense says the more that goes in, the more that will come out in the middle of the night.

By way of encouragement, Lois, I like your style. You're not letting your world crumble because of a bed wetter. But I still have to come back to the key issue, which is that each person has to control his bladder. You may not agree with me, but I'm not at all sure your son isn't pulling your chain a little bit. I could be wrong, but I've seen it so many times. I once counseled a boy who wet the bed at home but not away, and then his father finally said, "I've got an idea. If we really believe he can control his bladder and that he doesn't wet the bed at his friends' houses but only at our house, then he can sleep in the bathtub."

And that's what this eight-year-old kid wound up doing—sleeping in the bathtub. It was the last time he ever bed wet in his own home. I'm not recommending that you bed your boy down in the bathtub, but what I am saying is that sometimes parents have to do a little rug pulling to get a child to really come to grips with his problem. The thing to keep emphasizing is that everyone beyond diapers on planet Earth is responsible for his or her own bladder. There is no way a parent can be accountable for a child's bladder—it's up to the child.

□ ○ △ □ ○ △

How do I deal with older siblings who tease the child who bed wets?

DENISE: Our youngest child is nine and he still wets the bed regularly. He's got an older brother and sister, and they tease him and make fun of him. I've often heard both of you say on the air that you believe in letting siblings work out their own problems, but in this case I'm not so sure. Our nine year old feels badly enough about bet wetting, but when his brother and sister get on his case, it just devastates him. He goes into a rage, starts hitting and throwing things. When we try to calm him down he goes up to his room, slams the door, and won't come out for hours, sometimes not even for meals. We're a Christian family and I feel terrible about this, but I'm not sure how to handle it.

RANDY: There are exceptions to any general rule, and in this case I think you need to intervene to get the older children off your youngest boy's back. Bed wetting is a big enough problem without having his brother and sister teasing and ridiculing him.

KEVIN: I agree. Call the older kids together without your younger son there and talk to them about how he really feels and how their teasing has got to stop. Let them know that teasing and ridiculing their brother for bed wetting is not acceptable, no matter how embarrassed they are to have a brother who does this. Point out that teasing him isn't going to help him stop; in fact, it may only contribute to having him continue because of all the anxiety he feels.

DENISE: But what if my older children don't stop?

KEVIN: Then bring Reality Discipline into play. Don't give any warnings about what will happen if they don't stop, but if the teasing continues, all of a sudden certain privileges are revoked. All of a sudden the car isn't moving when the older kids need to be driven somewhere. Don't lecture your older kids about how unloving or un-Christian their behavior is, but hold them accountable for that behavior.

□○△□○△

Does diet or nutrition ever play a part in bed wetting?

BONNIE: Our son is almost twenty now, but he had a severe bed wetting problem from age seven up to about eleven or twelve. For years we sought an answer and finally my aunt, who is a teacher of special education with the developmentally disabled, came up with something that worked for us. Our son was especially sensitive to sugar, and after eating sugar he would become hyperactive while he was awake. But, when he finally went to sleep, it was almost as if he were drugged and we couldn't wake him. So he, too, was a deep sleeper and never aware of his bed wetting incidents.

RANDY: So what did you do?

BONNIE: We cut down his sugar intake throughout the day and after 3:00 P.M. cut out any kind of sugar completely. We also gave him protein snacks in the evening to help counteract any effects the sugar might be having on his body. Then, when he did sleep, it was a more normal sleep. We set an alarm clock for 2:00 A.M. and he was able to wake up and get to the bathroom and back to bed. After a few weeks of controlling his sugar intake and using the alarm clock, his bed wetting was over.

RANDY: So changing his diet actually did help him with his sleep patterns?

BONNIE: Absolutely. In her work, my aunt has always seen correlation between behavior and diet. If our son stuck to cutting down his sugar intake, he didn't have any trouble.

KEVIN: Sounds like reality to me. If he ate sugar, he had to pay the natural consequence.

BONNIE: It was the answer for us, but over that four or five years, I thought it would never end. I had nightmares of having him cleaning off his mattress at age seventeen. But once he realized he had to control his sugar intake, the problem came to an abrupt halt. Yes, there is life after bed wetting!

□ ○ △ □ ○ △

What is a good way to handle a child who wets his pants during the day?

ALISHA: My six year old has been potty trained for over three years, but he still wets his pants quite often, especially when he's out playing. Any suggestions?

KEVIN: The Reality Discipline "standard order of procedure" is to give the child one pair of underwear a day. If he gets them wet, he comes in and the end of his day draws nigh, no matter what time it might be. He puts on his pajamas or his robe and he is to stay in the house. The idea is not to be punitive but you firmly but gently tell him his day has come to an end.

RANDY: The one pair of underwear a day approach often works, but not always. Some friends of ours had a child who would wet his pants during the day, particularly when he got excited at school. They tried Reality Discipline and gave him only one pair of underwear a day. He didn't like that, but it still didn't change his total pattern. He'd still wet his pants fairly often.

So, they took him to a pediatrician who checked him out for any neurological impairment, which often is tied to lack of bladder control. There wasn't any, but then the doctor suggested that they look at any stress the boy might have in his life. They pinpointed his routine at school and made an agreement with their son's teacher that he be permitted to take regular breaks during the school day to use the rest room. This helped the problem, at least while he was at school.

Another thing the doctor suggested was to try to have their

son hold more urine in his bladder before going to the bathroom. In this way he could stretch the bladder so that it would actually hold more and he'd have a greater sense of control. The bottom line is that their child is simply going through a stage. They have learned to take it in stride and the problem has decreased quite a bit.

KEVIN: I've also counseled kids who continued to wet their pants, even though the one pair of pants a day rule was invoked. But I still think that's the place to start. Then, if they need to change their routine, for example going to the rest room more often during the day, that's great, but the point is, they are becoming responsible for their own problem.

CHAPTER 8

■●▲■●▲

HOW DO I FIND GOOD CHILD CARE?

RANDY: Imagine it, Kevin, the baby-sitter has arrived, you are ready to walk out the door with your wife and you're saying . . .

KEVIN: "We're free! We're free!"

RANDY: Then you look back over your shoulder and, as you wave to a smiling fourteen year old, you think, *She is awfully young. I hope she can handle those two little ankle biters.*

KEVIN: How old should a baby-sitter be? How do you find a good one? Should she clean up the kitchen? Will the kids get to bed before the 11:00 news? These are all pertinent questions for parents who want to get out now and then for a little R&R, without worrying about the house burning down.

RANDY: And we have with us in our studio today a mom who has grappled with all those questions, and more. Dawn, you have an eight year old and a five year old, and to begin we'd like to know what's your greatest concern when you walk out the door and look back over your shoulder at the baby-sitter?

Should baby-sitters be required to keep the house picked up?

DAWN: First, the safety of my kids. But my next concern is, "What am I gonna come home to?" Even though I might know the girl personally, it worries me sometimes as we're driving home. Are the kids still in their clothes rather than in their pajamas? Are there dirty clothes and wet towels lying all over the floor? Did she make fudge and leave a mess? Did she . . .

KEVIN: You're a firstborn child, aren't you, Dawn?

DAWN: Why, yes, I am. However did you guess?

KEVIN: Well, you did give us a few clues. I think being worried about making a mess with the fudge clinched it. Seriously, there are not many women—of any birth order—who enjoy going out to dinner with their husbands and then coming home at midnight and walking into a dirty, disheveled kitchen. Most women will just sigh and, dead tired as they might be, they'll clean it up then and there because they can't stand the thought of getting up to that dirty kitchen in the morning. But I'm sure that's only one of many concerns you've had to deal with . . .

□ ○ △ □ ○ △

What's the best age for a baby-sitter? Do some baby-sitters start too young?

DAWN: One thing I worry about is that a lot of the sitters available to baby-sit are getting younger and younger. I wonder if the demand is forcing baby-sitting upon them before they are really ready. Or do we just accept the younger baby-sitter because of changing times?

KEVIN: I think the answer is simple. It has to do with the opposite sex. We're talking about the hormone set and I'm convinced the best baby-sitter you can find, if Grandma is not available, is a young sitter who has not yet discovered the opposite sex. And how old are these young sitters today? They are twelve, thirteen, maybe fourteen. Now I realize that there are plenty of capable sitters who are baby-sitting at fifteen, sixteen and seventeen, but I don't think their tribe is increasing.

KEVIN: What do baby-sitters make these days, Dawn?

DAWN: During the early '90s I've been paying $2.00 to $2.50 an hour in our area for a sitter for our two children. I can't speak for other communities throughout the country, but I do know that sometimes baby-sitters charge according to how many kids: $2.50 for one, $3.00 for two, $3.50 for three, and $4.00 for four, for example. Of course this can vary a bit, depending on the going rate, with some charging as much as $5.00 per hour. But I think whatever people pay per hour, they need to choose carefully to get their money's worth.

RANDY: I think trust is a big factor. It helps to know the person who is baby-sitting, if she is a neighbor, for example. Ideally, it's great when you can leave the kids with the grandparents or their aunt or uncle. Donna and I have done both, especially when going someplace overnight. It is a big relief to know your kids are in the hands of someone who cares, someone who is part of your family.

DAWN: It's also very valuable for children to have those experiences with the extended family, but I think you're one of the lucky ones, Randy. So many people get transplanted throughout the country that they wind up thousands of miles from extended family, and they basically have to rely on hiring strangers. I've been lucky to have had three next-door neighbors who have been baby-sitting age. But all of them have had short careers, maybe a year, and then they're gone, getting better paying jobs, or getting interested in their peer group. They get to the point where they don't want to tie themselves down if you call several days ahead. I recall contacting one girl who lived a few doors away and she kept saying, "I will check and see what is going on, and if nothing is going on, I can sit." When a mom needs a baby-sitter on Friday night, she doesn't really want to wait until Friday afternoon to find out if she has one.

□ ○ △ □ ○ △

Are twelve year olds capable enough to handle all baby-sitting responsibilities?

RANDY: Sometimes you're really stuck. The sitters you know aren't sure they can sit, and you wind up with a stranger recommended by someone you know. For Donna and me there were many evenings affected because she was worried about what the baby-sitter was doing. We have April on the line. What's been your experience with picking baby-sitters?

APRIL: I agree with Dawn. I use neighbors primarily for baby-sitters, and the older they are the more trouble we usually have. When they're fifteen, sixteen, or seventeen, they're on the phone a lot, or more interested in watching TV than doing anything with the children. Actually, I have had the best luck with twelve year olds. They are excellent baby-sitters, because they are more interested in playing with the children and actually being with them rather than thinking about their social life.

DAWN: I can see your point, but I wonder if we need to lower our expectations when we're dealing with kids around twelve. Can we expect as much from them as far as housekeeping and that kind of thing?

APRIL: You have to look at their home life and if they have siblings. If a twelve year old has younger brothers or sisters, she's probably fairly experienced in caring for kids and helping in the kitchen. One twelve year old we've been using has a younger sister who's around five, so she has a lot of responsibilities at home. She's more mature, perhaps, than the average twelve year old.

KEVIN: I think you've pretty well summed it up, April. For my money, the best baby-sitter you can buy for $2.00 or even $3.00 an hour is, in fact, a twelve year old, firstborn daughter in the family. She is the one who has already gotten lots of responsibility and experience in care-giving to younger brothers and sisters, and, if she is a firstborn, she'll probably be very attentive to detail, which firstborn parents like Dawn are looking for. For that matter, babies of the family like myself don't mind that either.

□ ○ △ □ ○ △

What is the best way to tell a baby-sitter what you expect—your rules and regulations?

DAWN: No matter who your baby-sitter is, I think it's important to have written rules so she knows what to expect, or at least sit down and talk with her. I prefer leaving a written checklist which I post on the refrigerator. Whenever I try to just tell the sitter what I want, it seems as if it's going in one ear and out the other. Sometimes things don't get done or they're done wrong.

KEVIN: What are your rules like, Dawn? Read a few of them for us.

DAWN: My first rule is that if the sitter has any problems or questions, she is to call whatever number I leave where I can be reached. If we're going to a movie, then I give her a backup number of friends who will be home that evening. I also leave emergency numbers, such as 911, plus our own address and phone number and directions to our house if she needs to give these to police or firemen.

In addition, I want the sitter to be sure all doors and sliders are locked and to draw all the drapes at night. I don't want someone looking in, watching my children and the sitter and realizing they're home alone. Also, she should be sure the garage door is closed. If any food is taken out, it should be returned to the refrigerator in the proper container. One time I had a next-door neighbor sitting and I had laid out the luncheon meat that I wanted her to use for sandwiches. I came home and found the remains of a giant bowl of chocolate pudding, which is all the kids had that day. The meat was still sitting there on the counter wrapped.

KEVIN: It would have never lasted on our counter because Cuddles, our ravenous cockapoo, would have devoured it.

DAWN: Some other points on my list are being sure the kids' dirty clothes are put in the laundry hamper, and that all the damp towels and wet washcloths are hung up to dry. And another one I really like is to check to make sure the kids haven't taken the receiver off the hook. Sometimes parents try to call home and the line is busy, and when they ask about it later, the sitter tells them, "Oh, the kids must have left the receiver off the hook." But if you leave them strict instructions to be sure this hasn't happened, then you can pretty well know why the line is busy if you try to call—it's the sitter talking to a boyfriend or girlfriend, or whoever.

□ ○ △ □ ○ △

What should I do if a baby-sitter doesn't obey the rules—for example, she leaves the place a mess?

ELLEN: I also have a list of rules posted in my kitchen that my sitters are expected to follow. My first rule is that the sitter must play with our daughter, who is six, and I give them ideas on what they can do all day. Another big rule with me is that the sitter is not to allow the children to watch any MTV or other unsuitable trash on television. In fact, I usually try to spell out what programs the children can watch that day or that evening, and limit the programs to things I know are suitable. And, oh, yes, another one of the points on my list states that if the house is a disaster or other rules have been broken, we will deduct from the baby-sitter's pay.

RANDY: Wow! How much do you deduct?

ELLEN: I tell the girls to read the entire checklist, and that deductions will depend on the disaster. In our area right now, sitters get $2.00 an hour. If the house is totally a mess, I deduct a whole hour's pay, because it will take me that long to clean up. I've only had to deduct one sitter's pay. When I wrote out her check, I told her she was losing money because the house was a mess. I used the girl another time after that and the house was beautiful when I came home.

DAWN: Good for you, Ellen. I've talked to several friends, and we've all come to the conclusion that the only way to be sure sitters will stick with your list of rules is to hit them where it hurts —in the pocketbook. I tell my sitters that if they keep all the rules, they will make a full $2.50 an hour, but if they don't, they'll only get $1.00 or $1.50 an hour.

RANDY: Thanks, Ellen, for the good input, especially on docking pay if house rules aren't kept. Don't you just hate it, Kevin, when the baby sitter eats the last piece of banana cream pie? After all, there are limits!

KEVIN: At our house, a felony would be eating the last piece of chocolate cake. But seriously, Randy, I think what Dawn and Ellen have shared with us is excellent stuff because it helps people remember how to leave the baby-sitter with clear expectations of what should be done.

□ ○ △ □ ○ △

Should a baby-sitter have permission to spank the children?

TINA: On any checklist of expectations that I might leave for my baby-sitter, where does discipline come in? Is it okay for a baby-sitter to be allowed to spank if the kids really act up?

KEVIN: Absolutely not. Kids should be spanked only by their own parents, or possibly grandparents who give them a lot of regular child care. What do you think, Randy?

RANDY: I agree. There are other disciplines that baby-sitters can use. Besides, I think telling a teenager that she is to decide if a child needs a spanking is putting too much responsibility on her shoulders.

DAWN: I've never allowed any of my baby-sitters to spank my kids. I instruct them on my checklist to use the time out method —the offender has to go to his or her room for a while, or maybe go to bed early if they really act up. Mainly, however, we expect the baby sitter to give us a report on any misbehavior and we do the disciplining after we get back.

□ ○ △ □ ○ △

What's the best way to find adults who are willing to sit for several days at a time?

RANDY: We've got Janice on the line with a good idea for how to find reliable child care if you're going away for the weekend or longer.

JANICE: We solved our problem for getting good extended child care by getting together with a few other couples and placing a blind ad in the newspaper. The ad asked for a married couple with emphasis on "married and must love to work with children." They were to send a letter with their qualifications or résumé to a box number in the ad.

KEVIN: You say you, as well as some other couples, placed this ad together?

JANICE: Yes, the other four couples were friends of ours, all of whom are Christians and share our beliefs. The ad got a fairly good response and we picked up all the letters at the post office box and reviewed them. Then we called the best sounding couples for personal interviews. Out of this screening, we found a wonderful, childless, Christian couple, and they have been babysitting for all five couples for about nine years now whenever any of us goes away for three to five days.

KEVIN: They are actually on a live-in basis then? How much does this cost?

JANICE: Yes, they come right to our house and stay there the entire time we're gone. In recent years, they've been charging $40 a day, but they aren't in it for the money. They see it as a ministry and they do everything from caring for the kids in our home to running them to their various activities, just being "Mom and Dad" for a few days.

RANDY: Sounds like a great idea if you have that much money in your budget for get-away times. It seems to me, however, that the key is really screening any couple that you hire through a blind ad.

JANICE: That's absolutely right. All the couples involved interviewed the couple that was finally hired, and their references were checked very carefully. Also, the first time we left the kids with them, it was only overnight—sort of a trial run. This couple is outstanding. They now sit for a lot of people in our community, and they are able to have a Christian witness in some homes that are not Christian.

□ ○ △ □ ○ △

What are some practical alternatives to going to the expense of hiring baby-sitters?

MARGO: We have a little girl, eight months, plus five- and seven-year-old boys. It gets expensive to hire baby-sitters and it's also hard to find someone who's willing to cover a baby and two little boys. So, we have been switching off with another family in our town. This way we are guaranteed one night a month out at no charge, and so is the other couple. Everyone looks forward to it. Our kids love to play over there, and their kids love to play over here, so this has worked out really well.

DAWN: Besides saving money, the best part of that idea is that you trust your children with an adult who is experienced in handling children of her own. A friend shared with me an idea that is somewhat similar. Her daughters and son are all married and live in the same community. The sisters and sister-in-law give weekends of baby-sitting to each other as part of their Christmas gift exchange. They put a nicely inscribed note in a Christmas card that says, "Part of your Christmas gift is that you are entitled to one free weekend of baby-sitting." So they swap kids that way and it works out really well.

□ ○ △ □ ○ △

What is a baby-sitting co-op and how does it work?

RANDY: Kevin, we've been picking up some great ideas to help people find good child care, but what we haven't talked about yet is something Donna and I were involved in when we were younger. Have you ever heard of a baby-sitting co-op?

KEVIN: A baby-sitting co-op? How does that work? Do you take your kids down to the local grain elevator and drop them off?

RANDY: Not exactly. I've arranged for Marsha and Gail to join us in a conference call to tell us how they run their co-op, which includes, I believe, some twenty-five women.

MARSHA: I've been involved with our co-op for about two and a half years, and, because I'm a stay-at-home mom, it's given me such peace of mind. I can get a sitter for a few hours to go to the doctor, or child care for a weekend, if necessary. It just takes away all the hassle of trying to find a teenager or somebody else to baby-sit.

RANDY: Gail, give us a picture of how this works on a practical, everyday basis. Does any money exchange hands? If not, how does a mom volunteer to baby-sit and how does she use the service if she needs it?

GAIL: No money is exchanged, only hours. We have a president and vice-president who hold office for a full year. We also have secretaries who keep track of who is available to sit and when. The secretary's job is so demanding, we have alternates and no one does it for more than a month at a time.

If you need a sitter, you call the secretary for that month and she lines it up. She has a list of women who are generally available for the time you may need a sit. Then the secretary contacts these women, so they still have the opportunity to decline or accept after hearing who it is, how many kids, etc.

KEVIN: If you don't pay for baby-sitting in a co-op, how do you earn baby-sitting time? *

GAIL: We simply exchange hours. For one child, you exchange one hour's worth of time. For two children, it is time and a half, and if you have three, it is double time. Each parent is allowed to be only twenty hours in the red or to save up twenty hours of baby-sitting time in the black. All these rules are written out and provided for all co-op members. We keep updating them from time to time to keep the organization running smoothly. About every third month we have a meeting of all co-op members so that we can get to know one another, especially when new members join the co-op. It's a great opportunity for fellowship, and that way we can become familiar with the parents we are using for child care.*

How are new members selected to join a baby-sitting co-op?

RANDY: Tell us, Marsha, how does one join your co-op? Is there a waiting list?

MARSHA: Yes, there is. In fact, our co-op has been going for almost ten years, and there was such a constant waiting list that we took the membership up from twenty to twenty-five members, because the drop-out rate was so low and the need for child care was so great. Essentially, a person has to be referred or recommended to join the co-op. And then, at a meeting of all the members, when that person is not present, her name is entered for consideration as a member. If there are no objections, the person

* For free information on how to get a co-op started, send a self-addressed, stamped envelope (first class postage), to Parent Talk, Box 37000, Tucson, AZ 85740. Request "Baby Sitting Co-op Information."

is put on our waiting list and, as soon as there is an opening, she is made part of the co-op.

What happens if a co-op member doesn't want her children cared for by certain people who are members of the co-op?

GAIL: A good feature of our co-op is that anyone can request certain sitters and anyone can also let the secretary know if there are certain families that don't blend well with his. For example, sometimes kids just don't match up well and there is squabbling and fighting.

What are co-op rules for pickup and drop-off times?

MARSHA: Suppose the secretary calls and says that Mrs. So-and-So needs a sit from 2:00 to 5:00 P.M. on Friday. If you agree to take the sit, you are then responsible to call the mother who is seeking the child care and let her know that you can take her kids. Then she reconfirms the hours that she needs her children watched. All members are asked to be as prompt as possible when dropping off and picking up their kids. The time starts from the time of drop-off to the time of pickup.

RANDY: Are co-op members allowed to build up hours because they know something is coming up when they're going to need quite a bit of baby-sitting themselves?

MARSHA: Yes, we call it "time in the black." I'm piling up some extra hours myself because I'm going to be moving soon and I will have some days when I need some heavy-duty baby-sitting because I don't want to pack and move boxes with my children around. I should have plenty of good, positive hours, so when I need all that baby-sitting during moving I won't find myself twenty hours in the red.

How do you handle co-op members who do not follow the rules?

KEVIN: Suppose someone gets over twenty hours in the red, or they break some other co-op rule. How do you handle that?

GAIL: It is the president's duty to sit down and confront the individual. Probably our most frequent violation of rules is people not using the co-op. If somebody doesn't use the co-op for three months, they are asked to either use it within thirty days or please drop out so somebody on the waiting list can join. But as for our other rules, we have almost no problems.

RANDY: What do you think, Kevin? Would you like to be president of a baby-sitting co-op?

KEVIN: I'm on record, Randy, as stating that babies shouldn't be presidents of anything.

RANDY: Well, how about secretary, then—you could keep track of all the hours?

KEVIN: Me? Keep track of all those women who are supposed to sit on certain days at certain times? I have season tickets to the Arizona Wildcats, and I can barely keep track of those.

What part do husbands play when their wives join a baby-sitting co-op?

RANDY: How do the dads respond when their wives join a co-op? Do they get involved? Do they have to be checked out before their wives can join?

GAIL: Sometimes a husband might be the kind of person that the other moms do not want their kids to be around (bad temper, bad language, etc.). When that happens, an applicant for the waiting list is turned down.

MARSHA: That doesn't happen very often. Usually most husbands are fairly comfortable with the co-op concept. Some husbands love to have kids over at their house all the time, and their wives accept a lot of evening sits, while their husbands are home. Some husbands, however, want to relax in the evening with just their own family and not have a lot of other kids around. So, their wives accept sits only when their husbands are out for meetings or during the day when they're at work.

Can working mothers be part of a co-op?

KEVIN: Working moms have more than enough to do, but I'm wondering—do you allow a working mom to be part of your co-op or is it strictly for stay-at-home moms?

GAIL: We have a few moms in our co-op who work part-time, but the majority are stay-at-homes. There is no reason that working moms couldn't be part of a co-op; perhaps they could form one of their own because their needs would be a little different. They probably would wind up offering baby-sitting mainly at night or on weekends. That could still be a big help to working moms who don't like to spend all the money they make on baby-sitters.

□ ○ △ □ ○ △

What is the minimum number needed to start a co-op?

TANYA: I'm calling to ask about the number of mothers I'd need to get a co-op started. I don't think we could find twenty right away.

MARSHA: I was in a neighborhood co-op once, and we had only six members, but it worked very well.

□ ○ △ □ ○ △

Do baby-sitting co-ops provide fellowship times for members, so they can get together to exchange notes, encourage each other, etc.?

MILDRED: I've belonged to co-ops for several years and I think being in a Christian co-op is certainly the ideal situation, but something that I think needs to be stressed is how important it is to have the members of the co-op build relationships with each other. Stay-at-home moms, in particular, can really get isolated from the rest of the world, and the co-op not only gives them an opportunity to meet other women, but also to have some time with adults.

RANDY: That's a good point, Mildred. Gail, what about your co-op? Do you have fellowship times and is there spiritual input?

GAIL: We don't have official spiritual input per se, such as a guest speaker giving a devotional. Our meetings are mostly practical, going over rules that we are all getting a little lax on, or discussing people who have been recommended to be put on the waiting list. Marsha, what do you think? Our meetings seem to be mostly a time to bring up needs in the group that should be addressed.

MARSHA: I think one of the most important things we do in the meetings of the co-op members is to pray for each other and give thanks for blessings we've received. This helps us become familiar with one another and get to know each other's needs.

RANDY: Giving each other prayer support is an excellent idea. It also helps you reach out to other people with a certain need. Have you had that kind of thing come up?

GAIL: Oh, yes, we have had women who have had to go into the hospital, for example, and all the members donated baby-sitting hours for their children.

And, oh, yes, we have a prayer chain so that when something comes up the president can start the calls, and the last person on the list calls the president so she knows it has gone all the way through the co-op.

□ ○ △ □ ○ △

What are the pros and cons of putting your child in a preschool?

JOY: My husband recently left me and I'm going to have to go to work. I have no family members living in town who can help me with my children, ages five and three. What are your thoughts on preschools? And what's the best kind of preschool to use?

KEVIN: I am on record on this program and in many of my books in saying that, if at all possible, moms should be home with their children and not out working. Obviously, in your case, Joy, you have no choice, but I think what you are looking for is a good child-care facility, not a preschool, per se. Preschools are usually staffed by professional educators trained in child development, and sometimes parents get tempted to put their bright little preschooler into what I call Kiddie Kollege or Urchin University, where they have all kinds of high-powered programs that are supposed to develop what the well-known author David Elkind calls "super kids." In his book *Our Hurried Children*, Elkind talks about too many preschoolers becoming the victims of overwhelming stress because they are being pushed too hard in their preschools!

JOY: Well, I'm really not interested in Kiddie Kollege or Urchin University, so I guess what I want is a good child-care facility. How do I find one?

KEVIN: You're going to have to shop around and see what's available in your community. Ask friends and neighbors what they think of certain child care facilities. You should soon be able to pinpoint one or two that might work for you with your schedule. Then make a personal visit and check the place out. Is it clean? Is the staff warm, friendly, and experienced? Ask them what kind of turnover they have on their staff, and beware of a place where staff members are constantly leaving.

Ask if they allow parents to visit at any time. If they don't, I would advise finding another facility. If they do and you decide to go ahead and put your children into their care, be sure to take advantage of the "visit us any time" policy, just to see how they operate when parents aren't expected to be around. And what is their sick policy? You don't want your children in a facility that has no policy about keeping sick kids away from healthy ones.

RANDY: Also, ask the supervisor of the facility to give you the name of the organization or bureau with whom the facility is licensed. Then later call that bureau to see if the facility has violated any rules over the past year. Also, be aware that you get what you pay for. Don't make price the absolute, primary factor. And don't necessarily choose a child care facility because it is handy to your route to work or nearer your home. Better to drive an extra few miles in order to give your child the best care possible.

KEVIN: And, one other thing about preschools. Sometimes the trained professional staff can get so enamored with "educating" toddlers, that the place is just too academic. One tip-off is to ask them if they use a lot of dittos or a lot of printed material, which suggests a very structured approach instead of providing lots of freewheeling activities where the child can be creative and work at his or her own speed. Wherever you place your child for care, you want the child to be safe, unrushed, unstressed, and as happy as possible while you're gone.

Finally, after asking all those questions, ask yourself one more: "If I were three or four years old, would I like it here?"

CHAPTER 9

■●▲■●▲

WHY ARE SOME KIDS SO HARD (OR SO EASY) TO LIVE WITH?

KEVIN: A lot of parents ask us to explain why they knock heads with one child in the family while they are able to get along with the rest just fine. And why are some kids so strong willed and oppositional, while others are compliant—and practically a piece of cake?

RANDY: And we always go back to how the personality is formed. Within the family, every personality is unique; everyone is different and personality conflicts can sometimes drive us right up the wall. The birth order system within any family is a major cause of conflicts.

KEVIN: That's because birth order creates so many distinctively different personalities. I think about our oldest child, Holly, who fits the firstborn typical profile to a "T." She's reliable, conscientious. She's exacting, always has to have all her little ducks in a row. She's always been a little worrier, doesn't like surprises, and, oh, yes, she's always tried to organize the whole family, especially me. Firstborns are known for being bossy little buzzards who love to run things. That's why so many of them turn out to be CEO's, presidents, and even astronauts. Out of the first twenty-three astronauts, twenty-one were firstborns and the other two were only children.

RANDY: We should probably point out that the only child is everything you said about the firstborn but in triplicate.

KEVIN: The motto tattooed across the brain of every only child says, "I am responsible." The only models an only child ever has are the parents, and he grows up as a little adult. In fact he gets along better with adults or with other children who are much younger. He often doesn't get along well with peers.

RANDY: What about the so-called middle children? What makes them different?

KEVIN: To begin with, being below the firstborn in the family. It's practically a Midas Muffler Guarantee of Birth Order that your middle child will be the opposite of whoever is above him or her in the family. Your typical middle child is squeezed between the firstborn Crown Prince or Princess and Little Snooky, the baby. Just ask any middle child who has the fewest pictures in the family photo album, and he'll tell you in a hurry.

In fact, after I wrote *The Birth Order Book*, I got a lot of letters from middle children who had actually gone to the trouble of counting the pages devoted to the middle child. They wrote, "Dear Dr. Leman: How come the fewest pages in *The Birth Order Book* are devoted to middle children?" I replied, "Dear Middle-Born: What did you expect? Love, the Doctor."

RANDY: But being squeezed and getting the short end of the stick has a positive side. Middle children are often good mediators and negotiators, and they make a lot of friends.

KEVIN: That's right, Randy, they're usually the first ones to go outside the family to make friends. I think one of the reasons many of them are so good at the art of compromise is that they learn to live with hand-me-downs. I can still remember counseling two young brothers, and the oldest snapped at the youngest, "Wait a minute, you don't get a new coat, you get my old one!" Now that's what I call being put in your middle-child place.

RANDY: And, finally, we come to the third major birth order category—the babies. Since you and I are both babies, Kevin, I'm sure we have a few good words to say here.

KEVIN: Naturally, we both think babies are special, Randy, but there are more reasons for that than our own prejudice. The baby of the family is very special because he or she marks the end of the trail. Because babies get so much attention, they are often affectionate, outgoing little charmers. They turn out to be super salesmen, and many babies are comedians as well. Billy Crystal, Eddie Murphy, Steve Martin, Goldie Hawn, and Joan Rivers are all the baby boy or baby girl in their respective families.

In the debates that were held before the '92 election, there were three opponents: Bill Clinton, a firstborn; George Bush, a middle child; but remember the other one—a little guy with the big ears and one-liners that kept millions watching on TV in stitches? Yes, Ross Perot is a baby of the family.

RANDY: But, Kevin, I'm wondering if some people might be wondering how we explain Ross Perot's success as a CEO of several big corporations—he even ran General Motors for a while. This is something you would normally expect a firstborn to be doing, not a baby.

KEVIN: Well, there are always a few surprises. With all of his deals and companies, Donald Trump sounds like a firstborn, but he's really a middle child. And that brings up one of the most important things to understand about birth order. There are variables that can change the stereotypical characteristics of a firstborn, a middle born, or a baby, and help cause that person to come out with certain traits or skills that don't seem to fit his birth order at all. I think you are a prime example of a baby who came out with a number of firstborn characteristics. That's why, while we are both babies of the family, we are very different in the way we operate. When we work together at a seminar, for example, I'm playing more to the crowd, noticing everything that's going on, and trying to get laughs—typical baby behavior—while you're busy keeping everything on track, very organized, very responsible and serious.

RANDY: One reason for that is that I am the last of three boys, and there were exactly six years between each of us. One of the basic rules of birth order is that when a child is born five years or more after the child above him, it starts the whole birth order chain over again. So I came along, six years after my brother, Larry, and that made me in some respects a "quasi-only child." Not only did I have my parents as models, but I had two brothers who were a great deal older. Warren, in particular, who was eleven years older, seemed more like my uncle, not my brother. When I grew up, I was trying to keep up with all these people who were so much more capable than I, and I think that's what helped plant those traits I have today of being responsible, organized, and having all my little ducks in a row, as you like to put it.

KEVIN: Another obvious variable in birth order is the sex of a child. It doesn't take a rocket scientist to figure out that if there is only one female among five children, she's going to be a Baby Princess whether she's born fifth or third, and if you have one boy and three sisters, he might be born third, but he is the firstborn boy, and that could send him in the direction of firstborn traits.

RANDY: There is also the variable of physical disabilities. Or physical attributes. For example, suppose you have a ten year old who is five feet tall and weighs about 79 pounds, while his "little" brother is eight years old, 5′4″, weighs 120, and answers to the nickname of "Moose." There could easily be a "role reversal" with the second born taking over from the firstborn.

KEVIN: That's right, and when that happens it can cause all kinds of rivalry and friction. When parents see something like this happening, they have to move in and be sure they treat the firstborn like the true firstborn—let him or her stay up longer, go places the other can't go, receive a larger allowance, etc.

RANDY: We can't go into every possible variable that might happen in the family constellation, but it's obvious that when you mix genetics with birth order and then add the atmosphere of the home environment—it all adds up to developing individual and unique personalities that have to live together in the family. From our Adlerian point of view, we call it "lifestyle development," the way each person in the family sees his or her world. A cardinal principle for Adlerians is that everybody wants to belong and all of us decide early in life the best way to do that. In our early years, we decide what our role in life will be as we learn what works best for us. Some people are very strong, some are charmers, some are pleasers, others are controllers. There are all kinds of labels we can use. And when you mix these various personalities into a family, interesting things can happen.

KEVIN: Interesting is right. What you have are some natural conflicts. All of us have those people in life who rub us the wrong way, and some of the people we bump heads with have our same last name. We see this in families a lot—the firstborn parent bumping heads with the firstborn son or daughter. Or you see the baby parent of the family bumping heads with his last-born. And at the other extreme, you see some parents overidentifying with certain children—favoring them, if you please, while they practically ignore others.

RANDY: It all adds up to the fact that for parents, some kids are easy to live with and some are very difficult. I'm sure our calls for today's show will bear that out. . . .

How can I discipline my strong-willed firstborn without breaking his spirit?

□ ○ △ □ ○ △

RUTH: I have a four-year-old boy and a girl, two. My son is a handful. I also have a strong will and I want so much for him to do the right thing. I want him to be responsible and obedient, but I don't want to press too hard.

RANDY: We find that with so many parents there is a tendency to overdiscipline the first child.

RUTH: That's true for me and my husband, and we've had to remind ourselves often that he is just a child and this is what he's supposed to be doing at this age. We find that when we remind each other about this, it's helpful in keeping us from going too far with discipline. But I'm still looking for ideas on how to control him without being too controlling. Nick is particularly good at saying no, and "I won't take my nap," and so on and so on. Also, he just gets into everything.

KEVIN: Sounds as if you might be tempted to think you should have named him Dennis—as in "Menace." One thing, Ruth, that helps sometimes is to try to distract the child before the wrong behavior starts. Sometimes you can see something coming, and the best way to stop it is to just get down and play with the child for just a few minutes, or involve him in what you are doing. A lot of the time misbehavior is simply the child trying to tell you he wants to do something with you—that he needs Mom.

RUTH: That's a good idea, but what about the times I don't get a chance to distract him and he does misbehave? If I just raise my voice to Emily, our two year old, that's all that is usually necessary to correct her, and if I ever have to give her a swat, it's just about the end of her world. But with Nick, swats have never had much effect. He just turns around and laughs at me or looks up at me as if it had no effect at all.

KEVIN: Have you tried any other discipline with Nick that works better?

RUTH: What works with Nick is to send him to his room—to isolate him for a little while. He comes out after a few minutes and is a much better boy, but I am wondering if this is just breaking his will or if it's bad for his spirit?

KEVIN: It sounds as if you have found the key to disciplining Nick. Don't worry, you're not breaking his spirit. You're just making him accountable for bad behavior and he's learning that when he behaves badly he has a price to pay. It's also good that you've seen that swatting some kids just doesn't work. At "Parent Talk" we stress the idea of not treating all your children alike. We are all individuals and we all respond differently. So often parents get into one mode of discipline. They say, "This is the way it was done to me by my parents, and this is the way I'm going to do it." I think you're doing a great job, and my only suggestion is to sit down and talk with Nick a minute or two after he comes out of the isolation to let him know why he was isolated, and that you still love him very much.

RANDY: Right, and I would just add that you have to do more with some kids than just send them to their room. Sometimes they get in there and have a big time playing with their toys, and it's not much discipline at all. But if you isolate them on their bed with the restriction of "No toys," that does the trick.

□ ○ △ □ ○ △

Do firstborns tend to be the most oppositional and strong-willed, or do some kids just naturally oppose everything?

JUDY: As I listened to the last caller describe her kids, I realized I've got the same package. Our oldest son, who is seven, has always been a strong-willed, stubborn little guy. His little sister, who is four, is much easier to deal with. Are firstborns always like this? Is this why he's such a handful?

RANDY: Firstborns have to take the rap for a lot of things. But being firstborn doesn't automatically make you oppositional or compliant. I was talking to a client the other day and he mentioned that he was the firstborn, and his response to his father's authority was to be a very congenial, adaptive, and conforming kid. His dad would just have to look at him, or even threaten a spanking, and he would shape up. On the other hand, his little brother was something else. The story in their family goes that the first time little brother got spanked—and he was only around five years old—he turned around, looked at his mom and said, "You big poop!"

KEVIN: Now that is what we call an oppositional child!

RANDY: And then some! In the family where I grew up, my oldest brother, Warren, would have definitely qualified as the strong-willed child. On the other hand, I was the baby of the family and I was more compliant. So, the point is, birth order doesn't necessarily determine if a child will be compliant or oppositional. It plays a part, but it isn't the final answer.

□ ○ △ □ ○ △

How do I deal with a firstborn child who never stops talking?

REGINA: I'm the mother of three children, ages eleven, eight, and six. I'm rather reserved and quiet and our eleven-year-old daughter has a completely different personality. She's an outgoing, giggling, humming, singing, laughing chatterbox and she's driving me crazy. I'm getting to the point where I can hardly stand to be around her for very long because she never shuts up. If I ignore her, I feel guilty; if I give her undivided attention, she prattles endlessly. With her younger sister and little brother, there is give and take. But with my oldest daughter, all you do is listen.

KEVIN: A child who never shuts up, who is always talking, singing, and giggling, is doing more than the normal amount of attention-seeking. I think we're talking about a powerful little buzzard who's going to *make* you pay attention to her, probably because she feels insecure. The purpose of her behavior is to keep you involved with her and keep your attention off of her younger brother and sister, who may threaten her in some way.

RANDY: You can almost always pinpoint the purpose of your child's behavior by noting how that behavior makes you feel while it's going on. If you feel merely annoyed, it is probably attention-getting. But if you are moving from annoyed to irritated or even angry, it's a good bet the child is probably on a real power trip. It sounds to me as if you feel irritated and even angry sometimes with your daughter.

REGINA: Well, I'm afraid that's true. There are times when she just plain gets on my nerves.

KEVIN: The powerful child is the one who says, in one way or another, "I only count in life—I only matter—when I am the boss, when I am in control." What children are going to do through their power trips of one kind or another is to try to convince us parents that they are in control, but that is not the way God designed the family. Parents are to be the boss—in healthy authority over their children. So, Randy, we need to give this mom some ideas of how to quiet her daughter down without being too authoritarian in the process.

RANDY: Since your daughter is eleven, I think you can be rather direct and "grown up" with her about the problem. Sit down with her and point out that you really do want to talk with her, but you have many things to do and you just can't spend as much time as you would like with her. Agree with her that you will set aside time once or twice during the day where the two of you can sit down together and talk about the things she is interested in.

When you have these brief chats, help your daughter learn some control by being very interested in what she is saying, but after a few minutes start to wrap up the conversation. Set an agreed upon time limit and let your daughter know that there is one more story, one more joke, or one more point that she can make, but after that Mom has to get involved with other things.

Then be firm and insist that she find something to do by herself or with her brother or sister and do whatever you have to do. If she persists in wanting to talk, you may have to send her to her room for a "time-out" or what you might want to call a "quiet time." The point is, don't buy into having your child continually control you with her tongue.

KEVIN: Speaking of confronting the child on a little more adult level, Randy, Regina may also want to try saying, "Honey, if you have to talk and talk like this, pretty soon the kids at school won't want to spend time with you. You should really practice on being quiet and letting other people talk. I know it's hard, but you can do it if you really want to."

If you wish, Regina, you could share a true story I know about the mother of one of my best friends. This woman is now in her eighties, but she still remembers having her first birthday party at age ten. She also was an incessant chatterbox and she bugged all her friends so much about being sure to come to her party that nobody came. Even today this woman has painful and vivid memories about how crushed she felt. Tell your daughter that you never want her to have to feel like that, and the best way to be sure to be a person that others like to be around is not to talk all the time. Learn to let others talk and be *interested* in what they have to say.

□ ○ △ □ ○ △

What's the best way to discipline an only child in a balanced way—not too strict and not too easy?

ASHLEY: We have a six-and-a-half-year-old boy, and he's an only child. I just finished reading one of your books and you say I should go easy on a firstborn or an only child. What I want to know is, where do I go easy and where do I really clamp down?

KEVIN: Number one, as parents of an only child, you and your husband are probably brave enough to admit that you have rather high expectations for your son. By six and a half his personality is pretty well formed. He's probably six and a half going on nineteen and he loves adults. So, the more you back off and don't put too much pressure on him, the better.

ASHLEY: Well, I'm having trouble with backing off because I'm a compliant person, and when I do I seem to lose control.

KEVIN: You mean you tend to let him run over you?

ASHLEY: Well, yes, he has a problem being sassy to me and not obeying. In fact, even when I discipline him and send him to his room, it's a struggle because he'll just come back out. Then I have to do something else—it's a challenge. Everything is a challenge.

KEVIN: Okay, but my point is, we don't have to make everything a challenge. Let's say you put him in his room and ten minutes later he's back out again. You can try one of two approaches: you can meet his challenge and say something like, "Excuse me, but you are to be in your room and I want you to be in there *now*!" Then you can do everything—from forcing him back into the room, to holding the door shut—you name it. But I don't think that's working very well.

ASHLEY: No, it isn't, so what do you suggest?

KEVIN: When he comes out of his room without permission, you don't make a big thing out of it. Just wait until he asks you for something. Start denying him privileges or treats, or whatever hits him where it really hurts. After you deny him things a few times, he'll finally start asking, "Well, what's wrong with you?" Then you can say that he should know what's wrong. He disobeyed you when you asked him to stay in his room, and you can tell him you're disappointed and angry and upset. If he refuses to cooperate with you, you have no choice but to refuse to cooperate with him.

ASHLEY: You're saying that if he comes out of his room, don't force him to go back. Just let him get away with it.

KEVIN: The last thing I'm suggesting is that you let him get away with it. But it sounds as if you're the kind of person who will allow your son to go too far to begin with and you need to develop some new ways of holding him accountable. So, if he has something special planned, wait for him to get ready to go, and then let the air out of his tires. Other examples would be not allowing him to watch a favorite TV program (one you approve, of course), not allowing him to go to a friend's house, not letting a friend come for dinner, or not going to the park or to the beach.

ASHLEY: That seems awfully mean.

KEVIN: Mean? On the contrary, you're being very respectful of your son. I know it's hard to stick to your guns, but that is what

Reality Discipline is all about. And I'd like to give you one reminder of the crucial role you have as a mom because you represent womanhood to your son. You can do him a great justice for holding him accountable for things that he says or does to you or with you. You can teach him to have a healthy regard for women. In fact, you can do your future daughter-in-law a great service by standing in healthy authority over your son now as he's growing up. The more he learns to respect women, the better husband and daddy he'll be someday.

How do I stick to my guns with a charming, fun-loving child who manipulates me when he's being disciplined?

LOIS: I'm a firstborn and I'm having a power struggle with my firstborn son that's a little different. We have a very loving relationship and have a lot of laughs together, but he goofs around and jokes with me constantly and I have a hard time being consistent in discipline. I find myself backing off when I ought to be more—as you put it—in healthy authority.

RANDY: What kind of a kid is he? Is he causing a lot of problems?

LOIS: It depends. He and his teacher at school are butting heads, and the teacher just thinks he's being defiant. It's hard to tell; in certain situations he can be a wonderful child, and in other situations he can be difficult.

RANDY: When he is wonderful you have a good time with him and when he is needing discipline, you feel as if you can't be firm enough?

LOIS: Yes, that's often true, but then when I finally do get angry enough to discipline him, I have a hard time remembering that I am angry at what he did and not at him.

KEVIN: What you're saying is, it's difficult to separate the act from the actor. That's true for most parents no matter what age their kids are.

LOIS: Sometimes I wonder if he goofs around and is affectionate with me just to yank my chain, and I really don't want to get to the point where I think that every time he's affectionate or fun that he's just manipulating me.

KEVIN: Does he hug you when other people are around?

LOIS: Yes, he will do it in front of anybody.

KEVIN: That is the greatest testimony you can give about your relationship with your son.

RANDY: It sounds as if you could be honest with him, and I suggest that sometime when you're having some fun, sit down with him and say, "Listen, you know there are times when we are not going to have fun. There are times when I have to enforce certain discipline. But I want you to know that I love you then just as much as I do when we're having fun together."

KEVIN: Randy, I think part of the problem here is that we're talking about a mother and her son. Sons are very, very special to moms to begin with, so moms tend to be softies a lot of the time.

What's the best way to deal with a manipulative child who lies?

LOIS: I am getting accused of being a softie by my son's school. He has been caught in lies by his teachers, and there have been other behavioral problems. His teachers are telling me, "You really need to get on him and do this and do that." They see my relationship to him as all fun and games, and that I'm not administering any discipline. They think I'm protecting him and always taking his side.

RANDY: It sounds as if you are aware of your problem and what you need to do. If there are issues that need to be dealt with, such as playing fast and loose with the truth, you need to be firm and direct in holding him accountable. Develop a strategy that doesn't give him as much opportunity to be charming and manipulative. When you catch him lying, point out that if you can't trust him to tell the truth, you can't trust him to go to his friend's house, or engage in some other activity that he enjoys. Always tie the consequence for lying to an activity that he dearly loves. Another thing you may want to try, but I suggest it with caution, is to set up situations where he can experience fairly minor disappointments that let him know how it feels to be lied to. Don't do this with a promise to go to Disneyland or some other fairly big outing, but instead, offer or promise something like an ice cream treat, but then don't come through with the goods. When he asks why, say, "You know we have a policy in our family to always tell the truth. This time I was not truthful with you on purpose because I wanted you to know how it feels to be lied to." To use this strategy, you must really know your child and be *sure* he'll get the right point. You want him to understand that being lied to is very disappointing, and even painful. You do not want him to learn that "it's okay to lie." Be sure that you make it clear you're not at all in favor of lying, but that you did it only to give him a taste of how you feel when he lies to you.

KEVIN: Also, go talk to his teachers. Let them know that you do want to discipline your boy properly, that you are definitely not an easy mark, and you want to work in cooperation with them, particularly concerning his lying at school. Find out what he's lying about—for example, why his homework wasn't done or who clobbered whom on the playground. Let the teachers know that you will back them 100 percent on any disciplinary measure they wish to use. Here's an opportunity for you to work in close cooperation with the school to help your boy with a serious problem that can only get worse if he's allowed to continue lying.

RANDY: And one more thing, Lois, you need to discipline yourself. You need to ask yourself if you are basically a permissive parent, and you're just using your boy's charm as an excuse for being permissive. If you allow him to get too familiar, it stands to reason he won't really respect you or respond to your authority. You have to treat a child as you expect him to behave, and it's important to remember that, while we want our children to like us, a parent is a parent first and a pal second.

□ ○ △ □ ○ △

What can I do when I see myself favoring one child over another?

FRANK: I find myself gravitating toward our six-year-old son who is easy to deal with and tending to spend less time with our nine year old daughter, who is very difficult and oppositional. What can I do to change this?

KEVIN: Well, you've already started by just recognizing the problem. I believe there is a real correlation between the opposite sex parent and the oppositional child. Often it's a good guess that the opposite sex parent is authoritarian, and this helps create an oppositional child. What is your parenting style?

FRANK: Well, if I lean in any direction, it's toward being too strict. I try to raise my kids according to biblical principles.

KEVIN: It's good that you can admit that. I think what's happened with your children is that you and your daughter have butted heads from day one, but when your little son came along, you had a fairly typical male reaction to having a son—"This is great!" So it was easy to start favoring him. In addition, keep in mind that in any family, the first two children are usually night and day different. Your daughter was the strong-willed, feisty one, so it was easy for little brother to take a clue from her and to go in a completely different direction.

RANDY: The question he's asking though, Kevin, is what can he do to remedy this? I think one thing that always helps, particularly in Christian families, is to realize that in the Christian community, the value system says that we should be against rebellion and supportive of those who are submissive or responsive. And often that means that children with an oppositional personality (which parents have helped create, by the way) often get labeled as "bad kids" or "problem children."

There is nothing bad, per se, about being oppositional. I have a pastor friend who preached about Jesus being an oppositional child in his family. Some of his church members got upset with him, but what he was trying to point out is that you don't always want to see opposition in a negative context. There is a personality strength in the oppositional child that helps that child make decisions and know what he believes and stand by it. Oppositional personality traits can be very positive when they're channeled properly.

KEVIN: That makes a lot of sense, Randy, and I'd like to suggest, Frank, that you back off a little on your daughter. Analyze why you are butting heads. Where is it necessary to really hold the line and where can you give in? When you have an oppositional child, you can spend all of your energy putting out the little fires, and never find time to build a better relationship. Why not invite your daughter out on a date now and then? She'll be thrilled to have a night out alone with Dad and you can get a better perspective on her in a positive setting, rather than always seeing her as someone opposing you—someone with whom you have to "battle."

RANDY: Something else positive you can do is check to be sure the family rules aren't slanted in favor of the younger son. Have family meetings and discuss the rules—everything from bedtime to allowances, from chores to homework. Give both children a chance to bring things up that might be bothering them. Remember, your daughter is the oldest and, if anything, the rules should slightly favor her—later bedtime, bigger allowance, etc.

□ ○ △ □ ○ △

What's the best way to discipline a strong-willed, oppositional child?

BARBARA: I have two oppositional children, seven and a half and fourteen months old. I don't want to be constantly after them, but they are a handful. If I back off too far, they steamroller me! But if I clamp down, it's always a running, pitched battle. Is there some kind of middle ground on how to deal with them?

RANDY: If I were able to observe you and your children through closed circuit television, what would I see that was strong-willed or oppositional?

BARBARA: You can tell the minute they are born almost. My fourteen month old, for example, is constantly climbing up on the table or anything else she can find to climb on. I put her down and she climbs back up. We go through that a hundred times a day. And my seven-and-a-half-year-old son is a whirling dervish—always moving, and always having to do whatever he's doing "one more time" after he's called. I'm constantly having to say, "Over here—stay over here with the rest of the family."

And I'm getting a lot of flack from Sunday school teachers

because he is always bouncing off the wall or hopping up and down, and they'll ask me, "Why don't you discipline him? Why don't you control him?" I try to explain to them that I do discipline him, but obviously they think that I'm too permissive and that he's out of hand. It's hard to know what to do.

RANDY: From your description of your seven-year-old, it sounds as if he might have what is known as Attention Deficit Hyperactivity Disorder, but only a pediatrician who specializes in that area can verify that. You might want to have your boy checked out.*

KEVIN: That's a good suggestion, Randy. The first thing to keep in mind, Barbara, is what's best for your boy. If you're doing the right thing, all of that judgment at church is irrelevant. I'd like to point out, however, that when your fourteen month old climbs back up on the table, that's not unusual. That's what fourteen-month-old children do. It's part of their job description.

BARBARA: Not always. We have another child who's between the two I'm describing—a four year old who has never been a problem. When he was a baby, I could sit him on a blanket and he'd stay on the blanket. My fourteen month old was walking at eight months and she's been in a dead run ever since.

RANDY: One thing to do when your fourteen month old starts climbing back on the table is to "remove the table," so to speak. At least remove access to the table. Put her in a play pen or somewhere where she can't get at the table.

* For a complete discussion of Attention Deficit Hyperactivity Disorder (A.D.H.D.), see Chapter Thirteen.

Are there any positive things I can do with a strong-willed child to avoid constantly having to discipline him?

BARBARA: My seven-year-old boy concerns me the most. It seems I'm always correcting him, always reminding him, always on his case. It's a pretty negative scene.

RANDY: It helps to remember that the oppositional child often draws strength from being opposed. Find some ways that you can change the atmosphere in the family. Try to make things a little lighter, more humorous, and be less confrontive with him. Realize that when you ask him to stop what he's doing, that you know he'll do it at least one more time—probably to just pull your chain. Be prepared for that and cut back on bawling him out or saying no so often.

KEVIN: I agree. Try to create a pleasant atmosphere between you and your oppositional child. You don't want it to be negative all the time. Keep in mind that it's so easy to get in a power struggle with this kind of kid, and it usually all starts because you're trying to exert too much authority. That's like waving a red flag in front of a bull. You want to be authoritative and in healthy authority, but not authoritarian and just naturally "provoking the child to wrath," as the Scriptures put it.

RANDY: One thing that I've noticed in working with strong-willed kids is that if you give them responsibility or a sense of control over their own destiny, the tension level usually drops. Try to get your seven year old to help you with things that are important around the house. Give him a sense of authority or responsibility. Try to take the focus off of "How do I discipline this kid?" and put the focus on "How do I encourage him to use all of his aggressiveness in a positive way?"

KEVIN: Also, what happens with an oppositional child is that he feels he doesn't have any power so he tries to be even more powerful. Often, parents don't trust a strong-willed child. They are suspicious that he is going to "get into trouble again." That makes them crack down all the more and then it just escalates into a power struggle. Don't ever fall into the trap of thinking that active children are "bad." Beware of comparing one child with another on the basis of who is harder or easier to deal with. Accept the differences in your children. God made them that way.

RANDY: Keep in mind that children who appear to be oppositional are sometimes simply bored. Instead of always thinking about how you can discipline your strong-willed oppositional child, concentrate on giving him a positive outlet for all that energy. I recall counseling one mother who was really upset because her little girl would always be painting or coloring on the walls of her bedroom. I suggested that she get an old bed sheet and hang it up on the wall and encourage the child to express her creative energy by painting or coloring on the sheet. It worked beautifully, and Mom and daughter were both happy.

□ ○ △ □ ○ △

Is it possible for a child to be too compliant—too good?

KATHY: I'm worried about my ten-year-old daughter who is what I guess what some people would call a "goody two-shoes." She keeps her room immaculate, she makes all A's in school, and whatever I ask her to do she does it immediately without sassing. She brings my husband his newspaper. She helps me with the dishes. I could go on.

KEVIN: We have the picture. Tell me, is this child for lease with an option to buy?

KATHY: Everyone wants to lease Amanda. We get tons of compliments about what a fabulous job we've done to rear such a polite, considerate daughter, but I'm worried because I know what this could be doing to her. I know from personal experience that sooner or later feelings of hostility do come out.

RANDY: Are you telling us that you rebelled after you grew up? Or possibly during high school?

KATHY: Exactly. I've got a daughter who is me to a "T." Everyone thought I was a perfect child, but actually I was holding in a great deal of hostility. I was told so often I was a "good girl" I was terrified to be anything but perfect. I felt under constant pressure.

KEVIN: All children want attention and recognition, but it sounds as if you took it to extremes.

KATHY: It was like an addiction. I absolutely had to hear my parents, aunts, uncles, teachers, even the neighbors, say regularly that I was a delightful kid. If I didn't hear that, I'd start feeling unliked and unloved. I did everything I could to please and comply with however people around me wanted me to behave, but all the while I hated the pressure. I played a role but I didn't feel real.

After getting out of high school and going off to college, I rebelled big time. I did everything I had never done while growing up—parties, skipping classes, gaudy make-up, dressing like a slob, I tried everything I could think of to assert my independence.

RANDY: And while all this seemed like fun for a while, I would guess you eventually discovered something.

KATHY: I thought I was getting even with my parents and everybody else who had boxed me in as "little goody two-shoes," but midway through my first semester I realized that nothing had really changed. I was still a compliant person, only now I was complying with the lifestyle my roommates wanted me to use. I was just as phony as I had ever been and it made me feel worse than ever too.

KEVIN: You mentioned that as a compliant child, you wanted to be a pleaser, to be acceptable, but I think there might have been another motive—am I right in guessing that you've never really liked confrontation? Is it fair to say that as a child, and even now as an adult, you've always tried to avoid hassles and face-to-face opposition?

KATHY: To be honest, yes. I never liked to argue with my parents and today I'm totally non-confrontational. I won't even complain about our newspaper being delivered late. I seldom argue with my husband or my friends. Fortunately, my husband, Jeff, is terrific. He's easygoing, gentle, and understanding.

RANDY: That's extremely fortunate. Many times compliant children develop unhealthy patterns that they carry over into adulthood and they wind up with abusive mates. The compliant pleaser feels that if she can just be a little nicer, a little more patient, a little more subservient, her mate will finally love her. The more she tries to please, the more he controls and bullies, and the cycle goes on.

How can I help my "too compliant" daughter be more assertive and able to stand up for herself?

KATHY: What can I do to help my perfect daughter, Amanda? As I've said, she's a carbon copy of me. She doesn't like to confront or be confronted. All she wants to do is please.

KEVIN: Always complying and avoiding confrontation are often ways of avoiding accountability. I have an idea you might want to try with Amanda: Suppose you ask her to be sure to make some new friends during recess because you know she fears rejection and doesn't like to be that outgoing. And suppose Amanda volunteers to stay inside for recess and clean the chalkboards for the teacher. Then when you ask her if she made any new friends that day, she will say, "The teacher needed someone to clean the chalkboards, so I couldn't get out for recess." This sounds noble, but actually it's avoiding confrontation and bypassing accountability. Instead of condoning it, it would be better to hold her accountable by saying, "That was very nice of you to help your teacher, but tomorrow I want you to get in line for the slide, or take your turn jumping rope so that you can meet the children at your new school. To make friends you must first be a friend."

KATHY: Interestingly enough, Amanda does have trouble making friends and she doesn't like to break into new groups. I will start encouraging her to be more accountable in this area. But I know how tough it will be on her because I know how tough it would have been on me as a kid.

RANDY: If you're going to ask Amanda to be more accountable, you will have to model accountability and assertiveness in front of her. You admit you're not confrontational. So how can you start being a little more confrontational and assertive? See if your husband can help you with standing up to certain people—store clerks, newspaper carriers, whoever it might be.

KEVIN: And be sure to resist the temptation to step in and help your daughter solve her problems. Go out of your way to let her handle things, even when she seems a bit at a loss as to what to do. Also, don't praise her for good behavior. I don't like the word *praise* anyway—I much prefer to "encourage" kids. Never praise your daughter for being a "good girl." Instead, make it a point to say things like, "You did that well. I'll bet you feel good about how you handled that!" (For more on the difference between praise and encouragement, see pp. 112–113.)

CHAPTER 10

■●▲■●▲

REALITY DISCIPLINE WAS MADE FOR THE LITTLE LEAGUERS

RANDY: Kevin, what do you see as the greatest challenge parents are facing in the '90s?

KEVIN: I think it's just a general confusion about their task and how to get it done. It is amazing how many parents come to my office and say things like, "How do we do this?" And I say, "How do you do what? What are you talking about?" And they explain, "How do you parent—how do you become a parent?" I tell them, "You already are a parent." And their answer is, "Yes, we know, but how do we do it?"

People are looking for direction. Many of them are desperate. Their own parents weren't any help, in fact, they were a negative model and people want to know, "How do I raise my kid the right way?"

RANDY: As I think about parenting my own kids, the biggest thing that comes to mind is consistency—trying to be consistent across the board with three unique personalities. All three of our kids need love and discipline, but Donna and I have to go about it differently with each child.

KEVIN: Randy, I think one of the most interesting times to be a parent is when the kids move into what I call the "Little League set"—they get into school, start to take part in Little League, Pony Softball, ballet, soccer, and a million other activities. We always say that by the time a child is five, most of the personality is there, and by age seven it is all over, but I don't know that that's necessarily all true. The cement is definitely setting by age seven, but there is still some moving around that can be done in those years when the child moves through the first through the sixth grades.

RANDY: I agree. Two of our kids are right there—Andrea is eleven and D. J. is eight. At this level, you really start to see the lifestyle played out in earnest. D. J. is our little comedian and enjoys lots of attention. He's very creative and spends hours by himself inventing contraptions that are supposed to fly to the moon. He always enjoys having us come and see what he has just made. Andrea is our middle child but also our firstborn daughter. She's very strong-willed, very bright, and loves to engage in verbal debates. Evan, our firstborn, has moved on into the hormone set that we'll be talking about later—he's fourteen. To Evan, life is *serious.* He has to have all his ducks in a row, and I think we have a budding controller on our hands.

KEVIN: Every Friday we throw our lines open—what we call "Open Phones"—and people call in with every imaginable question and problem. We get a lot of calls on the little ankle biters five and under, but there are almost as many on the Little Leaguers, ages six to twelve. We know that one call represents hundreds, if not thousands, of people who have the same problems. Here are some samples:

What is the difference between being authoritarian and authoritative?

MARLENE: I have a seven-year-old son who is, as Kevin puts it, a powerful little buzzard. I've heard you both say that when a parent is powerful back to a powerful child, it makes him even worse, and that I need to be authoritative with him instead of authoritarian. How do I know when I'm being authoritative or when I'm being authoritarian and too powerful?

KEVIN: That's a question we often hear from parents of strong-willed children. Here's the difference between authoritarian and authoritative: Suppose the child says something to you that he shouldn't—he's really smart-mouthing you. The authoritarian approach is, "*What* did you say? Excuse me, young man." Then you go over, grab him by the scruff of his neck, give him a swift swat on his tail, and send him to his room. Or maybe you ground him, take away his Nintendo for six months—anything you can think of that really shows him who's the boss. Now all you have done is show your powerful child you are being powerful back.

MARLENE: Okay, what's the authoritative way to go at it?

KEVIN: There are various ways to be authoritative, but the key to all of them is not to get angry and huff and puff at your child in an authoritarian manner. One of my favorite approaches is to just wait until it's time for the child to do something he wants to do or go somewhere he wants to go. Then he says, "Mommy, c'mon, it's time for you to drive me here or there." But you say, "I'm sorry, Honey, I'm not driving you anywhere." And your child will say, "Well, what's wrong?" And then you say, "Honey, I think you know what's wrong." Sooner or later the child usually gets the point. "Oh, you're mad because of what I said this morning." And you say, "Yes, that's true, I am angry." And then the kid will usually apologize, "Oh, Mommy, I'm sorry." And you reply, "Thank you, I'm thankful you can apologize for what you did." And then comes the real payoff when you have to stick to your guns. Then your kid will say, "Well, will you drive me now?" And that's when you say, "No." That is being authoritative and using Reality Discipline.

MARLENE: I'm not sure I completely see the difference. Isn't refusing to drive him somewhere being powerful? It almost sounds as if I would be getting revenge.

KEVIN: It depends on how you deliver the news that you aren't going to drive him. If you are still full of anger and not in control of your emotions, then you might be simply getting revenge. But revenge should never be your goal. You want to teach and to train your powerful child and yet you never want to goad or provoke him or her. I think the Apostle Paul said it very well in Ephesians 6:4: "And now a word to you parents. Don't keep on scolding and nagging your children, . . . [but] bring them up with the loving discipline the Lord himself approves, with suggestions and godly advice" (TLB). You have to walk the balance beam. And a key is not getting angry, not being powerful back. That makes all the difference.

RANDY: And yet you stay in healthy authority and you take action. Marlene, one good way to approach it is to know in advance what you'll do if your child misbehaves. When you've already thought it through and you know what action you'll take and you take that action, you probably will be acting authoritatively. But if you just react, especially in anger, and do whatever the moment seems to demand, you're probably being authoritarian.

KEVIN: And one other tip. If the discipline is not to take him to his Little League game, it's a good idea to call his coach and try to win his cooperation. Ask the coach to call the boy later and ask why he wasn't at the game and be sure the coach probes enough to get the entire story. Then the coach can reinforce to your boy that he was out of line and if he were his dad he would have left him home from the ball game too. Many times parents fail to solicit the help of other significant people in their children's lives

—coaches, teachers, assistant principals, or what have you—but these leaders are usually more than willing to help you enforce Reality Discipline because it makes so much sense.

□ ○ △ □ ○ △

How do I handle a super sensitive boy who dissolves into tears when corrected or disciplined in any way?

JUANITA: We have three sons and the youngest is extremely sensitive. He can't handle any kind of rebuke or discipline of any nature. The minute he feels we are angry or upset with him, he dissolves into tears. He is twelve and he's been like this since he was a toddler. This is frustrating to my husband and me—we just don't know how to handle him. When he starts crying, do we continue with whatever discipline is being enforced, or should we back off?

RANDY: This is a good question because we know all kids are different and, in using any kind of discipline, you need to be sensitive to the unique personality of each child. Tell me, Juanita, what kind of discipline measures do you use now with your son?

JUANITA: We have pretty much passed the point of corporal punishment—no more spankings or anything like that. Right now we revoke privileges, such as watching TV or visiting friends, things like that.

KEVIN: There are a couple of key points you need to consider: First, we're talking about your youngest son. The youngest child is most likely to be the manipulative one of the family. He is also most likely to be the most affectionate and sensitivity can be a big part of that. Whenever I hear a parent saying a child is "very sensitive," I usually put an equal sign after the word *sensitive* and complete it with the word *powerful.* Sensitive equals power.

Second, you're asking us if you should back off on the discipline when he starts to tear up or become sensitive. Absolutely not. Continue on with the discipline, making sure that you're holding him accountable for his actions. No matter how many tears, no matter how many apologies he's already given, you still go on. Give me an example of what you're doing right now when he starts to cry while being disciplined.

JUANITA: The last incident involved my scolding him for the condition that his dresser drawers were in—all the dirty socks I was finding in there and so on. My husband simply walked by the bedroom door, looked in, and that dissolved Brad into tears. He thought Dad gave him one of his "mean looks."

KEVIN: When a child tears up, it doesn't help to get flustered or stop what you're saying or doing. Instead, just reach over and touch the child anywhere—on the arm, on the knee—while not breaking stride with what you're saying. This is a trick I've used for years while counseling children, and it helps the child pull himself together.

JUANITA: By the way, Brad is listening right now to this program, and he just walked in and told me, "I do not cry *all* the time." He is very particular about keeping all the facts straight and, while he doesn't cry all the time, he has to agree with me he does cry a lot of the time when being disciplined.

KEVIN: I think we're definitely talking about a manipulative, powerful child, who also has a streak of perfectionism. That's unusual for the baby of the family, but it does happen. I'm not saying that Brad doesn't feel hurt or disappointed when he is disciplined, but you must understand that all behavior has a purpose.

RANDY: When we talk about the purpose of behavior, there are three levels—seeking attention, going on a power trip, or taking revenge. All kids behave at level one—to get their parents' attention—but it seems to me that with your son, there is also a power struggle. He likes to be right, to be correct, and he mixes that with being sensitive. There are no more powerful tools than tears and sensitivity. We're advising you not to be manipulated.

You are responsible to love your son and set the boundaries and hold him accountable. It sounds as if you are doing this, but he doesn't like it. The worst thing you can do is back off. Remember that he doesn't have to like anything you do as long as you and your husband do it with firm consistency and love. The power of love and limits can't be underscored enough here. Kevin, that twelve year old is sitting there with his ear to the radio. What do you have to say to him right now?

KEVIN: Brad, the jig is up. You have been confirmed as a powerful little buzzard who masks that power with tears and sensitivity. So lighten up and be thankful that you have parents who love you and really care about you.

□ ○ △ □ ○ △

How do I get a "silent" child to talk and open up to me?

VERONICA: My seven-year-old son is the second of four children. He's not a discipline problem, per se. He's motivated, does well in school, but he will not open up to me. If he's having a problem—a falling out with a friend, perhaps—and I ask him what's wrong, he just won't talk.

RANDY: How does your son react when you try to get him to talk? It's my guess he may have difficulty returning love and affection.

VERONICA: He just gets a grumpy look on his face and will either walk away or, if I'm putting him to bed at night, he'll just get a grumpy look and turn away from me. And, yes, I do have a hard time getting hugs out of him. Once in a while he may give me a hug, but he is very reluctant—almost seems bored.

RANDY: It's commendable that you're aware of this problem and want to help your son because this kind of child may grow up to have trouble communicating in marriage, for example. Different kids relate to others in different ways. We all have a unique temperament and by natural design some kids are just more closed and controlled than others. I see this in our own family where our firstborn son has the hardest time opening up.

KEVIN: In our family, it has been our second-born daughter. You have to wait for her to come to you—you don't ask her a lot of questions. And that's one of the things I'd suggest for you, Veronica. Stop asking your son a lot of questions and don't ask him for hugs. Let him know that you love him and that you're always there for him if he wants to talk, but don't stay after him. That will just make him clam up all the more.

RANDY: I'd like to know where Dad is in all of this.

VERONICA: Communication-wise, he's out of it. He has the same problem. I feel totally in the dark with him most of the time, and I spend a lot of time second-guessing if I'm doing the right thing. It's really hard to bring up conflicts with him because he won't talk about them, so I'm disappointed again and still don't get anything resolved.

KEVIN: So your son has had seven years of learning not to be open from the master non-communicator himself—his father. What about your other three kids—do they open up to you?

VERONICA: Yes, they're all quite open. They tell me their problems and I can talk with them about most anything.

KEVIN: Then I think you should go with what you've got. Share your faults and weaknesses, your successes and failures with your other kids and let them share with you. As your non-talkative boy hears you sharing with the other children, he'll learn that it is not the most threatening thing in the world to open up and tell people how he feels.

RANDY: Regarding Kevin's other suggestion about backing off and not hammering your boy with lots of questions—that's good, but at the same time, don't give up on letting your boy know you want to talk with him. Take opportunities to let him know how important it is to a woman that a man be able to communicate with her. I'm not saying criticize your husband in front of him, but simply let your boy know, whenever you can, that it's important to share feelings and let people know where you're coming from. Remember, too, that you told us your son is really a good kid—obedient and a good student. You want to let your boy know he's loved and prized as he is.

KEVIN: And one other thought. Obviously, you have some feelings toward your husband concerning his lack of communication. It would be easy to project those feelings onto your son. Try to avoid that whenever you notice you might be doing it. Accept your boy as the neat kid he is. Right now he isn't talking a lot, but that can change if you just have patience. Also, if you can get your husband to go to counseling with you, perhaps he can get insights on why he doesn't like to communicate and how he is being a poor model for his son.

RANDY: Remember, too, that not every child is going to be a good verbal communicator. Children can communicate in many ways, nonverbally, through writing, artistically, musically, to name a few. We all know people who express themselves in many ways that aren't necessarily verbal. Perhaps that's the case with your son. Be sure you look over the papers that he writes for classes at school. Or does he do artwork that expresses emotions and feelings? Go over something he's drawn or written and try to verbalize what you see on the paper, and ask him if that's how he felt. He can either confirm or deny the feelings that you are seeing there, but at least you'll be demonstrating to him that you know he does have feelings and that he may have ways of expressing them that are different from simply talking.

KEVIN: If you find that your son just doesn't want to talk, I have a suggestion. There is a real analogy here to the way that eighteen-month-old children act. Often if you come at an eighteen-month-old child with your arms outstretched and say, "Come to Mommy," he'll take off and run the opposite way. But if you back up with your arms outstretched, and ask him to come to you, he usually will. It's called the "oppositional factor." You can do the same thing with your silent seven-year-old son. Just say, "I know you find it hard to talk and share, but if you ever want to, I'm here." This is the way you back up psychologically and give your son space. And you use a very important principle of Reality Discipline—to ask for but also to give respect to the other person.

□ ○ △ □ ○ △

How do I say no in a positive way when my child wants to watch bad TV or movies?

LUETTA: I'm a single parent and I have my ten-year-old daughter living with me while my sixteen-year-old son lives with his dad. I need some guidelines on how to communicate my values, particularly about TV—some of the cartoons. How can I explain to her that they might look innocent enough, but they are really not good to watch? When I try, she simply says, "Oh, Mom, so what if there are some bad words? I hear this all the time at school. I don't see anything wrong with this program." I usually wind up just letting it go, and I don't know what to do about it.

RANDY: In other words, your ten year old is sort of running the house.

LUETTA: In some respects, that's true. Maybe I try to take it too easy on her because of the marital breakup and all the things she's been going through. I was divorced only a year ago, so she's still hurting. I'm having a difficult time staying in control.

KEVIN: Try to look at your parenting task as being in healthy authority over your child rather than being in control of her at all times, which is impossible. As the single parent, your job is to establish boundaries that are reasonable and firm and then hold your child accountable for staying within those boundaries. It's my guess, as a single mom, you are letting guilt influence a lot of your decisions. Guilt is making you too permissive and, Luetta, you can't let guilt rule your life and then give your daughter carte blanche as far as what she wants to watch on TV.

LUETTA: I'd like to throw this in to help you understand the situation. I've always been a pleaser. I do let my kids have their way because I think that if I don't they won't love me. I know that's not true, but that's how I feel.

RANDY: So you grew up being a pleaser and now that you're a single parent it's obvious that you can't put that pleasing nature and inability to confront on a back burner. You still want people to like you, particularly your daughter. But I think, Luetta, you have to realize, as a parent, your job is to love and discipline your child, not to be liked by your child. There will be times when your daughter won't like you—particularly if you make her change the channel. But your job is to set the boundaries in love and her job is to respect you and obey you. In the long term, you hope that she will love and like you for what you did.

LUETTA: But how do I explain *why* I don't want her to watch certain programs and movies?

KEVIN: You have to be sure of your own values and stick to your guns. If a program has bad language, just tell her, "Look, I know you hear bad language at school, but that doesn't mean we have to hear it in our home. Let's find another program."

If there's too much violence, just tell her, "This show is too violent. The people who made this program want us to think that killing or hurting people is the way to solve problems."

As for shows that are sexy, this is a great opportunity to share your views about sex, dating, boys, men. Let her know that sex is something wonderful and these programs turn it into something cheap and dirty.

RANDY: The important thing, Luetta, is not to back off. Stand your ground and when in doubt, simply say, "No, we aren't going to watch this or do this because it simply isn't right or good. I love you too much to let you watch or do this." As a single mother who knows she's permissive, you have to keep working at being as authoritative as possible. You have no partner to back you up or provide a balancing style of discipline, so you have to provide that balance yourself. Just hang in there, Luetta; you and your daughter will be okay.

□ ○ △ □ ○ △

How can I get my child to pick up her clothes and put things away without having a constant hassle?

STEVE: I'm a single parent and my nine-year-old daughter and I have a running battle over her messiness. I'm always getting upset and yelling at her and this just doesn't work at all.

KEVIN: Tell me, are there other children in the family?

STEVE: Yes, I have a seven-year-old son, and I get along fine with him. He keeps his room neat, and is a very cooperative kid.

KEVIN: Tell me, are you a firstborn, Steve?

STEVE: Yes, I'm firstborn and so is my daughter, and we seem to be constantly locking horns.

RANDY: Well, that's not surprising—very typical of a firstborn parent and a firstborn child. Here are some things you can do. Realize that you're both firstborns and that your tendency is to get uptight, to get intense, to yell. Back off and don't yell at her. Instead, try using Reality Discipline. Hold her accountable for her messy room. If she won't keep her room clean, then maybe you'll have to hire her younger brother to do it and pay him part of her allowance. Or, maybe you'll have to pick up her room and pay yourself out of her allowance.

KEVIN: There are many ways to make her accountable. If her room isn't clean by a certain time, she can't go to a friend's overnight, can't watch her favorite TV show, etc. Find what really matters to her and use that as a way of holding her accountable for what she's supposed to be doing.

RANDY: Also, messy kids and messy rooms are a question we hear a lot from parents of all ages. Because you're a firstborn and obviously on the meticulous side, a clean room is important to you. But it may not be that important to your daughter. Make a deal with her. She has to at least "shovel out" her room every Tuesday and Friday. The rest of the time you will try to ignore the mess. Then, if she doesn't comply with the agreement, you can invoke Reality Discipline.

□ ○ △ □ ○ △

How do I deal with a child who constantly challenges my authority and always asks, "Why do I have to do this?"

SAMANTHA: My daughter is almost ten, and I have two boys, six and a half and three. My boys are usually obedient but my daughter is like me. She has difficulty respecting authority. She'll challenge me—every day it's a confrontation.

RANDY: How do you handle it when she's disrespectful?

SAMANTHA: It's fifty/fifty—sometimes I get angry and frustrated and tell her to go to her room, and say I don't appreciate her being disrespectful. Other times I'll say, "Honey, that is not God's way. You cannot act like this because it isn't God's best for your life." And very occasionally, I might spank her.

RANDY: I believe you said she's ten. When they get up around that age, the effectiveness of spanking starts to wane. What do you do, Kevin, with a child who is disrespectful?

KEVIN: One of the nicest things to do for a kid who is disrespectful is to, first, stop the initial knee-jerk reaction: "*What* did you say? Do you know *who* you are talking to? I am your *mother*!" As parents, we are quick to claim our authority, but by that time the battle is engaged. It makes more sense to just walk away. Now, you may think I mean let her get away with it. But that's the last thing I mean.

With a ten-year-old child, it works quite well to disengage from the immediate confrontation but to leave her with something to think about. Say in a straightforward, non-hostile way: "Obviously you don't want to do what I've asked you to do. That's too bad. We'll talk more about this later."

Then bide your time. Around 4:00 that day, she'll say, "Mom, I've got to go to dance practice in twenty minutes." And that's when you say, "Honey, I'm sorry, the car is not moving." The daughter will say, "But I *have* to be there; the recital is coming up and Mrs. Jones says *no one* can miss *any* practices." Then you say, "I'm sorry, Honey, the car is not moving."

Instantaneously your daughter will start wondering, *Why? What is Mom's problem?* And Mom can tell her that her problem goes back to 10:15 this morning when "You and I had some words and I didn't like what I heard. I said we would talk later and now 'later' has arrived. When you are disrespectful and refuse to do what I ask, then your privileges are taken away."

At this point your daughter may scream, have a little tantrum, cry, sulk, or, because dance practice is really important, she might become contrite and apologize, thinking that that will get her what she wants—transportation. It's then that you tell her, "Thank you for the apology, but today the car is not moving.

We'll see how things go tomorrow." It doesn't take too many encounters like this to get your point across, and I think your daughter will cut down on her challenges to your authority.

What does a firstborn mom need to remember when disciplining a firstborn daughter?

RANDY: Samantha, you and your oldest daughter seem to be a great deal alike. You're probably the firstborn in your family or the firstborn daughter. . . .

SAMANTHA: You're right. I am the firstborn in a family of four.

RANDY: Well, then it's natural for you and your daughter to butt heads. Maybe one thing you can do is ask yourself what worked or didn't work with you when you were that age. I also noted something else, Samantha. You mentioned that your two younger boys are very obedient and this means that you could possibly be inadvertently showing them favoritism, which your daughter may be noticing, and that's causing some of her stubbornness.

Another thing you said was that you were about fifty/fifty in how you respond to your daughter. Sometimes you're angry and sometimes you lecture her. If you want to see her behavior change, you need to develop a consistent strategy and stick with it. Don't preach, lecture, or get angry when she challenges you or disobeys. Simply pull the rug on her by taking away something that really matters.

We've already used the dance practice illustration, but there are many other ways to pull the rug: not letting her go to a friend's house, or assigning her to stay in her room until she decides to cooperate or do what you've asked. You have to analyze what will really work best with her. But instead of accepting her challenge, and letting her get your wind into her sails, learn to back off and let her experience the consequences of being disrespectful or disobedient.

□ ○ △ □ ○ △

What do I do with two little boys who never seem to hear what I tell them?

BETH: I've got two sons who are seven and five, and the only way I can get them to follow through and obey what I have asked them to do is stop them, look directly into their eyes, tell them what I want, and have them repeat back to me what I've said. This takes a lot of time, and I'm wondering if it's the only thing I can do. Do you have any other ideas?

KEVIN: You could ask almost any kid in America how many times does your mom have to call you for dinner? Most American children will say, "Three times. The first time is just sort of a general alert. The second time Mom raises her voice, and I know it's getting close to being serious. The third time, she adds my middle name and that's when I know I better get home *fast.*" With that kind of routine, parents *train* their kids not to listen.

BETH: You know, there's a difference between talking *to* your children and *at* your children. If I just walk by and say to one of my kids, "Time to pick up your toys," he just doesn't hear me. But if I turn around, look him right in the face and say, "Mother wants you to pick up your toys, now what did I just ask you to do?" then he will say, "Pick up my toys." And then I say, "Do I want you to do it now or in ten minutes?" And he'll say, "You want me to do it now," and he does.

RANDY: All this takes time, Beth, but it's just part of parenting this age level. It's amazing how children can go through screening at school for vision and hearing and come home and simply be totally deaf and blind as far as seeing the mess on the floor and hearing what Mom wants done with it.

KEVIN: The same thing can be said about husbands, I'm afraid. My firstborn wife had to train me to pick up my clothes after we got married. And there have been times when she's gotten pretty disgusted with all of us in the family over the mess. During the years we were raising our "first" family—Holly, Krissy, and Kevey—she got so fed up, she threw a banana peel on the floor and stood back to see what would happen. It almost blew her mind when every kid in the family walked right by it and, as I came through, I kicked it out of the way. The Cub got it from Mama Bear that day!

I have improved over the years, but I'm still getting used to the bit in my mouth. It just goes to show that you can grow up, get married, earn a Ph.D., and counsel people for a living, but deep down the little boy you once were you still are, and you have to use a little Reality Discipline on yourself now and then.

RANDY: We would suggest that your strategy of stopping to look the child in the face and tell him what you want isn't bad, but along with that you could simply give your instruction once and then not go through the big routine of "What did I say, and when do I want it done?" Instead, simply walk away and see what happens. Later, if the toys aren't picked up, Reality Discipline goes into effect. A treasured toy disappears for a while. A privilege is revoked, or something the child wants to do or get becomes unavailable. If you do this consistently, your boy's hearing will improve a great deal.

□ ○ △ □ ○ △

How can I get my children to stop using the offensive language they pick up at school?

AMY: We have four children, thirteen, twelve-year-old twins, and a nine year old—all boys. All four, but especially the twelve year olds, are coming home using foul language, which is never used in our home. I don't know what to do with them. I threaten them; I send them to their rooms, but it doesn't help much. What is a good way to turn this around? I'm at my wit's end.

RANDY: Hearing their kids use foul and inappropriate language is a common problem for parents. One thing most parents do is overreact when kids do things that violate their parental values. And the bigger the deal the parents make out of it, the more it reinforces the behavior.

KEVIN: That's right, threatening them or sending them to their rooms is never going to work. When children use foul language in your presence and continue to do so when you clearly tell them not to, I think you as a parent have an obligation to get what I call "the long jaws." In other words, look offended because you are offended. Look concerned because you are concerned.

Don't threaten, lecture, or preach. Just let them know this is not acceptable, and then wait for the proper time to revoke a privilege or refuse to do them an important favor like drive them to the movies, or to school. When they want to know, "What is it with you?" tell them that they know perfectly well what is wrong. You are hurt by their filthy language and until it stops the car isn't moving to haul them around, or other things aren't happening. Make mental lists of things that are important to your kids, and use those things to discipline your kids with love.

RANDY: Another approach you may want to take, Amy, is to sit down with the child, one-on-one, and let the child know that you are well aware of what these vulgar words mean. Then explain the definition of these terms to them, very specifically and graphically. Let them know how inappropriate and gross they really are and that's why you are offended.

Another way to use Reality Discipline would be to tell your child he will be left out of going out to restaurants or going over to other homes for dinner with the family, because you aren't sure of the kind of language he will be using. Also, your twelve year olds and your thirteen year old are on the phone a lot, and you might let them know that if the vulgar language doesn't cease, the phone will be off limits, too, because that kind of talk over the phone simply can't be tolerated either.

Shouldn't Christian children be reminded that God disapproves of bad language or bad behavior?

AMY: Does Reality Discipline ever allow for bringing God into the picture when kids are doing something wrong, like using foul language? We are trying to raise our kids as Christians and it seems to me it would make sense to point out that what they are saying is offensive to God as well as to us.

RANDY: I think there is a tendency in many Christian homes to preach at children whenever they do something wrong. It's correct to tell them it's offensive to God, but it's so easy to go beyond that and use God as a club to beat them over the head. Too many parents get angry and wale on their kids with statements like, "Christian children shouldn't talk that way. God will punish that kind of talk . . ." and on and on. At the same time, parents have a responsibility to explain why they don't like certain behavior or certain language, for example.

KEVIN: Instead of telling kids how angry God is about bad language or bad behavior, take the tack that you love God and want to please him and do what the Bible teaches because you know that's the best way to live. It's much more productive to use these incidents where kids use bad language or whatever to teach them why you have certain values and why these values are so important in your family.

Moms should start early planting seeds with their children about what abusive language really does. I haven't run on to many women who say, "I love abusive language. I love filthy talk. I want to hear it all the time." When you analyze filthy language or filthy jokes, who gets the brunt of the humor? Generally speaking, it's the women. When kids use bad language or filthy expressions, their parents, especially Mom, can let them know that this is a very degrading thing for women to have to hear, particularly in their own home. Then, at an opportune time, sit down and show your kids what God's Word has to say about keeping your thoughts and your speech clean.

□ ○ △ □ ○ △

If I haven't used Reality Discipline before, can I just start "cold turkey," or should I ease into it slowly?

ANN: I have two boys, nine and seven, and a little girl, three. I can see using Reality Discipline with her, and I've already started, but what about my boys? They're the typical, strong-willed type. They are constantly giving me a bad time, particularly with not wanting to get ready for school. Both of them are night owls—bedtime is a battle, too, and when it's time to get up, they just don't make it and every morning it's a hassle.

KEVIN: You can start "cold turkey" and you can start without apology. You might say this much to your boys: "Boys, things are going to be different from this day forward." End of explanation. Don't give them a lot of warnings about if they misbehave they're going to have to pay the consequences, if they don't get up on time, they're really going to get in trouble, and so on. When Reality Discipline is used correctly, there are no warnings—*none*—because warnings are disrespectful acts.

RANDY: For kids who don't want to get up for school and morning is a hassle, we usually have one basic solution: be sure the child has an alarm clock and knows how to use it. Then tell him, "It's your responsibility to set your alarm and get up in time to clean up, get dressed, get breakfast eaten, and leave for school on time."

If your child says, "But Mom, aren't you going to help get me up the way you always have?" You reply, "From now on, it is your responsibility." And leave it at that. What your child is probably used to is having you poke your head in the door in the morning and say, "Honey, it's 7:20," and five minutes later you're back again saying, "Honey, it's 7:25." Then, when it's

7:30 your voice increases in intensity and instead of calling the child, "Honey," it's "*John Allen*! You've got to get up for school or you're going to be late." When the kid hears his middle name, it's probably the first time he even begins to stir. Now he knows that Mom is getting upset and that he's pushed her as far as he dares.

ANN: But what if I give him the clock, and make him responsible to get up and he doesn't? What then?

RANDY: Then he's going to be late. No rescuing him by driving him down to school. And no writing him an excuse. Send a note along, but simply have it say, "Dear Teacher: The reason why little Harlan was late today is because he didn't get himself up for school on time. We have made this his responsibility and he is totally responsible for being late today."

KEVIN: Letting your child be late for school a few times may be embarrassing. You might want to call the teacher and explain what you're trying to do and enlist her cooperation. When little Harlan starts realizing that you are not going to bail him out when he plays his usual game, that is when he will start feeling the pain and being accountable. He's going to have to explain to the teacher why he's late, and he'll have to accept the discipline she gives him—detention time at recess or staying after school, or whatever.

Reality Discipline is not just a technique to discipline children. It's really a way of life for all of us. It's respectful, action-oriented, and it gives you an out in so many situations where you might otherwise be pummeled by your powerful little buzzards. So keep in mind the goal: *To raise adults, not children.* Someday they are going to leave your nest and no longer be under your protection. Hold them close in the early years, but bit by bit always look ahead to when you must let them go. Reality Discipline is the way to give them new challenges and responsibilities, so that someday they will be able to make the kind of decisions that life requires of them.

CHAPTER 11

■●▲■●▲

"MOMMY, WHERE DO BABIES COME FROM?"

RANDY: Our topic, Kevin, is, "Mommy, where do babies come from?" Are you ready?

KEVIN: I certainly am. With all that we've had happening at the Leman household, I'd like to have the answer, Randy. Where *are* all those babies coming from?

RANDY: Well, if you haven't been able to figure it out by now, this is your chance. Our special "over the phone" guest is Dr. Grace Ketterman, who is a practicing child psychiatrist and author of numerous books on children, including *How to Teach Your Child About Sex*, and that's the focus of today's program. Welcome, Grace, to "Parent Talk." Tell us, what kinds of questions do you get from moms who are concerned about this whole issue of explaining sex and sexuality to their children?

DR. KETTERMAN: First, most moms want to know *when* to tell their children about sexual matters. Second, they need help with *how* to help their children understand sex in a natural and wholesome way.

RANDY: Why do parents shy away from talking to their kids about this very natural part of life?

DR. KETTERMAN: In past generations, sex was made out to be something of which to be ashamed. It was to be hidden, and not talked about in a comfortable, matter-of-fact way. Even today many parents have inherited this sense of embarrassment or shyness about sexual issues. We have made some progress in overcoming this attitude, but in the process some people have swung too far the other way and have talked about sexual matters in a rather coarse and unwholesome fashion. Maybe someday we'll find the middle ground.

KEVIN: I agree. I'm afraid what we have done is allow the world to define what the word *sex* means. As we all know, there isn't one word in Scripture that says sex is nasty, dirty, or not good. There are a lot of references to why sex is wrong outside of marriage, but within marriage, sex is good. It is God's gift, and it is our challenge as parents to present this essential part of life to our kids in a positive way.

At what age should I start introducing sexual concepts and principles to my children?

DR. KETTERMAN: By the time parents start thinking about introducing sex to their children, they have already been doing it for quite a while. They do it through their inner attitudes toward sex and sexuality. They do it, for example, when they change the new baby's dirty diaper. If the parent grimaces and acts as if there is something ugly, dirty, and awful about that part of a child's body, the child doesn't understand that what the parent is really grimacing about is the smell. Instead, the little baby picks up the message that there is something bad about the genital area.

Also, parents may communicate their attitudes about sex when children discover their genitals. Isn't it interesting when children discover their fingers or ears parents get all excited and call Grandma about this wonderful new development, but when children discover their penis or their vagina, parents don't call Grandma. They are more apt to brush the child's hands away as if this is something bad or a cause for punishment. It is ironic that in a world that is so sexually preoccupied we have such unhealthy attitudes, which teach children that sex is very negative or "bad."

□ ○ △ □ ○ △

How much should I tell my toddler about where babies come from?

RANDY: Our producer, Kay, went out and talked to some five year olds about where babies come from, and here are their answers:

KAY: Glen, where does a baby come from?

GLEN: From inside a Mom's stomach.

KAY: What about you, Karlie? What do you think?

KARLIE: Babies first come from heaven.

KAY: That's right. Tell me more.

KARLIE: When it comes from heaven to its mom's tummy, it is ready to come out. But when it comes out, it doesn't feel that good because it is warm inside Mom's tummy.

KAY: Anybody else who wants to tell me where babies come from? Cassie, what do you think?

CASSIE: An egg. Daddy puts the seed in there and it kicks when it wants to come out of the mommy's tummy.

KAY: And how long does it take for the baby to come out? Do you know how many months or how many days?

DEBRA: A hundred—millions, trillions.

KEVIN: To some moms it seems that long, doesn't it? Just ask my wife, Sande. But I have a personal story about when and how to tell a toddler where babies come from. When our firstborn, Holly, was three and a half, she and I decided to drive down to get a hamburger at one of the finer places to eat in Tucson. It was so fine that it has been torn down for several years now.

As we drove along, Holly asked a very simple question: "Daddy, where do babies come from?" I remember thinking, *This is the BIG ONE. Sande, I am coming home!* For a few seconds, I was sort of shocked, and then I thought, *Well, you'd better follow your own advice, Leman, and do what you say in your books.* So I said to Holly, "I will tell you the truth. The daddies plant a special seed in the mommies, and that little seed grows, and it takes a while, but before long—about nine months—there is a full-grown baby ready to come out of a very special place in the mommy."

You see, my advice to parents is to simply tell the child what you think they are asking and what they need to know, and let it go at that. There is no need for a full-blown course in Sex Ed 101. Holly seemed satisfied with my answer. Normally my little firstborn might tell me, "You're kidding?" or "That's a lie. I don't believe it. I'm going to call my attorney." But she didn't say a word, so I let it go. We got to our hamburger joint and we were standing in line waiting to place our order. Just as we got up to the cashier, Holly decided to continue our conversation as only she could at the tender age of three and a half, and she yelled out,

"*But Daddy, how do the daddies get the special seeds in the mommies?*"

I'm sure you've all seen the ad about "Our broker is . . ." The whole place froze. The cashier, the head cook, and all of the customers waited for Daddy Leman's reply. I did not flinch for a second and simply said, "Holly, that is a very good question. We'll talk about it with Mommy when we get back home."

RANDY: Great answer, Kevin. Daddies aren't obligated to conduct sex education classes while standing in line for a hamburger. But I think Kevin's story raises a great question, Grace. Can we be guilty of telling our children too much too soon?

DR. KETTERMAN: I think we can, but I also think we do need some preparation to tell them at least what they are asking, as Kevin did. I also think it's perfectly okay to postpone giving children answers, particularly when the child asks an inappropriate question in public, as Holly did. Whenever that happened to a friend of mine, she would tell her child, "Honey, there are some things we talk about anywhere and there are some things we talk about in families, so when we get home I will be glad to sit down and explain this to you."

That kind of answer does three things: It allows the child to learn to wait; it saves saying something in public that is a bit awkward at best; it also gives you time to think about what you are going to say! Yes, there are times when a little postponement can be wonderful. As for answering the basic question, "How did the daddies get the special seeds in the mommies?" most little kids understand that daddies have certain body parts and Daddy's penis puts that tiny seed into Mommy's tummy and that is where it grows. Usually, that is enough. Three year olds don't need to know a whole lot more than that.

□ ○ △ □ ○ △

When is a child old enough to watch her baby brother or sister being born?

CONSTANCE: I had my third child at home by choice because I wanted my other children, who were two-and-a-half and four at the time, to be able to be part of my pregnancy and even the delivery. So, from the very beginning the two older kids were really in tune with how the baby got in my tummy and how it was developing. My midwife, who welcomes older siblings to watch when she delivers children, gave me a book that illustrated very clearly but tenderly how babies were born and what to expect, so that my children wouldn't have any fear or anxiety about it. I felt that was important.

RANDY: Did both children watch the birth?

CONSTANCE: We gave the kids the choice of whether or not to stay in the room as I gave birth. As it turned out, my two year old decided this wasn't for her, and she took off.

RANDY: Grace, what is your opinion about allowing a child to watch the birth of a baby brother or sister?

DR. KETTERMAN: My general feeling is that it is a little much for most children to handle unless they are seven or eight or older and can understand what is happening. It is a rather frightening sight to a small child who does not understand about the bleeding and the fluids, and whether or not Mommy is being hurt.

And, with small children in the room, the person doing the delivery may have more on his or her hands than can be handled very well. I certainly do respect, however, those who have chosen to let their older children watch the birth because they feel that it brings the family together. It is one of those issues on which many of us may disagree, and I respect that.

KEVIN: One thing about the Leman family, we have had a chance to test almost every theory I have ever had. Our little special child—our fifth—will be coming our way in August, so we have a chance to put this kind of question to ourselves. We don't want Hannah, our five year old, in the delivery room, but we do want her to come in right after the birth of the child. We thought that would be appropriate.

RANDY: Kevin, are you going to be in the delivery room, camera in hand?

KEVIN: I'll be there, but I am not into photographing births. As Grace said, there are some things we kind of keep "in the family."

DR. KETTERMAN: I like the idea of having children available to walk in after the baby is born. That happened when my youngest grandchild was born. There is such a bonding and a beautiful, almost ecstatic, sense of intimacy. There is really much to be said for allowing the older children to come in and see the baby right after he arrives.

RANDY: When our producer talked with those five year olds, she asked some questions that fit right in with babies being born, for example:

> KAY: Can anybody describe to me what a lady looks like when she is going to have a baby?
>
> BRETT: Fat tummy.
>
> KAY: When your little brother was born, Heather, how did you know it was time to be born? How does a baby know?
>
> HEATHER: I don't know, he just wants to get out and he kicks because he wants to see his mama.

KAY: What do you think the baby is feeling when he kicks inside of Mommy?

HEATHER: The stomach???

KAY: And if the baby could talk, what would he say?

HEATHER: "I want out, Mama!"

KEVIN: "I want out, Mama!" That's what Hannah, our little five year old, wants to know. When is her little brother or sister going to come out of there? Oh, boy.

RANDY: That's right. You are right in the middle of all this, aren't you, Kevin?

KEVIN: Indeed we are. But enough about that, back to the phones . . .

□ ○ △ □ ○ △

Can parents afford to avoid or refuse to explain sex to their children? What are the dangers?

DOLLY: In my church, I find a lot of people who are ready to switch off "Parent Talk" whenever you talk about sexual subjects. They say, "That's personal. It's nobody's business but our own." But yet I'm quite sure they aren't telling their kids much of anything about sex—they're just letting them find it out on their own in classes at school, in locker rooms, or on the playground. How do you feel about this?

KEVIN: Yes, we've gotten letters from people who have said they aren't listening to "Parent Talk" anymore because they heard us talking about sex, and that we even mentioned a bra once on the show. We realize that these people love God, and they want to do things right, but they are making a terrible mistake when they absolutely turn off at even the mention of the word *sex.*

DR. KETTERMAN: Kevin, I agree. There are a lot of people like this, and I truly respect them, because I grew up in that same era when it was just not permissible to talk much about sex. I think, too, it's easy for many people to believe that this is just a natural part of life and, just like eating, sleeping, and taking care of other bodily functions, it will "just happen." But I urge these parents to look around and see that we do not live in a world where this kind of shelter or protection is possible anymore for even 1 percent of our young people. TV, radio, films, and other media have seen to that.

Unless parents start teaching their children about sex and the proper use of sex from early on, they are running a tremendous risk of losing them to sexual misbehavior, venereal disease, early pregnancies, and any number of tragedies. Statistics show that 45 percent of church young people are sexually active before they finish high school. I'm talking about *church* young people. To me, that says we have hidden our heads in the sand too long and we need to wake up. Even if it's a little embarrassing, we must teach our kids the truth and the right way to use it.

□ ○ △ □ ○ △

How do we explain to our adopted child the sexual part of how he got here?

RON: We are building our family through adoption and we'd like to have some ideas on how to explain the sexual act in a positive light to our adopted children. How do we explain that sex happens between unmarried people? We don't have a problem explaining adoption, but we don't quite know how to tell our adopted child that we didn't participate in bringing her into the world.

DR. KETTERMAN: For a very young child, I would not try to make this distinction unless you really feel a compelling reason to do so. When they get a little older, nine, ten, and into pre-adolescence, they can better understand how people engage in sex, for a variety of reasons.

I think it's much more important for adopted children to know that their biological parents really did love them, but they could not provide the kind of care that was needed. A lot of adopted children feel they were abandoned, or thrown away, or are "no good." So I'd begin by explaining to your children that they are very valuable and very loved, not only by you and your wife, but by the parents who brought them into the world as well. You could put it this way: "The mommy and daddy who made you loved you so much that they gave you up to a family that could take better care of you—us. That was very hard for them to do, but that shows how much they loved you." At a later time, explaining the sexual act of intercourse and conception can more easily fall into place.

□ ○ △ □ ○ △

What is the best approach to telling my seven-year-old daughter about sex?

HAZEL: My daughter, Lisa, is seven and a half and in second grade. We have always been very open about body parts and calling them by their right name, and such, but even at seven and a half she has really never asked me, "How does the baby get in there, Mom?" She doesn't ask any questions along that line at all. I think it's time to talk with her and I want to know how to go about it. Do I wait until she brings it up? Do I bring it up myself? If so, do I try to read her books on this subject, or what?

DR. KETTERMAN: This is a common question. Whenever the opportunity seems natural—perhaps the pet is having babies, or maybe a friend or relative is having a child—you can ask her if she has ever had any questions about all this. Tell her you would be happy to talk about it. As for finding a good book on the subject, there are many of them out there. One that I have often used is called *The Wonderful Story of How You Were Born.* If you go to your local library, I'll bet you'll find it listed in the card catalogue or reference computer. Or there may be other very excellent books for you to choose from that give basic facts without going into too much detail.

RANDY: And, Hazel, just in case you don't have any pregnant pets or relatives, there is a simple way to open up the subject of sex with your daughter when you don't quite know how to get started. When our oldest child, Evan, turned ten, he still hadn't asked us anything about sex, so I took him for a ride in the car on an extended trip across town, which I knew would take almost an hour. Riding in the car is a great place to talk to your kids, because you can both sit there looking straight ahead, instead of being eyeball to eyeball while discussing something that could be embarrassing.

As we drove along I said, "Evan, do you ever wonder about the difference between men and women, and how babies are conceived and born?" He said, "Yes." And so I said, "Would you like to know about it?" All he said was, "Yes," again, so that was the opening I needed to talk to him, and we had a great conversation for the rest of our trip. A simple question that basically asked Evan to say, "Yes," or "No," was all it took to get started.

DR. KETTERMAN: That's an excellent approach, Randy, and I hope Hazel will try one of our suggestions with her seven year old. You can't begin too soon. I've had mothers of children as young as six and seven tell me that kids are learning just incredible things from school mates who talk about very negative and perverse sexual acts. Our little children are just totally unprepared for how to cope unless we teach them the truth.

□ ○ △ □ ○ △

How do I go about warning my kids against experimenting with sexual information?

ROSALIND: We have children six, four, and two, and I am expecting again, so the subject of where the baby comes from has come up recently. We're very open about explaining this, but I'm getting concerned that the children may try to go off and experiment to see "how Daddy puts his penis into Mommy's special place." I could use some good advice.

DR. KETTERMAN: This is an excellent question and what I suggest is that parents always teach from the very earliest time in the child's life that sex is something that mommies and daddies do after they grow up and get married. This way the children can understand that sex is something they should not be doing, because it is for adults—married adults.

RANDY: That is really true with anything in life. We sometimes are concerned about talking to our kids about drugs because we think they might go out and experiment with them, but we really can't come at the problem in that way. Children need information, lovingly provided by their parents, and we need to be honest and open and tell it like it is—what is right, what is wrong, what is pure, and what is impure.

KEVIN: I agree. About the only warnings many kids hear about sex are statements like, "Now don't you go out and get somebody pregnant," or "Be careful! It's always the girl who has to pay the price." What our kids need to hear, from a very young age is: "God made sex for mommies and daddies who are married because he wants little children to be born into families that love them and will care for them."

□ ○ △ □ ○ △

What should I say to my little boy now that he has discovered his genitals and enjoys playing with them?

PEARL: I have two sons, three and twenty months. My three year old has discovered his penis and he even knows that this is what he is to call it. He touches himself a lot, usually when he's taking a bath, but today I was taking the two of them out in the stroller and, while the little one was sitting in front of the three year old, the three year old said, "Lean back against my penis." I'm a little embarrassed and I wonder what this means and how I should react. Also, what should I tell my son?

DR. KETTERMAN: That reminds me of my grandson when he was about two and he found the sensation of playing with his penis very delightful. As I mentioned earlier, some parents want to slap the child's hands and somehow make the genitals shameful. Instead, I said, "Jimmy, that feels good, doesn't it? And that is why God made that organ—it does feel good. But we play with toys, we don't play with our bodies, because bodies are not for playing with." Try saying something of that nature to your boy—"Yes, it does feel good to touch your penis, but let's play with something else instead."

RANDY: Grace, what I notice as you have been talking is that you can present sex sensibly and as such a natural part of life. I think that's what parents need to learn.

DR. KETTERMAN: When we make sex a hidden and secretive thing for children, it can become exciting when they become older because the forbidden always seems exciting, particularly if children are rebelling to any degree. That's why it's so important for parents to have a sensible, wholesome attitude toward sex from the very start.

KEVIN: That is why we talk about sex on "Parent Talk." Let's face it, if it weren't for sex, we wouldn't need a "Parent Talk" program, would we? I think the question for all parents is this: Someone is going to teach your children about sex. Who do you want that person to be? Do you want to do it, or do you want someone else to do it?

RANDY: That's a very good question, Kevin. Nothing is more precious than our children, and on this subject, maybe they should have the last word. One of the questions that Kay, our producer, asked that group of kids was, "Before you were born, what did God know about you?" Their answers pretty well sum up why parents don't want to leave the teaching of sex to chance:

> STACY: God knew that I was going to have blue eyes like my mommy's.
>
> BRUCE: He knew that he wanted me to be born in the right mom's stomach.
>
> KRISTY: He knew which mom would take care of me.
>
> ALAN: He already knows all about us, because he loves us.

CHAPTER 12

SCHOOLWORK: WHO IS RESPONSIBLE—YOU OR THE KIDS?

RANDY: Okay, Kevin, parents all over the country are asking the question "How in the world do I get my kid to care about school, homework, and getting a passing grade?"

KEVIN: Can't you just hear Mom? "Is your homework done, young man? If it's not, I'm telling you, you're not going anyplace; you understand me? No place, period!"

RANDY: If we had to pick the top three areas where we get the most questions from parents, one would be regarding school: How can I motivate my child to do his homework? How can I get a bright child who is flunking to work up to his potential? When should I hold my child back, and for what specific reasons? And on and on the questions go. Getting kids to do their schoolwork is a big headache for parents, Kevin. They want to know how much responsibility they should take and what in the world they can do to help motivate their kids.

KEVIN: To begin with, Randy, I think that it's really important for kids to start off with a good taste in their mouths about school, and for that they need parents with an optimistic attitude, not parents who will hover over them and hound them. I think the key is that the kids have to know that their parents care about them—that's number one. A good relationship between the parent and the child is fundamental. Then, when school and homework are important to the parents, they are far more likely to be important to the kids.

RANDY: But who, Kevin, is really responsible to be sure that the schoolwork gets done? The child or the parents?

KEVIN: Ultimately, it must be the child. You don't want to run interference and snowplow all the roads of life for your children. You have to hold them accountable for what they do or don't do, because that's the job God has given you. But it's the child's job to get his schoolwork done.

RANDY: As we could have easily predicted, the board is lighting up. There are parents out there who are at wit's end corner because their kid is flunking, has no interest in school, just doesn't care, and what have you. I'm not talking about kids who have learning disabilities. I'm talking about average children who can get the work done, but they simply aren't doing it. And here's our first—and foremost—question. . . .

How do you motivate a child to do his homework?

EUNICE: My son is in second grade this year and I'm having the same problem we've had since kindergarten—motivating him to want to do his schoolwork. We've tried bribes and threats to no avail. So I've just been talking to him, trying to encourage him. I tell him that his job in life right now is school. He seems to agree with me. He says, "Oh, yes, Mom, I'll do better."

KEVIN: He throws you a fish to quiet you is what he does.

EUNICE: He sure does. I've had him tested and I know he's a bright kid. He could probably be in a gifted program, but he's had this problem ever since kindergarten when I think we started him too early. I don't think he was quite ready. He never has liked schoolwork so he doesn't do it.

RANDY: Maybe he's bored. Bright kids can get bored with school.

EUNICE: His teachers have tried to encourage him to work up to his potential, but he just doesn't want to. If this goes on through high school, I think he's gonna' put me in my grave.

KEVIN: First, Eunice, let's look at what you have here. Bribing, threatening, and pleading don't work, and apparently your boy got off on the wrong foot with school because he was started a little too early. But you've had him tested and you know he's bright enough, so there's not much point in continuing to talk about mistakes of the past.

EUNICE: So what can I do? I am out of ideas.

KEVIN: Now you want to take a new proactive approach. You do that by making a list of all the things and activities that are important in your son's life. Every kid has things he loves to play with or do. And when you have that list completed, you use it to discipline your boy in a very matter-of-fact way. You provide motivation in a very natural sense by telling him that when he completes his homework he can enjoy the things that he truly loves. What does he like to do in life?

EUNICE: He loves to play soccer; his team practices twice a week and plays once on Saturday.

KEVIN: Let me ask you, what should happen if his homework isn't done and it's time for practice, or even a game?

EUNICE: I guess he shouldn't go, but . . .

KEVIN: What's the "but"? I'm dying to hear the "but" because this is what gets you into trouble.

EUNICE: I understand that, but my husband is not in agreement with keeping him out of soccer for not doing homework.

KEVIN: There is your problem. The child is driving you up the wall because you and your husband are not on the same wavelength.

EUNICE: Well, it isn't just my husband. Even the teacher he had last year said we shouldn't take soccer away from him.

KEVIN: You tell the teacher that I disagree—big time!

RANDY: The only way to motivate children is through things that motivate them. You can't be constantly beating them over the head, so to speak, but you do have to hold them accountable and let them know that school is more important than soccer or Boy Scouts or Girl Scouts or whatever. We've done that in our own family, and it has worked. In our case, it was taking away Little League and gymnastics class, and it motivated our kids, no question about it. The point is, however, you have to follow through. When it's time to go to practice and the homework hasn't been done, you have to be willing to say, "Sorry, no homework, no soccer." If you just warn him and threaten him, and then don't do it, he'll just continue to pull your chain.

KEVIN: But what happens, Randy, if our little guy perceives that Mom and Dad are in disagreement over taking soccer away? What happens then?

RANDY: The kid knows he can just put a wedge in there. We've been through that in our own family and it's something Eunice and her husband will have to resolve. Eunice, sit down with your husband and try to convince him that Reality Discipline is worth a try. Nothing else is working, and, besides, we're not suggesting the end of your son's soccer career, only missing a few practices and maybe a game. We're willing to bet he'll come around on the homework.

□ ○ △ □ ○ △

What do you do when homework becomes a power struggle?

ISABEL: We have three children. Our oldest daughter is in high school and does very well in all her subjects. Our youngest child is in fourth grade and he gets better than average grades. But our middle child, who is eleven and in sixth grade, is failing three of her subjects. She's very disorganized and has never done well in school. She also gets very rebellious when I or my husband even ask her about her homework.

RANDY: She sounds like a pretty strong-willed child.

ISABEL: She's a lot like I am—very strong-willed—and we are in a power struggle. I am a teacher myself, but I'm just working part-time right now in the mornings. I am usually home when she gets home from school, but she's vehemently against having me even look at her homework because she knows I know too much about what she's supposed to be doing. To tell you the truth, she feels that the school and her mom are her enemies.

KEVIN: One question, Isabel, who is the perfectionist, you or your husband?

ISABEL: I am. When my husband tries to help her, I'm always telling him, "Ask her about this" or "Get her to do that." But she won't let him help either. It is all very difficult.

KEVIN: So we have a second-born daughter who is disorganized and rebellious, and we have a Mom who is a perfectionist and can spot a flaw at forty yards. Might I guess that you're a firstborn?

ISABEL: Well, not exactly, I'm second born, but the firstborn girl. My daughter and I are very much alike.

KEVIN: I don't really think we have just a school problem here; it's also a personality problem. You have to own up to trying to be Super Mom and Hover Mom—old Mother Hover is what we could call you. You just hover over Jennie like a space craft, and when she doesn't measure up, you zap her with your picky-picky gun. It's not too hard to understand why she is rebellious.

RANDY: What about Jennie's relationship with God? Is she rebellious in that area as well?

ISABEL: No, as a matter of fact, she's been very active recently in her Sunday school class and at Awana. I think the Lord is in her heart, but she's just confused and worrying about not being able to measure up to her sister, who's a freshman in high school, getting good grades, and playing in the band.

KEVIN: I had an older sister like that, and an older brother, as well.

ISABEL: I suppose it's possible that Jennie feels she can't compete, so she's just given up. I can just feel it in the air that she resents her older sister for doing everything so well.

KEVIN: Being the middle child leaves Jennie on the outside of all the glory looking in. It must be tough for her, especially if you compare her at all to her older sister.

ISABEL: I try not to compare the children, but I'm afraid I really do. We've had Jennie tested and, according to her scores, she could easily be a "B" student, but, you're right, I need a new approach. What do you suggest?

KEVIN: I suggest you start by apologizing to Jennie. Make your own speech along these lines: "Hey, I am sure you are as sick of all this as I am. I am here to tell you that I am laying down my arms and I am not going to fight anymore. I'm not going to bug you about your schoolwork. That doesn't mean that you don't have to do your work, but from now on you are totally responsible. I am quitting the sixth grade."

RANDY: Why don't you try setting a standard but lowering your sights? In our home, 'C' grades say the children are doing average work and at least passing. Yes, they may be able to pull 'A's' and 'B's,' but that's really up to them, not us, their parents. We don't get on any of our children for bringing home 'C's' and we never ever compare. We talk to each child individually, but we never discuss in the family who got what grade.

ISABEL: But if I "resign the sixth grade," and I'm not bugging her about her schoolwork, how can I set any standard, even if it's a lower one than we've had in the past?

RANDY: Try saying something like this, "Look, we're not asking for very much—in fact, this is your problem and you realize you're failing three of your subjects. So why don't you shoot for bringing home 'C's' at least? You're easily capable of that." Be sure she has a good environment for study—her own quiet spot, a desk, a good lamp—then it's up to her.

KEVIN: And she chooses whether she will do the homework. But at the end of the week, if homework hasn't been turned in, then weekend activities don't start.

ISABEL: But isn't that going right back to bugging her and being on her case?

KEVIN: Not at all. It sounds to me as if you've been hovering over Jennie, wondering if her work is done, pushing her to try harder, but you're going to stop all that. At the same time, however, you're going to tell her that if she doesn't try to make a basic effort of which she's perfectly capable, then she's going to pay the price—and it's her choice. You are not going to bug her.

RANDY: And while you're doing all this, make a real effort to focus on Jennie's strengths and capabilities. What we've always tried to do in our family is focus on the uniqueness of our three children. All three have different strengths and capabilities, and I make it a point to talk about those and encourage the children in those areas. What makes your younger daughter different from the older one? What are some of your younger daughter's strengths? It could be sports; maybe it's a certain hobby she has or the ability to express herself. Maybe she really cares for people or maybe it's the pets in the family that she makes her special responsibility. Whatever it is, let her know that she's special in that area and that she doesn't have to be just like her older sister.

Are all five year olds necessarily ready for kindergarten?

SHEILA: I'm calling to talk about my son who is six years old right now. He started kindergarten at age five last year in a Christian school and was doing very poorly. We were spending an hour to an hour and a half with him every night on homework. I talked to his teacher and she claimed that he was just not trying. I waited a few more weeks and then went to the school and sat in on the class. As I observed him, I saw that he was really in outer space. I came home and told my husband, "We are wasting our money. This is crazy. The kid just does not understand what's happening—he doesn't have the slightest idea."

RANDY: Where did you go from there?

SHEILA: We talked to the principal and his teacher and decided to pull him out of school. Everyone was upset with us, especially his grandparents.

KEVIN: I suppose they thought their grandchild had flunked kindergarten.

SHEILA: That's just about it. But we went ahead and did it anyway and started working with him at home, just an hour a day, if that. We made it fun trying to teach him his numbers and his ABC's, and that is all we tried to do. This year we started him in kindergarten in a different school, and he's at the top of his class.

RANDY: What do you think made the difference?

SHEILA: I'm sure the one-on-one stuff helped, but I think the big thing was that he wasn't mature enough for a full-blown kindergarten class last year. I'm sorry we made Mark go to kindergarten when he was too young. I'm afraid we just knuckled under to grandparents who kept saying, "Well, the boy is five years old. He should be in kindergarten." We practically felt compelled to send him.

KEVIN: If you think about it, that makes about as much sense as telling the grandparents that turning sixty-five means they should move to Florida.

RANDY: According to some of the latest research, holding a child back should be done at the earliest age possible. Beyond second grade, the impact can be too negative because the child is more aware of what his peers think of someone who "flunked." Holding a child back should be done for the right reasons. Is it an academic problem? Or is it a behavior problem due to immaturity? Sometimes all that's needed is some extra tutoring. In other cases, maybe some counseling would help. Also, how does the child feel about *himself*? A happy-go-lucky baby of the family can usually handle being held back better than a serious-minded firstborn.

KEVIN: But I like what Sheila did, Randy. She was a smart mom and took her son out of kindergarten because she could see he was a guppy swimming with the sharks. She went in and observed for herself and made the assessment that he was in way over his head. Then she took the appropriate action, which was to take him home and work with him there. Now, a year later, he's doing very well. This makes good sense with boys, especially, because they often mature a little more slowly.

RANDY: I think the message in Sheila's story is that kids should get off to the best start possible in school. Some of them really aren't ready for formal schoolwork at the age of five, or even at six. Parents need to really know their kids and work in close cooperation with the teachers and school officials so they can do what is best for their children. One friend of mine, who is a school psychologist, said holding a young child back often means that you're giving that child "the gift of time." You're letting him catch up, so to speak, and he has a much better chance for success.

Should kindergartners have homework?

GRETCHEN: I have my kindergartner in a Christian school and he's had homework every night since they started in September. I'm having a real hard time getting him motivated to do it.

RANDY: Homework for your kindergartner? Is it because he's not getting his work done at school, or do they really want him to work at home?

GRETCHEN: All of the kids in his class have homework. We do six to fifteen minutes' worth every night, and he's tired of it.

KEVIN: I don't blame him. What kind of homework is it?

GRETCHEN: Basic concepts concerning shapes, numbers, and problem solving. I don't understand why kindergartners have to do all this. He's getting irritated with me because I make him do it, and now the teachers are telling me that he doesn't want to do much in class either.

KEVIN: Unfortunately, this is all too typical. Kids are naturally curious, and learning is one of the most natural things in the world. Kids are always asking questions, Why? Why? Why? But by third or fourth grade, we've beaten the natural curiosity out of them. And I think it might start with assigning homework in kindergarten. I want to go on record that this is a bad idea.

RANDY: My feeling is that kids should be able to get their regular schoolwork done in the three hours or so that they are at kindergarten class. If a teacher wants to send home some papers for kids to work on because they choose to do it, I think that's fine, but required homework in kindergarten? I'm also opposed to that.

GRETCHEN: What can I do about it? How do I deal with this? All three of the kindergarten teachers in the school assign homework. It's a uniform policy. I don't want him to get bad grades, so what do I do?

RANDY: Specifically, you should talk to the principal as well as your son's teacher and find out their rationale for this policy. Discuss the why's and wherefore's of the need for this kind of homework, and let them know this is turning into a power struggle between you and your son. Then I would be pleasant but firm and say, "In our home, we have our own schedule and routine for our family. While it may be your policy to ask children in kindergarten to do homework, the fact is our child will not do homework, and if he gets a lower grade because of that, it will be our responsibility."

KEVIN: That a mom has to be concerned about her five year old getting bad grades in kindergarten is, if I may be frank, a sign of a sick society. This isn't worth the bruised relationships between you and your son, Gretchen. If the school isn't willing to make the homework optional for your son, at least for a while, I'd consider finding a kindergarten that isn't a Kiddie Kollege. Kindergarten should be fun—not an ordeal for a child and his mother.

Why do schools seem to think all children learn in the same way?

LORNA: We have two children, a girl and a boy. Our daughter went to this very structured, back-to-basics school and did beautifully. Two years later our son started kindergarten in that school, and we had to fight with him to get him to go. He would be wiggling and playing with his pencil and just would not try. He struggled through the year, but his teacher said he wasn't really a stay-back case.

So I worked with him over the summer, and I thought first grade would be better. But it was more of the same. His teacher thought he was frustrated, but he still wasn't a candidate for staying back. She called him "borderline." By the next year I found an entirely different school that stresses hands-on learning, which means that children get involved in experiments and other activities in which they apply what they learn in the classroom. I put him in there, and his self-esteem came back immediately as he began doing much better.

RANDY: One of the most serious mistakes schools make with children is to assume they all learn the same. The truth is, every child has a little different learning style. Some are more visual, which is the predominant style used by most schools. But others are more auditory, and some are tactile, which sounds like your son. He likes to put hands on and that's how he learns. What kind of learner are you, Kevin?

KEVIN: I think I lean toward the auditory. I am blessed with a great memory. When I hear something—a phone number, for example—I can usually remember it.

RANDY: Clearly, we can structure a system so tightly we don't let the individual learning style and abilities of the child come to the surface.

LORNA: It was all so frustrating because he was in school with children of several of our friends, and these kids were even younger than he was and they were doing great. I thought I was the only one with a problem. I'm glad we found another school with teaching methods that suited his learning style.

□ ○ △ □ ○ △

Is a point system a good way to motivate a child to do his schoolwork?

MABEL: I've got an eight year old who will do almost nothing at school, but when I work with him at home he puts out the work like a trouper.

RANDY: What you're saying is that he will do schoolwork for you but he won't do the work for his teacher at school, correct?

MABEL: Well, it's interesting, because he did pretty well at school last year. He got a lot of "100's" on his papers, so when he makes up his mind to do it, he can put the work out. But this year he'll work only for me at home, and he's doing nothing down at school.

KEVIN: This is good news and bad news. What's your secret to motivating him at home?

MABEL: I have worked out a reward chart with points. He gets so many points for not having any detentions, so many points for getting so many pages of math done, and so on. At the end of the week, we add the points. A certain amount means he gets a little toy at K-Mart; a larger amount earns him a trip to Chuck E. Cheese.

KEVIN: I have been to Chuck E. Cheese. It's a great place for kids, but I'm not sure about adults!

MABEL: Well, it's working fine right now—next year, who knows?

RANDY: Where do you go after Chuck E. Cheese?

MABEL: To McDonald's? Burger King? The amusement park?

KEVIN: I know it's very tempting to use rewards because they often work on a short-term basis. Parents see the kid responding and think, "Aha, I'm on the right track." The problem with rewards is that, in the long run, they don't make a lot of sense. Do you really want your child to learn and do well in school in order to get points so he can get rewarded with quarters or brown sugar or Chuck E. Cheese, or something else? I don't think so. The more natural the learning is, the more real the learning is going to be for the child, and the more the child is going to grow and tell himself, "I am a competent person."

RANDY: Kevin, if you were going to give Mabel one single bit of advice to help her seemingly unmotivated son, what would it be?

KEVIN: First of all, I'd back off and make sure that going to second grade is *his* experience. In other words, Mom, stay out of the second grade. If there's going to be a power struggle, let it be between the teacher and your son, rather than your son and you.

MABEL: Am I hearing you say that I should stop the point system and, if he's going to fail, I just let him fail?

KEVIN: Yes, I would be first in line to say that that is very good advice. And what happens to your child if he does fail? What are we afraid of?

MABEL: I guess I'm afraid of the same thing anybody else would be afraid of—he would have to repeat second grade.

KEVIN: I would have no problem with your son repeating second grade. I would take that chance so he can become motivated about school for the right reasons.

RANDY: I think we should be careful to make a distinction here, Kevin. You're not saying you're disinterested in the child. You're not saying, "I don't care if he fails or not." You do care about his failure, but you are willing to hold him accountable for that failure because it is his choice.

KEVIN: Exactly. I would simply tell him, "Honey, I want you to do well in school but I can't remind you to study all the time. I can't make you remember to hand in your assignments. I can't make you pass second grade—that's your job."

MABEL: In other words, make it his responsibility, his job, his decision.

KEVIN: Right! Oh, Mabel, it works. It has worked for four of mine, and I know it will work for our Number Five when she heads off to school.

□ ○ △ □ ○ △

When is a child old enough to be totally responsible for his own homework?

JOANNA: I have three children, nine, six, and four. Our nine year old is in third grade and does very well in school. When she gets home, she's required to practice the piano and get her homework done; then she can go out to play or whatever. I have to do very little reminding or checking on her. But I am wondering about my two younger ones. Our son, who is six, is in first grade and just starting to get homework assignments. Should I make him responsible for his own homework too?

KEVIN: A lot of parents have the rule that kids can't play after school until their homework is done. Personally, I prefer the opposite. The kid comes home, puts his backpack down and goes off to do what he wants. He can do his homework when he likes—after dinner, for example.

JOANNA: I don't prefer to operate that way at my house. We can't wait until after dinner because my husband works late and we always have a late dinner.

KEVIN: Okay, I understand that you have a different situation, and you can do it any way you want. I'm just saying that the key to making a child responsible is not to hover over the child and always be giving him a lot of direction and reminders. As for your first grader becoming responsible for his homework, he won't start learning any younger. When he comes home and says, "Mom, I've got homework," then you should say, "Well, Honey, you better get to it, because your teacher is going to ask you for it in the morning." Right from the beginning you don't get sucked into saying, "Oh, my goodness, you have homework! Just a minute, I'll stop everything and help you get it done." You don't cast your plans aside and set up this little schoolhouse in your home. Do you see what I am saying?

JOANNA: Yes, I believe I do, but I'm still concerned about Kurt because he's only six and he's not as bright or as disciplined as his older sister. He has a little tougher time with school.

RANDY: Joanna, I don't think Kevin is saying you don't help your little first grader at all with homework, particularly when it's all so new to him. Some kids need more guidance and encouragement than others, so it's perfectly okay to sit down with him and be sure he understands his homework assignment. Get him started and give him some encouragement, but don't give him so much guidance you practically wind up doing the work for him.

□ ○ △ □ ○ △

Is there anything you can do to help a child who can't keep her mind on her homework?

ROSALIND: I have a ten-year-old daughter who's bright enough, but she's having trouble with her fourth grade work because she can't keep her mind on what she's supposed to be doing. Her mind just wanders—at school or at home.

KEVIN: I've got the same problem. My mind wanders all the time.

RANDY: Did it wander in school?

KEVIN: Oh, yeah, I used to sit in class and look out the window and just be enamored with anything that was going on outside because I was bored inside.

ROSALIND: I don't think my daughter is necessarily bored. But she is a little social butterfly. She started reading at a young age and loves books. But when she brings home a reading assignment, she can't stick with it very long. She'll read two or three pages and then she's got to be up doing something else.

RANDY: I think your daughter is typical of many bright children whose minds run in many different channels at one time. They get bored with what they're doing, and their mind is off on something else. We have found that when our children have concentration problems, they need a place where they can go to do homework that has the least amount of stimuli possible. It should be a spot where they can sit and work individually away from the confusion created by the rest of the family. There shouldn't be any TV or radio, and there shouldn't be a lot of toys around. We tell all three of our kids—who are now fourteen, eleven, and eight—that they are required to go in their rooms and, when their work is done, they can come out. They can sit and daydream all they want, but they don't come out until the work is done.

KEVIN: That's a good point, Randy. A lot of parents are going to wonder, *What's going on in there? Are they doing the work?* They'll be tempted to play hover parent and check on the kids every five minutes. But now is the time to bite the bullet and trust your children to be responsible and accountable. The point is, they are in there for as long as it takes—fifteen minutes, half an hour, or an hour. You give them every opportunity to do what their teacher has asked of them, and when their work is finished, they can come out and do other things.

ROSALIND: So you're saying she should be made to stay in her room and get her work done? She doesn't do that right now, not even for reading, which she loves to do. She likes to be out in the family room where all the action is.

KEVIN: I believe you said she's a social butterfly. Randy and I both have kids like that.

RANDY: Andrea, our eleven year old, who is probably listening right now, would be just as happy doing her homework sitting on my lap because she loves to be around the family and be involved in all the conversation and activities. That's great, and we love being with her, but when she needs to do her homework, we tell her, "Andrea, you can go into your bedroom or my office, and when your work is done, bring it out so we can take a look at it."

Sometimes when she shows us her work, we may see a section that was not done correctly. Instead of pouncing on that, we say very gently, "Honey, you've done a lot of really good things here, but I did notice a couple of areas you should go back and check again if you want to get them all right." We always put it back in her lap, and we don't tell her she has to correct the work —it's up to her. She usually goes back and does the incorrect parts over because she does want a better grade—but that's her decision, not ours.

□ ○ △ □ ○ △

Is there another way to motivate a child to do homework besides "taking away his privileges"?

KATE: I'd like to put emphasis on finding out what the problem is rather than taking things away when kids don't do homework. I have a stepdaughter who doesn't live with me, but when her mother dropped her off for her summer visit, she told me she was concerned about Rebecca's math and spelling. So that summer I worked with Rebecca on her math and I found that she could do it, but she had a problem with concentrating. Instead of thinking it through and getting the correct answer, she would write down any old thing just so she could give me the paper back and get out of there.

I knew she didn't have a learning problem because she was too bright, so I told her, "Look, I know you can do this. I know you're just writing down anything because you hope that I'll accept it and you can go play. Well, that isn't going to work. Tomorrow you're going to sit at your desk all day. You will stop for breakfast, lunch, dinner, and to use the bathroom. But you're going to do math until you get them all right."

RANDY: And so what happened? Did you follow through?

KATE: I did indeed. She went into her room, did all the math problems, and brought them to me. They were all correct! I got her to do her math, but not by withholding privileges. I guess her real mom had been holding her out of gymnastics, but I don't think that's what works with Rebecca. The divorce has put a lot of stress on her, and that's partly why she doesn't want to do her homework.

KEVIN: You make a good point, Kate, for using different kinds of Reality Discipline. One way to approach a child is to say, "Hey, listen, I'm on to you. I know you're trying to give the work just a lick and a promise and then turn it in, but I know you can do it right." You're encouraging her by telling her that she's capable of doing the work, and you're holding her accountable as well.

KATE: Once I gave her the ultimatum and she knew she'd be there all day if she didn't go ahead and do it; it made all the difference in the world. At the same time, I was sensitive to her and let her know that the divorce had been tough and I appreciated how she felt about that. That helped soften her anger, and she was more willing to do the math. And you know what? Now she usually finishes any math assignment in less than an hour!

KEVIN: That's a great combination of love and limits, Kate, saying to the child, "Yes, I know life has kicked you in the teeth, and I'm sorry, but the math is still going to get done!"

RANDY: I like the way Kate handled this situation, too, Kevin. But I think we need to add a word of caution because maybe we've implied that Reality Discipline will solve every homework problem.

If you use Reality Discipline for a period of time and the children are still getting poor grades or simply not getting the homework done, maybe you have to look at a deeper level. Perhaps your child has a learning disability or an emotional problem and needs professional help. Or sometimes there can be a physical problem. I have a friend whose son was having all kinds of trouble in school, as well as being a messy kid at home. They finally took him in for an eye exam and discovered that he had a visual problem that was causing a lot of other problems.

The point is, when you use Reality Discipline, you are concerned first with the person and then the performance. As you said at the beginning of this program, kids should feel good about themselves and school. One of the best ways to help a kid feel good about himself is to teach him how to be accountable and responsible for getting his own work done. We're raising independent adults, not dependent children, and school is a great proving ground for doing that through Reality Discipline.

CHAPTER 13

■●▲■●▲

"DENNIS THE MENACE," OR A.D.H.D.?

RANDY: Attention Deficit Hyperactivity Disorder. Many "Parent Talk" listeners have struggled with this complex problem, not always sure of what they are up against. Sometimes the signs are there when a child is very young, but most parents either ignore these signs or misunderstand them. They may think the child is "just going through a stage." Or, at the other end of the spectrum, they may label the child as a "Dennis the Menace," the kind of kid who just naturally attracts trouble.

KEVIN: I knew a kid like that once. When he went in to see his high school counselor about trying to get into college, the counselor told him that he couldn't qualify for reform school.

RANDY: Yes, I think I know who you're talking about—he's in radio now, a psychologist with a doctorate, telling parents how to handle their kids.

KEVIN: You know, Randy, I'm convinced that I had Attention Deficit Hyperactivity Disorder as a kid but back then very little was known about how to read the symptoms. Maybe the first question we need to deal with is . . .

What are classic symptoms of Attention Deficit Hyperactivity Disorder?

RANDY: Over the years, the experts have used different terms for what we're talking about today. Through the '70s they spoke of the "hyperactive child." In 1980 they came out with the term "Attention Deficit Disorder" (A.D.D.) to emphasize that in many cases the child's problem wasn't that he was hyperactive, but that he just couldn't maintain his attention for very long. In 1987 a new term was introduced—Attention Deficit Hyperactivity Disorder—which has become an umbrella label to cover anything that has to do with lacking attention, being hyperactive, or being impulsive.

KEVIN: Thanks for the history lesson, Randy. It's my guess a lot of people are still using the term A.D.D., but I see you have the diagnostic statistical manual in hand. How does it describe A.D.H.D.?

RANDY: It has taken A.D.D. symptoms and lumped them together with symptoms of hyperactivity and impulsiveness to come up with fourteen signs of the overall problem—which these days is called Attention Deficit Hyperactivity Disorder:

Does your child fidget with his hands or feet? Does he squirm in his seat?

Do you have trouble keeping his attention?

Is he easily distracted by any outside stimulus?

Does he have difficulty waiting his turn in games or group situations?

Does he sometimes blurt out answers to a question in class before the question is even completed?

Does he have difficulty following through on instructions from other people?

Does he have difficulty sustaining attention—often shifting from one activity to another?

Does he find it hard to just play quietly?

Does he talk excessively? Does he interrupt or intrude on others?

KEVIN: You've given eleven so far and, during my earlier years, I think I would have been ten for eleven, at least . . .

RANDY: Here are the last three:

Does your child not seem to listen to what is being said to him or her?

Does he often lose things necessary for a task or an activity?

Does he often engage in physical or dangerous activities without considering the consequences?

KEVIN: Chalk up three more. That's thirteen out of fourteen in all for the Cub when he was a kid.

RANDY: Some people around here—our producer, for example —would say you still show several of the symptoms today, but, Kevin, seriously, A.D.H.D. is difficult to diagnose and more difficult for parents to cope with. Sometimes it shows up at home and in other cases it shows up only in the classroom, causing the parent to complain, "What's the matter with these teachers? My child is fine at home." Of course, sometimes there really is a behavioral problem, which is not Attention Deficit Hyperactivity Disorder at all. We know there are many parents who are struggling with this problem. In fact, we have Dale on the line right now. Her boy is twelve and still has A.D.H.D., but her story goes back to when he was much younger. . . .

How early can A.D.H.D. be detected?

DALE: We noticed that Jonathan was different from other kids as early as a week old. He seemed more bright, alert, looking around, and lifting his head even though it was very wobbly. He didn't go to sleep easily and when I nursed him, I had to go into another room and have everything totally quiet so he was able to pay attention enough to eat.

KEVIN: In other words, Dale, as early as infancy, you could see that Jonathan was easily distracted—a hallmark of A.D.H.D.

DALE: That's true, but he could go to the other end of the spectrum, too, and become so engrossed in what he was doing that the house could have burned down and he wouldn't have known the difference. A.D.H.D. kids can go from one extreme to the other. If it's a task of low level interest, he won't stay on it for a minute, but if it's high level interest, you cannot pull him away from it. For example, when he was able to sit in a high chair, we'd put food in front of him but he was more interested in the mechanics of the chair than he was the food. When we gave him a tricycle to play with, he preferred to turn it over and play with the wheels and gears, rather than get on it and ride.

Why do parents sometimes mistake A.D.H.D. for "going through a stage"?

KEVIN: Dale, what did you and your husband tell yourselves about Jonathan when he displayed these symptoms as a small child?

DALE: We continued to see signs, but we didn't want to think that anything unusual was wrong. As a toddler, Jonathan had difficulties getting along with other kids, and he was always getting in trouble around the house—fighting with his brothers and sisters. When he got into the four- and five-year-old department at Sunday school, he couldn't stay on any task very long at all. But we felt that these were just stages that kids go through and that he would outgrow all this. We thought what he needed was more discipline and we tried it all. We spanked, we had a lot of time outs, a lot of grounding, and a lot of taking things away—making him go without a meal, or without a particular thing he wanted to play with. We tried just about everything, but nothing did much good.

RANDY: So you and your husband were telling yourselves that somehow you could fix his problem by being more strict?

DALE: Well, at first that is what we thought, because as he got into school he didn't do well. He was also something of a behavior problem. For example, the teacher would be giving the class instructions and, if Jonathan thought he saw something out of order in the class, he would just get up, right then and there, and go take care of it. He'd have to straighten up all the desks in his row to make sure they were in a perfect line, or he'd take out his pencil box and rearrange it. Then five minutes later he'd take it out and rearrange it again. He was more or less in his own world. If the teacher told him to write his name at the top of his paper—and she'd even draw a sample on the chalkboard of how to do this—he'd write it at the bottom. We also saw a lot of reversals when he would write his letters.

RANDY: What did you make of all these signs?

DALE: It was puzzling because, although he did poorly with written work, his teacher could ask him something and he could give her an answer. Also, he was beyond his years in his sense of humor and ability to communicate.

Why does the school system sometimes mistakenly label an A.D.H.D. child as a behavior problem?

RANDY: Obviously, Jonathan's teachers noticed his strange behavior and his low grades. What happened next?

DALE: His teacher recommended him for testing by the Special Education Department. We didn't know much about Attention Deficit Hyperactivity Disorder and we thought Jonathan had some kind of information processing problem, but when we suggested that to the school, we were told that that was normally what they heard from parents. They put Jonathan through a series of tests but, frankly, they had more or less decided he had a behavior disorder problem, and that's what they told us when they had what they called a "staffing." That's when a group of teachers and other specialists would get together to decide if a child should go into special ed classes or not. We were invited to sit in when they talked about Jonathan.

KEVIN: How did you enjoy the staffing experience?

DALE: We didn't know much about learning disabilities or Attention Deficit Hyperactivity Disorder, and it was very intimidating to have a group of professionals sitting there telling us that if we did not put our child into a special class for behavior disorder, he was going to be robbing banks by age thirteen.

KEVIN: If we want to make anything clear, it's not to let the experts run your life. You have to take charge as parents. You're responsible for your child and should never be intimidated.

RANDY: I am disappointed but not surprised by what you went through with your local public school. A minute ago we referred to the diagnostic statistical manual that is the handbook for all of us in the mental health profession. We call it the DSM-III-R for short. If you look in there, you will find a whole section entitled "Disruptive Behavior Disorders," which lists all kinds of interesting things such as Conduct Disorder, Oppositional Defiant Disorder, Separation Anxiety Disorder, and, of course, Attention Deficit Hyperactivity Disorder. It's not unusual for one expert to disagree with another about what kind of disorder a child has. That's probably why people in this staffing meeting that you and your husband had to undergo were telling you that your son could be in jail by the time he is a teenager.

What is the best way to find out if your child really does have A.D.H.D.?

RANDY: If you could go back, Dale, to when your son was showing early signs of A.D.H.D., even as a toddler, what would you have done differently?

DALE: I would have gone to a pediatrician sooner—but one who specializes in A.D.H.D. diagnosis. We finally took Jonathan to a pediatrician when he was seven and learned that he was indeed A.D.H.D. The A.D.H.D. child shows three kinds of behavior: (1) hyperactivity, (2) distractibility, and (3) impulsiveness. Jonathan showed all three signs.

KEVIN: That's what we always recommend. The pediatrician is the one who should make the diagnosis, not a psychologist and certainly not a staffing done at school.

DALE: Right, but it's important to find a pediatrician who is well-versed in Attention Deficit Hyperactivity Disorder or other neurological problems; otherwise, he or she might just do some basic elementary tests and miss what is really going on.

How effective is medication for the A.D.H.D. child?

RANDY: You say that your son was diagnosed at seven and now he's twelve. When he was diagnosed, was he put on any medication and, if so, what effect did it have? Do you find that as he's gotten older some of the symptoms are subsiding?

DALE: Yes, he's been on Ritalin since age eight, but it hasn't been the whole answer. The mistake a lot of people make is that they think that getting their kids on medication will be the answer to everything, but there are a lot of things Jonathan still has difficulty with. For example, he finds it hard to stay organized and get things done. Part of this is his own nature, because he's super perfectionistic. He'll spend four to five hours an evening on homework, and then won't be satisfied enough to turn it in.

KEVIN: Why do you allow him to spend that much time on homework?

DALE: He gets extremely frustrated. In fact, he just blows up if we tell him to let the homework ride. We don't make him do it. He's hard on himself.

KEVIN: In my opinion, someone is missing the boat here because one of the goals with an A.D.H.D. child is to give very little homework.

RANDY : Dale, I'd like to have you stay on the line while we talk to some other moms about A.D.H.D. questions that they have . . .

My son has some A.D.H.D. symptoms, but how can I be sure I actually need to have him checked by a doctor?

SHANNON: My five-year-old son has some of the symptoms that you have on your list, and we're getting frustrated because of discipline problems. The preschool teachers at our church say there is simply no way they can control Tyler. He disrupts the class and destroys other kids' papers.

RANDY: What's he like at home?

SHANNON: He's destructive there too. He's taken scissors and cut up one of the quilts. He's cut his sheets. We don't allow him to have scissors anymore, period, but he'll still climb up and get hold of them if he really wants to.

RANDY: Does he fidget around a lot at home as well as at church?

SHANNON: Well, he can sit there and watch cartoons or a video, but only for ten or fifteen minutes at a time. He has to get up and go do something, then come back and start watching again.

RANDY: Does he get lost in his own world—as if he doesn't know you are there?

SHANNON: Sometimes it seems that he's ignoring us, but when we yell at him he'll finally recognize us.

RANDY: When he's in a more confusing situation, such as in church where there are lots of stimuli around, do his symptoms get worse?

SHANNON: Yes, they do. He is a lot more fidgety and restless at church than at home.

RANDY: That's a key sign. When an A.D.H.D. child gets into an environment like a classroom where there are a lot of other stimuli—a lot of other kids, for example—he can get easily confused and more hyperactive than ever.

SHANNON: Up to this point we've been thinking Tyler is just being a typical little boy, but from what everyone is saying I guess we'd better have him checked for A.D.H.D.

DALE: We thought that for several years too—Jonathan was just an active boy and, because our firstborn daughter was obedient and responsible, we just wrote it off as "There's a big difference between a boy and a girl."

RANDY: It sounds to us, Shannon, as if you should definitely take your son to a pediatrician who specializes in A.D.H.D. If Tyler does have the problem, you need to know it so you can work with him more effectively.

What is the typical reaction of the A.D.H.D. child to siblings?

SHANNON: One more question. Tyler's older sister is in kindergarten, and when she's not at home, he's a lot easier to live with and more attentive. For example, we make bread and cookies together while she is gone, but when she gets home from school he starts to whine or cry and nothing seems to go his way. When they are together, it all seems to get out of control. Is this another sign of A.D.H.D.?

RANDY: Let's have Shannon talk with Dale who is still on the line. Dale, is what Shannon saying sounding familiar?

DALE: It is very typical for A.D.H.D. kids not to get along with their peers, particularly brothers and sisters. The A.D.H.D. child has tunnel vision, and he can only see things from his point of view. They always want things their way. When our Jonathan went on Ritalin, he got a little better, but even today he works better by himself or one-on-one with an adult or one other child who is a good friend. Keeping him separated from our other two children is, frankly, quite often the key to harmony in our home—which we achieve sometimes for as much as five minutes a day!

□ ○ △ □ ○ △

Does a child eventually outgrow A.D.H.D.?

GEORGIA: My son is seventeen and he's never really given us any real problems, but his teacher told me that sometimes he'll get up while she's teaching a lesson, walk around the room, and then sit back down. She doesn't understand why he does this, and neither do I. He is doing rather poorly in school but he wants to go to college. If he has A.D.H.D., will he outgrow it, or, can he get some help?

KEVIN: To answer your first question, yes, up to 50 percent of A.D.H.D. children have decreasing symptoms when they reach adulthood. And during their childhood and teen years, they can be helped to function without hyperactivity, being distracted, or being impulsive. To answer your second question, there are programs on college campuses to address the needs of students who have learning disabilities. But it always starts with testing. My suggestion is to have him tested by a doctor and possibly other learning specialists.

GEORGIA: He always feels badly because he doesn't do well in school. He'll work on a subject for as long as two weeks, and then come home and tell me, "Mom, I really don't remember any of it."

RANDY: It may not be A.D.H.D. in his case. He might just have difficulty processing information, or it could be some other problem that is lumped under another broad term called Learning Disabilities (L.D.). That's what makes A.D.H.D. diagnosis so complicated. You really need to start with a medical doctor who understands A.D.H.D. and get some testing. That's the place to begin.

□ ○ △ □ ○ △

If you face a "staffing" at school because your child has been displaying A.D.H.D. symptoms, what can you do to feel less intimidated?

GARY: I'm a school psychologist, and one of the comments that I heard earlier is that people in the Special Education system can be very intimidating. Since I'm involved with Special Ed every day, I can say that sometimes this is true, but in many other cases it can be a very valuable learning experience for parents if they know how to take advantage of it.

RANDY: What would you say then, Gary, to parents who have a child who is displaying A.D.H.D. symptoms? What if they are facing a "staffing" at school and feel very intimidated by that?

GARY: If there is a staffing scheduled, they should prepare as many questions ahead of time as possible. It also helps if they can bring somebody along who is familiar with the process—another parent, possibly, who has had an A.D.H.D. child.

RANDY: What kinds of questions should they ask of school personnel?

GARY: Anything that has to do with the process. What tests have been done and what are the results? What specific treatment or approach is recommended and why? How much and what kind of experience have the teachers at the school had in working with A.D.H.D. kids? What kind of success rate have they had with these children? I sit in on these staffings all the time and the schools I work with are never trying to cover up information. As the professionals, we want to give the parents as much information as possible about their children. As a parent, I'd take all this information to an outside source—like my pediatrician—for verification and testing.

KEVIN: Where do you think pediatricians fit in with what the school does?

GARY: I think pediatricians have their place, and maybe parents should start there, but they should be sure to choose one who is trained in recognizing A.D.H.D. symptoms. In addition, however, the school psychologist is the one who can best figure out if the child has learning processing weaknesses. Pediatricians don't typically test in that particular area. It's my impression that pediatricians will see a child in their offices and it's a one-on-one setting that's not a typical classroom situation. In many instances, some A.D.H.D. symptoms don't necessarily come out until a child gets into a classroom situation.

RANDY: I think you'd agree that there will always be conflicts among professionals in diagnosing the A.D.H.D. condition. That can leave parents even more intimidated by the process.

GARY: Yes, that's true. In fact, there is often a big difference of opinion right in the middle of a staffing that can be pretty confusing to people. With human behavior there are not always absolute answers.

KEVIN: Gary, I'd like to know how many students you have to cover, and how many evaluations you will do this year.

GARY: I cover five elementary schools, around two thousand children in all, and I do somewhere between eighty and one hundred evaluations regarding A.D.H.D. or L.D. problems in a year.

KEVIN: Suppose you had a son or daughter you suspected had an A.D.H.D. problem. How would you have your child tested? Would you find a fellow school psychologist, would you do it yourself, or would you go to a professional in the private sector?

GARY: I would feel confident to test my child myself because the tests have a certain number of standardized measurements that don't allow for too much subjective opinion. But just to be sure, I would also have him checked with another school psychologist for balance.

RANDY: Thanks, Gary, for your call. As we go through this program, there is a growing appreciation for what parents go through when they think they may have an A.D.H.D. child. I think the message is that every parent is responsible for being informed and for getting help for his child—literally, to become his child's advocate.

KEVIN: And don't let the experts run your life. Use their knowledge, but remember they aren't God.

□ ○ △ □ ○ △

Can I use Reality Discipline on a ten year old who has Attention Deficit Hyperactivity Disorder?

EUNICE: My ten year old was diagnosed with A.D.H.D. two years ago by both a psychiatrist and a child behavior therapist, and he's been on Ritalin ever since. His grades have improved and his behavior is fine—as long as he's on the drug. But I've never been completely at ease with his taking medication.

RANDY: Remember, he will eventually not need the medication. Why are you uneasy right now?

EUNICE: It's hard to pinpoint; maybe it's the social stigma associated with drugs. I also know that his doctors said that it is very hard on his body. The trouble is, the minute he's off the drug, or even at the end of the school day when the drug effects are wearing off, he can be a handful. One of the side effects of the Ritalin is sleeplessness, so we don't give him any more for the rest of the day or evening. We also don't give it to him on weekends or during the summer. But when he's off Ritalin, he immediately goes back to the typical A.D.H.D. behavior—not paying attention, acting as if he didn't hear. He's constantly getting in trouble, particularly with me.

RANDY: Are you his main disciplinarian?

EUNICE: Yes, I am, because his father isn't home a great deal and when he is here he's very permissive. I don't get a lot of follow-through from him. He spoils the kids, basically, and doesn't like to discipline. He didn't have to be disciplined when he was growing up, never had to get a spanking. On the other hand, I was always getting spanked as a young girl.

RANDY: Do you ever spank your son?

EUNICE: He doesn't respond well to spanking—it actually causes him to throw a temper tantrum.

KEVIN: He sounds like a powerful child, so our advice is not to use spanking. He's getting too old for spanking anyway.

RANDY: What you need with an A.D.H.D. child is structure. Undoubtedly, you've been told he needs a consistent schedule. He needs his own desk, his own light, his own space if at all possible.

KEVIN: And above all, you need to give the A.D.H.D. kid focused attention if you want to help him. You have to go eyeball to eyeball with him to be sure he understands what you have said.

EUNICE: I try to explain to him that he must be accountable for his actions and there will be consequences if he isn't. He somehow doesn't seem to understand this.

KEVIN: Don't believe it. A.D.H.D. kids are perfectly capable of understanding that if certain things are done or not done, there will be consequences. You need to spell these consequences out as briefly and clearly as possible, and then leave it up to the child. If there is misbehavior, you need to use action, not more words. All kids pay more attention to action than they do words anyway.

RANDY: When you use Reality Discipline with an A.D.H.D. child, you want to have plenty of structure and to keep things as simple as possible. Don't get into a lot of arguments or explanations or you will be in a power struggle, which is always a losing proposition. Keep the consequences simple and very direct. If he does not get his homework done, he loses a treasured privilege. If he is loud and disrespectful, he must spend so much time in his room. When you invoke these consequences, however, be sure to be loving and positive, not punitive or harsh. You are already dealing with a child who has problems suppressing his emotions and, when you treat him harshly, it really beats on his already battered self-esteem and intensifies the problem.

Set your A.D.H.D. child up for success rather than failure by building on his strengths and minimizing his weaknesses. Something as simple as the chores that you assign can make a difference. Don't give him jobs where he'll probably goof up, but don't excuse him from chores either. Think through what he can handle. For example, draw him a sample table setting and then let him set the table.

KEVIN: Sports are another area, Randy. Parents need to think through what their children can do and can't do. An A.D.H.D. child may be a disaster at sports like baseball and basketball, which require a great deal of eye/hand coordination. Instead, he may do quite well at swimming, football, or track. Find a sport he can succeed in and it will do wonders for his self-image and confidence.

In addition, use simple strategies to avoid unnecessary tension. For example, if one of the problems is that your child seems to ignore you or doesn't pay attention, don't call to him from a distance or from another room. Seek the child out. And except for calling his name, don't begin speaking until you have established eye contact. Then tell the child what's on your mind. Again, it's focused one-on-one attention that counts. And always zero in on what interests your child. You definitely have to get on the A.D.H.D. child's wavelength. For example, with reading, don't give him a copy of *War and Peace* when he's into baseball cards. As Randy said, always set the kid up for success rather than failure.

CHAPTER 14

■●▲■●▲

HELP! THE KIDS ARE FIGHTING AGAIN!

RANDY: You know, Kevin, it seems that ever since the days of Cain and Abel, kids haven't gotten along very well with each other. Children naturally get into arguments, squabbles, and even knock-down-drag-out fights, and it all drives poor old Mom and Dad bonkers. You and I are both the youngest in our families. Were you picked on?

KEVIN: Indeed I was, by my big brother to whom I gave the nickname "God." It used to drive him nuts when he'd come home from school and I'd holler, "God's home!" I used to do a lot of "setting him up." I knew how to push his buttons, and I would just keep picking away until I provoked him to wrath.

RANDY: How did you set him up, besides calling him "God"?

KEVIN: He hated anything that challenged his authority. But I loved to poke him in the ribs when I walked by, or, if he asked me to get him something, I'd get it all right, and then I'd throw it in his face. Then he'd grab me and stomp me real good. He loved to sock me in the arm. Then I'd scream and yell and Mom or Dad would come in and say, "How many times have I told you to leave your little brother alone?" And there I'd be, crying, because he really did hurt me, but I'd still remember smiling on the inside and thinking, *Ha! Ha! Ha! Gotcha!*

RANDY: My brother, Larry, would sock me on the arm, too, and he would make faces at me to make me cry. Then my mother would come in and stand by my side. I think the moms of this world always want to defend the baby of the family.

KEVIN: Now wait a minute, I want to understand this. You cried because he made faces at you?

RANDY: Yeah, he would wrinkle his nose at me and call me names.

KEVIN: Sounds as if you were a big wimp.

RANDY: Maybe, but I wasn't stupid enough to take on a brother six years older than I was.

KEVIN: Well, I've got to admit that I was. Actually, he was only about five years older, but that didn't stop me. I guess he used to really bug me because he'd go off with his friends and, when I'd follow them, they would try to lose me in the woods.

RANDY: We know from our mail and the questions we get in seminars and over the phone that squabbling kids, politely known as "sibling rivals," are one of the biggest problems parents have.

So we may as well get started with the basic question we get asked the most . . .

How can you get your children to stop attacking each other with name-calling, put-downs, or even blows?

KEVIN: One of the features I like best about "Parent Talk" is that we often let parents talk to other parents and share ideas on what works and doesn't work for them. We have Thelma on the line, and she wants to tell us how she dealt with her kids when they got into squabbles . . .

THELMA: We had seven children, three of whom still live at home. Early on, my husband and I decided it was really important for our children to grow up and still want to be friends. Through numerous errors and frequent trials, we learned that children can be very adept at tearing each other down, particularly with their tongues. So we set some very strict guidelines.

RANDY: What were some of these guidelines?

THELMA: One guideline was that no one could assault another person and insult that person's character. They could not say things like, "You are stupid," "You are dumb," "You are fat," and things like that.

KEVIN: Could they say, "You are ugly"?

THELMA: About all we would allow would be things like, "That wasn't a real smart thing to do." That kind of remark allows showing displeasure, but it doesn't insult a brother or sister's character.

RANDY: What happens, Thelma, when the kids talk to each other in a bedroom, and then one of them comes out and says, "Susie (or Sean) just said such-and-such to me"? What would you do?

THELMA: When that happened, I'd sit everybody down and find out what went on. The person who had said "such-and-such" to someone else had to apologize for his actions. That was another rule—when you offend a brother or a sister, you have to apologize.

RANDY: How old are your children right now, Thelma?

THELMA: Four of them are well into their twenties, but we have three still living at home who are eighteen, seventeen, and eleven.

RANDY: And how do they all get along?

THELMA: They all get along beautifully now. But it wasn't always that way until we put our foot down and told everyone he or she would have to be accountable for what was said or done. We had five children in five years, and at one time we had five teenagers living in our home. Everyone learned that when he jumped on a brother or a sister, he'd have to apologize and be accountable.

KEVIN: Thelma, I'm wondering, with your teenagers, did you set a time limit on how long someone could wait to apologize? Two teenage boys can really go after each other once in a while and they need a day or two before they even begin to think about wanting to apologize.

THELMA: Well, that's true, I guess. But we didn't give them a day or two—maybe a few hours, and we didn't have a problem. We found that having this rule cut down tremendously on the fighting and bickering. It was just phenomenal.

RANDY: This is interesting, Thelma, because we've had this kind of bickering in our family. I've seen firsthand that just telling kids they shouldn't do something, and then apologize for it, isn't always enough to stop it. Sometimes it actually increases the fighting and bickering because there is a certain amount of attention being paid to them for the behavior. But what I hear you saying is that your kids must have picked up the message that Mom and Dad really mean this. This is serious and we are not going to tolerate this.

THELMA: We had a real problem until I read Kevin's book, *Making Children Mind Without Losing Yours*, when it first came out, almost ten years ago. What he said about Reality Discipline and being accountable made sense. We really went by his book. The kids knew that if they didn't apologize and they didn't stop that kind of behavior, there would be consequences. We became very good at revoking privileges.

KEVIN: Is *Making Children Mind* . . . almost ten years old? Time sure flies when you're having fun! Thelma and her husband made some rules, and then they backed them up with Reality Discipline. It makes sense to me!

□ ○ △ □ ○ △

What are some ways to stay out of the middle when children fight and want you to get involved and take sides?

COLLEEN: When my children would start fighting and then come to me and want me to referee, I just refused to get involved. I used something I read somewhere in a book, and it worked every time. For instance, Roger would say, "Raymond is hitting me." So I would say, "Raymond, Roger said you were hitting him." And when Raymond would say, "Well, Roger was pulling my hair," I would say, "Roger, Raymond said you were pulling his hair."

KEVIN: It sounds like Little Sir Echo.

COLLEEN: That was the idea. I would just repeat back what each one of them had said about the other, and pretty soon they both started laughing at each other because they could see how ridiculous it was. Then they would just go on and do something else and forget about their squabble.

RANDY: And you never took either side?

COLLEEN: I never did. And it always worked.

□ ○ △ □ ○ △

When kids start getting physical and come to blows, what's the best way to handle it?

ERICA: My brother and I used to get into fistfights and my dad would step in and stand us in front of each other and then say, "Okay, Scott, go ahead and hit your sister." Of course, he never did really slug me then. He'd just reach out and tap me, and my dad would say, "Go ahead and hit her, if you want to fight, go ahead and hit her." And then maybe he'd even shove him toward me a little bit. Then my dad would turn around and tell me to do the same thing—"Go ahead and hit your brother." I usually wound up giving him a little tap or a little shove, but that was all. The effect was that we both lost our interest in fighting. I suppose some people might think this was sort of harsh, but it worked with us, and I just wonder what your comments might be.

RANDY: I'm not sure it would work with every kid. Some kids are just waiting for Mom or Dad to say, "Go ahead and zap your sister." And they would! If parents doubt that this "reverse psychology" approach will work, they may prefer separating the kids until they cool down. Then bring them together to work out their problem and set two rules: no hitting and no name-calling.

KEVIN: That's true, Randy, but I still think Erica's reverse psychology idea can be effective with some kids. There's a very good principle here that reminds me of when I was in high school and a fight would break out in the hallway, in gym class, or where ever. The teachers grabbed both participants and put them in the gym wearing big sixteen-ounce boxing gloves. I got in a few of those fights myself, and all I can remember is those gloves felt like a ton after we boxed for just a little while. The other thing was that there was no audience. We had to duke it out in there alone, and that's the key. I never heard of anyone really going after the other guy when they had to put on the gloves and fight without an audience.

□ ○ △ □ ○ △

What are some good ways to get kids to settle their squabbles themselves?

GRETCHEN: We have a seven-and-a-half-year-old boy and a two-year-old girl. As soon as our little girl hit two and got ideas of her own, we started having problems between the two kids. It got to the point where they were fighting constantly, and I realized a lot of it was their trying to get me involved. Also, Kevin mentioned pushing his older brother's buttons. That's so true. I was shocked when I saw my two year old pushing my seven year old's buttons. In fact, you could see it happening at eighteen months—her little wheels going around as if she were thinking, *I'm going to get him.*

RANDY: What did you try to do to change things?

GRETCHEN: First, my husband and I decided that instead of just scolding the kids and spanking them, we would figure out ways to separate them. Secondly, we sat down with our seven year old because we thought he was capable of reasoning things out with us. We let him know that we were concerned about how he was not getting along with his sister, and how the two of them were doing so much fighting. We asked him what kinds of behaviors he felt deserved a spanking, a grounding, taking away a privilege, and so on. We worked out an entire plan with him concerning what we expected from him. We just made a list together as to what he was allowed to do and not do—no yelling at his sister, no name-calling, no hitting, etc.

KEVIN: Did you give him an idea of what to do if his sister attacked him?

GRETCHEN: He was not to hit back or say things back. We told him that he should tell her, "When you behave like this, I am not allowed to play with you." We thought this was appropriate because that gave her the message that she wasn't succeeding in pushing her older brother's buttons; all she was accomplishing was having to play by herself, which she hates to do.

RANDY: Your ideas sound excellent for a short-term solution, but as your two year old gets older, I think it would be a good idea to start putting the spotlight on how the two of them can get along and resolve conflicts between themselves. I don't think it's a long-range solution to just sit kids down, separate them, and not let them have disagreements.

GRETCHEN: One thing I should clarify is that we do not separate the kids for every little squabble. We step in only when the biting or hitting starts, or when the anger really elevates. Our system has been working well, and it seems that it has all evolved to where they both respect each other and want to play together. And I agree, as Amy gets older, she'll be able to understand the ground rules better, and they can resolve their own conflicts without our help.

□ ○ △ □ ○ △

Our firstborn has a learning disability. How can we get our second-born to stop calling him, "Stupid"?

JUANITA: We have two sons, twelve and thirteen years old. The older boy has a learning disability and his brother likes to egg him on by calling him stupid or dumb. Our firstborn is tolerant for a while and then he'll turn around and call his younger brother stupid or dumb. Then the second one comes up to me and says, "Mom, he called me stupid!" They've been doing this since they were little boys, and I just don't know how to stop it.

KEVIN: The most important clue in what I have just heard, Juanita, is that the boys have been doing this since they were small. That means that there has always been some kind of reward or payoff. Now how do you suppose they have been rewarded? I'm wondering if maybe Mom hasn't spent a lot of her time going in to smooth things over and play Judge Wapner in her own version of "People's Court."

JUANITA: I'm afraid you're right. I've always wound up the referee. I used to just give the older boy advice and tell him not to fall into his younger brother's trap. But lately the older boy is getting more belligerent and now I don't know what to say to the younger boy.

KEVIN: The healthiest situation is not to say anything to either one of them. What you should start to do is hold them both accountable for what goes on in their relationship. If one brother calls the other brother stupid, don't wait for it to escalate to where you have to play judge and jury. Just move in with Reality Discipline on the spot. If they do it at the dinner table, they're both gone with no dinner. If one says, "That's not fair, I didn't start it," just tell him that you're not going to play God and decide who started what or whatever. The point is, if either one of them calls the other names, they both have to pay the price. Let them figure it out from there.

□ ○ △ □ ○ △

How can I get my four-year-old twins to quit fighting in the back seat of the car?

ROSEMARY: We have four-year-old twins, a boy and a girl, who seem to wait until they get into the car to go a little crazy. We are all rushing to get to church, and my husband and I put them in their seat belts in the back seat. Then we get in front, and while I'm checking to be sure I've got two earrings and matching shoes, the twins go wild. First, they don't want to stay in their seat belts. Brad might be playing with his toy and Brenda will reach over and grab it. Then they start screaming and fighting. I turn around and start yelling and trying to swat them but I can't quite reach them. It's incredible. Here we are, a Christian family on the way to church, and we are all going down the street as if we are all insane.

RANDY: I think a lot of parents can identify with your insanity.

ROSEMARY: Have you ever tried to bite your sunglasses in two because you are so frustrated?

KEVIN: It's probably less painful than biting your tongue. Quite a few years ago, the cars were equipped with a foolproof solution to your problem, but not anymore.

ROSEMARY: What was that?

KEVIN: When the kids would start fighting, you could just drape them over the front fenders, the way hunters used to bring deer home, but with the newer cars that won't work anymore.

ROSEMARY: Let me give you our latest scenario. My husband runs the book table at our church, and last night, as he was finishing up, the twins and I went out to the car to wait for him. In just a minute or two, they were going nuts in the back seat, yelling and screaming, and hitting each other. Brad finally crawled up to the front seat and hung on to the rearview mirror. I just got out of the car and stood in the parking lot, waiting for my husband. I didn't need that.

RANDY: We always look for the purpose behind a child's behavior, and one of the best ways to tell is to monitor how you're feeling at the time. Because you are getting angry with your twins, that means they are definitely on a power trip.

ROSEMARY: I am definitely angry with them, and I want to know what I can do about it. It is driving all of us nuts.

KEVIN: Well, one practical step would be to separate the kids. Put one of them in the front seat, and leave the other in the back seat.

ROSEMARY: I do that sometimes, but we have a car with bucket seats and it isn't too comfortable with a squirming four year old on your lap.

RANDY: I think what you're missing, Rosemary, is failing to have a real consequence involved when the twins misbehave. For one thing, you can just pull over to the side of the road and say, "This car isn't moving until you calm down."

ROSEMARY: I'm not sure they would care, unless we were going down to get an ice cream cone, or something.

RANDY: You'll have to make the reading on that, but it is a way to get kids to settle down when they are getting wild in the back seat of a car.

KEVIN: Another obvious thing is that you are putting your sails in the twins' wind. They are both back there huffing and puffing and carrying on and having a great old time and you just get all involved with them, sputtering around, screaming and hollering and yelling—what I call raising your sails right into their wind. You need to make them each accountable for their behavior. They have to have a privilege revoked—something that will really get their attention and convince them when they do act that way, there won't be any payoff but there will be consequences.

RANDY: There is one other possibility, Kevin, and that's stopping the car, taking each child out carefully and firmly, and giving each child two or three good swats on the popo. Then put the children back in the car, buckle them up and say, "No more fighting." If they continue to fight, repeat the procedure.

KEVIN: You're right, Randy. From what we've been hearing, these kids are being deliberately defiant, and maybe some swats are what they both need. Rosemary will have to decide that.

□ ○ △ □ ○ △

How can I get my two daughters to share a bedroom without fighting all the time?

ESTHER: We have a blended family. My husband had two kids, a girl, eight, and a boy, five, and I had two also, a girl, seven, and a boy, four. We have a three-bedroom house, so the girls have one room and the boys have another. The boys seem to get along fine except it's hard to get them to go to sleep at night. But the girls are constantly fighting because they have to room together. They argue over everything—who has what space, who is messiest, who wants it quiet for homework, and it just goes on and on. Do you have any ideas on how to get them to cooperate with each other?

KEVIN: You have to realize that you have two firstborns who are butting heads for territorial rights. They both want to rule the roost, and they're going to have to work it out. Do they get you involved in their hassles right now?

ESTHER: I'm afraid they do. I'm constantly being called in to settle disputes and rule on who gets what space and who wore whose sweater when they weren't supposed to. You name it, I settle it.

RANDY: Then you need to stop playing Solomon immediately. I think the best thing for you to do is to have a meeting with the girls and help them work out some kind of agreement with rules that are written down—the whole bit. Work out boundaries, whose space is whose, and have them come to some kind of agreement on how neat the room must be. Are they both typically messy, or is one neat and the other a slob?

ESTHER: I'm afraid my daughter is the slob, and my step-daughter is the neatnik. There is a lot of friction over that.

KEVIN: The Leman family is proof-positive that a slob and a neatnik can live together. But I will admit that Sande had to give me some lessons on how to hang up my clothes when we were first married.

RANDY: I think what you have to do with your daughters is to have them agree on whose side of the room is whose and, if your sloppy daughter wants to keep her side sloppy, that will be her prerogative. The neat daughter can keep her side neat, but she'll have to live with the other side being messy. The point is, they can work it out, and once they have their rules written down, be very firm on one point: *You are not going to referee.* They will have to settle their disputes between themselves, and if they can't, there will be consequences.

KEVIN: And be sure the consequences apply to both girls. Don't get sucked into deciding that it's one girl's fault, and she has to miss a favorite club or team or event. Both girls will have to miss things they want to go to or things they want to do. That's how they'll learn to live together.

□ ○ △ □ ○ △

When someone picks on my child, should I tell him to fight back or turn the other cheek?

SYBIL: Our seven year old is on a Little League team, and the other night at practice a nine year old, who is quite a bit bigger and stronger, picked on him. Grant didn't try to protect himself and he ended up getting choked and punched. When my husband heard about it, he told Grant, "When some kid picks on you, you've got to be aggressive. Punch him in the face and don't let him take advantage of you." My reaction was, "Grant, you should turn the other cheek. You need to tell him what the Bible says. If you're going to have friends, you have to be friendly."

RANDY: So now your son doesn't know whether he should pray for the kid or punch his lights out.

SYBIL: That's right. I don't want my boy getting beaten up, but I don't want him beating up other people, either.

RANDY: This happens a lot with kids at school or on teams. My wife and I have told our children that if they are being swung at or thrown at, or attacked in some way, they have to protect themselves in a defensive mode. They have to hold the child away, or get out of the way of the punch . . . .

KEVIN: . . . or bleed all over them!

RANDY: I don't think it is very good advice to punch back. I know what your husband is thinking. You have to teach a child to defend himself, and I think that is important, but punching back is not the first line of defense.

KEVIN: What I heard your husband saying was a lot more than "defend yourself." He was saying to get in the other kid's face and punch him out. I have this picture of your seven year old going up against a big, husky nine year old. He's probably a good head shorter, and he is going to lose. He's going to look like a goalie, and chances are you don't even have a hockey team in your town.

RANDY: I think your husband would do better to teach your son how to defend himself and get out of the situation. There's always someone bigger, stronger, and meaner who is going to punch his lights out, so the best offense is a good defense. We have told our kids to go get help when this happens to them. They should find the teacher or coach or playground supervisor and say, "I'm being hit and punched and I don't like it. Will you take care of this?"

KEVIN: I'd always tell Kevey to play dead. Just fall to the earth and play dead. Make them think they really hurt you bad.

RANDY: This is a difficult area, Sybil, because kids are always getting into scuffles. But I think the basic principles are, one, teach your son not to punch back, two, have Dad teach him how to fend off the blows and get out of the situation . . .

KEVIN: . . . is he a fast runner? Running is a great way to get out of the situation.

RANDY: Three, go report what's happening to a teacher or coach or supervisor. If your boy does punch the other kid back, he'll only wind up in the school office to be disciplined for fighting, along with the kid who is really the bully.

KEVIN: As Randy says, this is a tough area. Even today I can remember the fear in my heart as I'd walk around the corner, hoping that the big kid from down the block wasn't going to be there—but he was there, and he'd beat me up but good. I went to his house and told his father what happened, and all his father said was, "What do you want me to do about it?"

I only tell that story because I want to add this advice for kids: If a guy is a *lot* bigger than you are . . . and he looks as if he's going to kill you . . . RUN!

CHAPTER 15

■●▲■●▲

STAYING SANE DURING MEALTIME MADNESS

RANDY: How do you get kids to eat the yucky green stuff, that yellow stuff, and some of the white stuff, too? How do you get them to eat the things that are "good for them"? What were the yucky foods when you were a kid, Kevin?

KEVIN: Well, I remember green beans. I used to gag on them. Today I would like to hear from some parents who are willing to tell us what they used to gag on, and what it's like now when they try to get their gagging kids to eat.

RANDY: Kay, our producer, went out and talked with some first graders about food. Here's some of that conversation:

KAY: Tell me, what kinds of food do you not like to eat? What is your most unfavorite food?

FIRST KID: Squash. It tastes yucky, so does spinach—it looks like seaweed!

SECOND KID: I hate corn because it looks like old teeth, and broccoli because it takes like green weeds.

THIRD KID: I hate zucchini, peas—and chicken.

KAY: Chicken? Why?

THIRD KID: Because my mom puts onions in it, that's why.

KAY: What would you say if your mom served you chicken with onions tonight? What would you tell her?

THIRD KID: I don't want to eat this!

KAY: What would she say?

THIRD KID: You have to.

KAY: Then what would you do?

THIRD KID: I would just plug my nose and eat it.

KEVIN: I'm glad to hear that the old "hold your nose" trick still works, but you know, Randy, those are pretty bright kids and at least one of them could grow up to be president.

RANDY: Which one?

KEVIN: The one who hates broccoli!

What do you do with a picky eater who takes forever to finish?

RANDY: Strange, but I didn't hear anyone mention hating banana splits or chocolate sundaes. Today's program is sparked by one of our faithful listeners, Bonnie, who wrote us not long ago saying she tries to use Reality Discipline, but sometimes reality doesn't seem to be enough stimulus to change the behavior of her three-and-a-half-year-old son who is driving her a little crazy, with his picky and poky eating habits.

BONNIE: I am pretty frustrated because my three and a half year old is not only a picky eater, but he takes forever to eat. At breakfast this morning, he took an hour to eat a bowl of cereal, one piece at a time. I didn't have any place to go today, so, okay. But sometimes I do have places to go and I can't wait for him to take an hour to eat.

RANDY: What would happen if you told him that he has fifteen minutes for breakfast, and wherever he is at the end of fifteen minutes, the bowl disappears? What would he do?

BONNIE: He doesn't eat any faster. I put him on a thirty-minute timer for dinner, but he pokes and picks then, too, and never finishes, so that means he can never have dessert. That's our rule.

RANDY: Does he look as if he is not being well fed?

BONNIE: Not really, but awhile ago I was really worried because he had grown two inches and hadn't gained any weight. I thought the kid was starving to death. I took him to the doctor for a thorough checking out and, after examining him, all the doctor would say was, "He's a very healthy boy—don't worry about his picky eating." But I can't help it. I still don't think Zacchary is getting enough to eat.

RANDY: One of the most powerful things a child can use against us is food. For some children it grows into a serious eating disorder. For most, it's just part of a universal problem that most families have to face to one degree or another. What parents need to ask themselves, is, "How important is it to make food a battleground?" Bonnie, would you say your problem is that your little guy hates most foods, or he's just slow about eating?

BONNIE: He likes a few things, like cereal. But he's just so slow. It is very wearing three times a day to have him sit at the table forever and ever and ever. There are other things I want to do.

RANDY: I think little Zacchary knows that because, as we often say, children know just how to pull your chain. It sounds to us, Bonnie, as if your son is taking a power trip on you.

KEVIN: Poky kids are poky for a reason, Randy. They're getting paid off somewhere by the extra attention or whatever. Since he eats most things, it might be a good idea to just back off. One of the reasons for a person developing an eating disorder is that somewhere along the line as he or she grew up, too much attention was paid to food. I don't think it is wise to become overly involved in what the kids eat.

I know it is tempting to push kids to get them to eat because you want them to get plenty of vitamins, nutrition, and all that. But you really will be better off by just letting nature take its course. Holly, our firstborn, was a picky eater and Sande was worried sick about her. She would go to the pediatrician and he would say, time and again, "Don't worry about it. She will not starve." He was right. Today she is a slender, very healthy young lady of twenty-one.

BONNIE: But it is hard to pretend that you don't care when meal after meal you child doesn't get dessert or a snack because he didn't finish. I mean, I am his mom and I do care. Even though I'm not supposed to show it because it is a battleground.

KEVIN: But that's his choice, isn't it? You mention giving him a reasonable length of time to eat, then the food is taken away. Your timing consequence is the best thing you have going for you, and I suggest being consistent with that at every meal. Just because you have a little extra time some morning, don't give him an hour to piddle with a bowl of cereal. Let little Zacchary learn that he has to be accountable and that he can't control the whole family by piddling around over his food. In other words, we all sit down and eat our meal. Then all four, or five, or six of us, whatever, help clean up the table and that is the end of dinner. It is just sort of a natural thing and the more natural you can make it, the better off you are.

RANDY: You told us in your letter that you are a firstborn perfectionist. How do you think that fits into your parenting style regarding this particular problem?

BONNIE: Oh, I want him to be perfect about eating and finish everything on his plate without dawdling. I fight against that tendency and I am sure it makes me even more anxious about his eating because that's the way I want it to go.

RANDY: You have the battle half won, Bonnie, because you recognize that it's more important for you that Zacchary eats than it is for him. If you have had him checked by a medical doctor who says he is fine and not suffering from malnutrition, then your challenge is to develop a strategy to learn how to back off and deal with his little power trips at meal time.

Are small helpings a good idea for poky eaters?

What you may want to try in addition to the time limit consequence, is giving Zacchary about one-third the amount of cereal you usually serve him for breakfast. It's discouraging for a child to have more on his plate or in his bowl than he can eat, so give him a lot less. Then keep the timer rule in force and take away his bowl when the time is up. Do the same for lunch—a smaller portion—and no longer than twenty or thirty minutes to eat that. He will probably be hungrier at dinner because he hasn't eaten much at breakfast or lunch, and he may eat a little faster if he is hungry. But, if he is not hungry, when time is up, take away that plate also. Keep using Reality Discipline in a consistent way, and be content with having him eat smaller meals right now. He'll have another growth spurt in a few weeks or months and probably start eating more, and he will probably eat faster because he is hungry! But, the key to everything I have just said is that he has *no snacks between meals* until he starts eating faster and finishing his meals.

□ ○ △ □ ○ △

Does the "if-you-don't-eat-it-now-you'll-get-it-for-the-next-meal" strategy really work?

CLARICE: When our kids were small, I was just like Bonnie and worried about nutrition, particularly for our oldest child because she really had picky eating habits. Early on, my husband and I were unwise in picking our battles and our daughter learned quickly that she could put us over a barrel. She knew we wouldn't sit there all night in order to make her eat. We even put food in her mouth, but we couldn't make her swallow it. So it was a frustrating time.

When our twins came along, we decided to change our strategy and pick battles we knew we could win. We decided that for each meal there would be at least one item the children liked and would eat. For nutrition's sake, we wanted them to have other things and they would get a small portion of those items, which they were also required to eat. We told them, "It's your choice. If you choose not to eat, then you don't have to eat, but you will get the same plate with the same food on it for the next meal—cold."

KEVIN: And did they call your bluff?

CLARICE: We weren't bluffing. The twins were younger than Bonnie's boy is now when we started this new program, and we enforced it with the older daughter, too. They all learned that cold oatmeal isn't necessarily very tasty for lunch, and it's even less tasty for dinner. But when they went hungry long enough, they finally would eat. They learned that when they sat down at the table, they had better eat what was on their plates because it was much better when it was warm.

RANDY: How old are your kids now, Clarice?

CLARICE: The twins are ten and our daughter is fifteen. They all have good appetites and eat almost anything that I put on the table now.

RANDY: I don't blame them! There's nothing worse, Kevin, than cold oatmeal that is two days old.

CLARICE: We would let them watch us save it, wrap it, and put it in the refrigerator, and we never warmed it up in the microwave. They ate it just the way it came out of the refrigerator.

KEVIN: You are a mean mamma!

CLARICE: Oh, I was horrible, but I think it's called Reality Discipline, isn't it? And you know what? We won the fight every time. Yes, they lost a little weight in the beginning because we made sure they didn't eat snacks or even fruit between meals. We'd give them drinks like milk and water, but nothing with sugar in it. We knew they had to get hungry sooner or later, and they would have to eat.

RANDY: I think I might have been inclined to mix Reality Discipline with at least warming up the leftovers, but you make a good point, Clarice. We have to choose our battlegrounds carefully because there are going to be plenty of them while parent.

CLARICE: Kids learn real fast how to pull your chain. Even though they're too young to tell time, they can sense when you are in a hurry and you can't wait around forever for them to eat. I think Bonnie has a good idea with leaving only so much time to eat, and then everyone is finished, everyone clears the table, and dinner is over. We did pretty much the same thing except we would save what they hadn't eaten and they'd get it the next meal.

RANDY: Clarice, did your kids use creative ways to make you think they had eaten the food when they had actually hidden it?

CLARICE: Oh, yes, our oldest daughter would hold it in her mouth until she could leave the table and spit it out in the bathroom, but she made the mistake of letting us see her do this once, and so we got wise to that one. As for our twin boys, they took an easier approach, they just hid food in the pockets of their clothes!

□ ○ △ □ ○ △

Should I always demand that my children finish everything on their plates?

NAOMI: We have a three and a half year old and a six year old. When our six year old was very young, we made a rule and have stuck with it: They get small portions of everything we have on the table for the meal and they have to take two bites of each food on their plates. After the two bites, they get to choose what they want to finish. They are pretty good eaters. Sometimes there will be something that they absolutely detest. That's fine, as long as they take their two bites, they don't have to finish it.

RANDY: How does this work out overall? Do they leave a lot of food?

NAOMI: They end up finishing almost everything. Once in a while they will hit something and say, "I don't like this!" What is funny, though, is that the things they hate change from day to day. One day they will absolutely detest broccoli and the next time we have it they will eat a large helping.

RANDY: Do you ever try to get them to eat by talking about the starving people in Africa or the Far East?

NAOMI: No, I never have, because my folks tried to use that on me and I would simply go over, scrape my plate in the garbage disposal and say, "Here, they can have mine."

RANDY: I think our generation used to hear that more when we were kids. I doubt that many parents do that very much any more because it just doesn't answer the problem.

□ ○ △ □ ○ △

What if a picky eater eats what he likes and then waits for Dad or Mom to say, "Dinner is over and the rest goes in the garbage disposal"? Doesn't he win?

CLIFF: Kevin, I have heard you say many times that when you have a finicky eater, just scrape his plate into the garbage disposal and make the child wait until the next meal before he gets anything to eat. This has been working pretty well, but our four and a half year old has decided to eat one or two things on his plate that he really likes and, when all the rest of it goes down the garbage disposal, that's fine with him.

KEVIN: The question we must ask, then, is how does all that food get on his plate? Do you put it there to begin with?

CLIFF: Yes, we do, because we want him to get a balanced meal.

KEVIN: I'd like to suggest that you take the risk and let the child put on the plate whatever he wants to eat. I realize this is a theoretical problem for many parents because of what you just said, you want the child to have a "balanced meal." But I really think that in the long run we would do away with a lot of meal-time problems if we would just put good, well-balanced food on the dinner table and encourage kids to take what they want. Once they put it on their plate, they have to at least taste it. They don't have to finish it. I like that rule: put it on your plate and you at least have to taste it.

RANDY: But at our house, at least two of our kids would pass up the beans, the corn, and the salad, and take chicken or beef night after night. There would never be any vegetables flowing through their little veins. Isn't there a basic question here by a lot parents who are thinking, "Now wait a minute, this is not teaching our children about good eating habits and being responsible if we just let them pick whatever they want to put on their plate."

KEVIN: Again, I want to go back to what we've put on the table for the meal. If all we would have would be bowls full of candy, then I might see that point. But if what we put on the table is basically good food, then I think allowing the children to take what they want to put on their plate is a healthy thing and a good way to teach them personal responsibility and making their own choices. And don't misunderstand me, I want kids to get a balanced diet. I like the idea of kids trying new things, just taking a bite or two, and once they do, get off their case and see what happens.

RANDY: Reality Discipline always wants the child to learn how to make good choices, but I think, Kevin, that many parents would be uncomfortable with letting a child choose one or two things, meal after meal, and never try anything else. Perhaps what you can try, Cliff, is what Naomi just told us about. If every night you can't bear to see the child choose just the chicken and mashed potatoes and no salad or steamed vegetables, for example, give him very small helpings of other items and insist he take at least two bites of each food.

Another thought would be to have the child take the two bites of the less desirable foods first, *before* the chicken, mashed potatoes, and gravy. It's easier for a kid to eat the foods he likes less first instead of waiting until he's filled up on the things he loves.

□ ○ △ □ ○ △

What if you "try everything in the book" and a child still eats almost nothing at all and every meal is a battle?

DAISY: We have three boys. Our first- and third-borns are fairly good eaters, but our second son will not eat much of anything. I nursed him, and that went okay, but when it came to solid food he looked at me as if to say, "Is this a joke?" From the age of eight months until now—he's six—we still struggle with getting him to eat. We have tried all the tricks and none of them has worked except for what we are doing now.

RANDY: And what is that?

DAISY: We are just chilling out. We put a taste of everything on each child's plate because I believe if you don't taste it you can't say you don't like it. Besides, I'm a strong believer that your tastes do change as the years go by. Anyway, I started by putting less than a teaspoon of each food on my middle boy's plate, and, of course, he balked. He literally would gag and vomit. So my husband would take the plate, rinse it off, and double that portion on the plate. He doesn't try to "vomit" his food anymore. He does eat and it takes him forever, but that's okay with us. We just go about our business and he is left there to finish the tiny portions of food that he is given. Once a week I cook him foods that he likes —macaroni and cheese, hot dogs, or pizza. He is not dying. He is a very healthy boy.

KEVIN: Are you and your husband in agreement on how you are approaching this?

DAISY: As a matter of fact, it was my husband, Herb, who finally convinced me not to worry so much about it. I used to get uptight and nervous to the point I didn't even want to cook food because my middle boy was always saying, "Yuck, this is gross," and, "Oh, I don't like that," and on and on. Then his brothers would often pick up on it and start saying "Yuck," and "Gross," too. So Herb said, "Fix what you want, and we will all eat it." And another rule now is that none of the boys is allowed to say anything negative about the food being served at any meal. If they do, they are excused from that meal and can have nothing to eat until the next one. No snacks to tide them over.

RANDY: That's a good use of Reality Discipline, Daisy, and it reminds me of one more thing of which parents should be aware. Many children say they don't like something because they have heard a sibling or friend say they don't like it. So, to be "cool," or to control, they decide they don't like it either. Some dislikes are for real, but a lot of these dislikes are decided or copied. So, if you sense that your kids are trying to be "cool" or control you with all of their likes and dislikes, again it's time to bring in Reality Discipline.

□ ○ △ □ ○ △

Do you have any ideas for "hiding" veggies in something my kids like?

RANDY: We have several moms on the line who want to share their best ideas for how to slip the kids nutrition in a painless, hassle-free way. So here we go. . . .

JULIA: I got this idea when I worked in a convalescent care center. I took a box of orange Jell-O and added about half a blender of carrots and then let it all set up. My kids slicked it all up, but when I told them there were carrots in it, they said, "We don't believe you." They wanted more and more, just as if it were dessert.

RANDY: And this just raises the point that kids have their likes and dislikes, and if we can find out what it is they like, and it is not terribly inconvenient to fit it into the meal, then go ahead and do it. Whatever works.

JULIA: Another recipe I tried was adding spinach to pistachio pudding. You have to experiment because spinach has a strong flavor and you can put in too much. But if you start with a little bit and the kids don't notice it, you can increase it next time. Other green vegetables work, too, and you can get a good amount of them in there without changing the taste of your pudding.

PENNY: My kids love chicken soup, but if I try to put in chopped carrots and celery for a little extra nutrition, they sit and pick out all the vegetables. So what I learned to do was to cook up the soup and then take some of the broth, put it in the blender, and add carrots and celery. Then I would blend it completely and pour it back into the soup. Finally, I would add the noodles. This way they didn't see the vegetables, and it still tastes like chicken soup. They love it!

STELLA: I've used my blender to doctor up a lot of different soups the kids like. Split pea is a favorite and all I have to do is blend in chopped onions, carrots, and celery to add a few more vitamins—and good flavor. Another good trick is using minced, dried onions in meatballs, meat loaf, or casseroles instead of trying to put in chopped fresh onions which my kids usually don't like to "see" in their food. The same thing can be done with tomatoes—or use pureed tomatoes or tomato sauce in place of chopped tomatoes.

RANDY: In the battle for better nutrition, it sounds as if the blender is an invaluable weapon!

But no matter what approach you use to get your kids to eat, mealtime will be much less of a hassle if you don't raise your sails into your child's wind. Set your rules and then quietly enforce them without getting grim, punitive, or hysterical. Getting kids to eat right is a little bit like potty training. Eventually they figure it out. But if you try to force them to do exactly what you want when you want it, you are in for a power struggle.

CHAPTER 16

■●▲■●▲

WHAT IF MY SPOUSE AND I DISAGREE ON DISCIPLINE?

RANDY: Disagreements between parents on how to discipline the children can have a profound impact on the entire family. Kevin, you are the great Kahuna of Reality Discipline. Does Sande ever disagree with anything you say?

KEVIN: Does she ever! Oh, yeah, I'm too hard on my son—I hold him accountable. When I'm too hard on him in her eyes, that sets her up to be too soft on him in mine.

RANDY: Why are you so hard on Kevey? Why not his older sisters—Holly or Krissy?

KEVIN: I'm sure it has something to do with the father/daughter relationship and the mother/son relationship.

RANDY: You mean dads tend to be soft on their daughters and moms on sons?

KEVIN: That's often true. Talk with any woman in America about her son—I mean this is her boy! She loves little Denise and little Danielle, but when it comes to little Dennis II, don't you dare touch him!

RANDY: I'll tell you where Donna and I disagree—on the little stuff. She's a neatnik while I'm a little bit of a slob, so she tends to crack down on the kids for being messy and I tend to let things go. Over the years there's been some disagreement, but Donna has become a little more lenient in that area, and I've tried to become a little more strict. I think we've moved toward each other.

KEVIN: That's great. I know that's true in our relationship. There's a lot of give-and-take between Sande and me. I'm the one who gets after the kids—I take the more active role in disciplining, which isn't true in many homes where moms have to be the chief disciplinarians. When I see Sande enforcing discipline that I know is hard for her, I'll say something like, "That was really a good job. I'm proud of the way you handled that problem."

RANDY: Speaking of handling problems, here come some now. The board is lighting up . . .

How can I get my husband to go with me to the parents' class I'm taking?

JOSIE: I've been going to parenting classes and have been learning a lot of different kinds of consequences you can give kids. I've tried to get my husband to come, but he simply refuses. Do you have any ideas?

KEVIN: It's doubtful. You see, he's smarter than that. He'll just stay home.

JOSIE: I want to get him more involved, because I'm tired of doing most of the parenting. And I also see that we go in opposite directions in the way we deal with the children.

KEVIN: Give us an example of something that happens at home, Josie. Something that goes wrong with the kids or whatever when you and your husband are both there.

JOSIE: For example, one of the kids would hurt himself and would come upstairs crying and I would . . .

KEVIN: Now wait a minute. Who do the kids go to?

JOSIE: They go to Mom.

KEVIN: I see. Is there a road map or something the children use to always find Mom? A second ago I might have sounded a little sarcastic when I said your husband was too smart to show up for those parenting classes. But think about it. He knows he doesn't need to show up because you're the one who deals with everything anyway. I suggest that the next time the kids come running to you to tell you how unfair brothers or sisters are, or whatever, that you tell them, "Go tell it to your father." Then you close the bathroom door and lock it behind you. Chances are your husband will become a little more active in parenting.

RANDY: There is also a cultural factor here that may be part of your husband's problem. Even in the 1990s many men assume that dealing with children is the woman's role. They've grown up in traditional homes where Mom did the parenting.

KEVIN: Right. All I'm saying, Josie, is that as soon as you see your kids charging relentlessly towards you, just step aside and say, "Let me introduce you to this man. He's your father. Some of you refer to him as Dad. He can handle your problem." Start doing that just a little bit and I think your husband will become a lot more interested in those parenting classes.

What if I don't like the way my spouse deals with the kids and I'd rather do it myself?

JOSIE: Sometimes I try to turn the kids over to my husband, but I have a problem with it because I don't like the way he treats them.

KEVIN: Ah—that's a whole other story. What's he doing that you don't like?

JOSIE: One major thing is that he just discounts their feelings. When they try to tell him how they feel, it doesn't matter. He just says, "You do this right now," and that's it. He is what you call "very authoritarian." What he says goes and it doesn't matter how the kids feel.

KEVIN: So what if that's the way he deals with them. I'm not trying to be flippant. I'm just saying, "So what?" If that's what he's going to do, let him do it. At least he is parenting the kids and you're not carrying the whole load yourself. Besides, kids are resilient little buzzards and they can learn. When they're around Dad and he says, "Do it because I said so and I want it done now," the kids will learn to jump to it. With you, they learn a different way of responding because Mom is obviously more understanding of how they feel.

JOSIE: Yes, but won't that breed what you always call inconsistency?

KEVIN: Yes, if it goes on indefinitely, it probably will. But right now we're talking about getting your husband involved. You're going to have to stand back and let some things go by that you're not real pleased with at first.

RANDY: That's right. In fact, you need to point your kids back to Dad when they come to you complaining that he doesn't understand or he's "mean." Say something like, "Honey, I understand you're upset and you feel as if Dad's not listening, but he's really the only one who can help with this one, so I suggest you go talk with him again." Then really encourage them to follow through. It's important for the children to start expressing to Dad how they feel about his discipline and his lack of interest in their feelings. If you really are concerned about something he's done, talk to him later when the two of you are alone. Or, write him a note, but don't start arguing with him in front of the kids about what he is doing.

KEVIN: Exactly. If you start letting him take a more active role in parenting, and then turn around and harpoon him from left field, he'll back off and hand all the parenting back to you. Take him aside and talk to him about the children's feelings and encourage him to try to listen to them a little more. But at the same time, let him know that you're glad that he's being a dad who wants to be firm and stick to his guns when trying to correct the children. It's a matter of give-and-take.

□ ○ △ □ ○ △

How can I get my husband to stop teaching our son the wrong values, especially with the TV programs he lets him watch?

FAYE: We have two sons, one is three years old tomorrow and the other one is two months old today. I just got the older boy into a Christian preschool but right after that my husband let him start watching the "Batman" series from the 1960s. I went along with it at first and made him a Batman costume with the cape and the tights, but I soon regretted it. My husband started letting him wear his tights to bed every night, and now every morning I fight with our son to wear other clothes. I'm so tired of it that yesterday morning I told him his tights were ripped and I was throwing them away. He could choose—wear regular clothes and go to preschool or stay home and go to bed. He chose to stay home and cry in bed from 9:30 to 11:00 and that meant he missed preschool on the day they were having a special party. He was very put out with that too.

RANDY: Is "Batman" the only TV show you and your husband disagree on?

FAYE: "Batman" is bad enough, but my husband even lets him watch *Star Wars.* My husband is not a Christian, and I just think those kinds of shows are too violent for a three year old.

RANDY: Faye, you're speaking for a lot of parents all over the country where the disagreement isn't so much about discipline but about values. And values usually come up when we talk about movies and television programs. You're caught in the old dilemma: a Christian woman is supposed to be "quietly submissive" to her husband, even though he's an unbeliever, but at the same time he's exposing the children to what you feel is harmful.

FAYE: How do I get it to stop? Tomorrow is my three year old's birthday and my mother-in-law is coming with presents. She has bought Batman *everything.* And I've decided I just want to put a stop to Batman costumes because it's such a battle to get our little boy to change clothes anyway. He wants to wear the same shirt over and over. When my husband is watching him on weekends when I go grocery shopping or to church, he allows him to wear whatever he wants.

KEVIN: I'm not sure if we have a discipline problem here or a marital one. Tell me, Faye, does your husband care about you? Does he care about what you think? Does he think that your opinions are important?

FAYE: We actually don't spend a lot of time talking because he has to work three jobs.

KEVIN: Well, it doesn't sound to me as if Batman is the real problem. The real issue is that your husband has one set of values and you have another, and apparently he won't respect your wishes. Your first step is to find some time to talk. I don't know how you're going to find it with a husband who works forty hours here and forty hours there—maybe you'll have to cast your body over the television set and say, "Would you please *listen* to me? It's very important to me that this Batman thing stops because I don't like it. I don't want our son being influenced by this at the age of three. It's causing me all kinds of grief, and I want to know if I can expect some cooperation from you on this."

RANDY: You see, Faye, your three year old is picking up on the power struggle between you and your husband, and now he's turning around and being powerful with you. In other words, the relationship between you and your husband is teaching your three year old *how* to be powerful. If you can stop the power struggle between you and your husband, then you can help the three year old learn that he doesn't have to be powerful all his life.

Is it worth taking a stand with your spouse on allowing the kids to watch "Batman" or other violent shows?

FAYE: I've come to believe that "Batman" is way over my three year old's head and I should try and stop it. It's gotten so it's all that he talks about, and he's starting to imitate Batman's gestures and his way of talking. "Batman" is a big issue with me, but is it big enough to confront my husband the way you suggest?

RANDY: I think it *is* a big enough issue because it's setting a pattern for other things that will come up later that will be even more of a problem.

KEVIN: I agree. Three year old's shouldn't be hooked on anything like Batman. You really have two concerns, Faye. "Batman" is a problem, but how you and your husband are getting along and communicating must be dealt with first. "Batman" is only a symptom. Try to talk with your husband and see if there's some place you can reach a middle ground. Go easy on preaching at him, however, because that will just make him set his feet all the more firmly. Try to find a compromise and work together to parent your kids.

Also, keep in mind that men are great problem solvers. They love to "fix the situation." At an appropriate time—and only you would know best what that time would be—drop the Batman thing in his lap by saying, "I'm really not sure how to solve this problem. I'm really concerned about "Batman", and I really think our three year old is too young to sit there and watch it. I don't know how to handle it and I need your help."

With a comment like this, you have put the tennis ball of life in your husband's court. If you and your husband have any kind of relationship at all, it would be rare for him to say, "Oh, what are you worried about that for? It's fine." When approached by their wives with tact and vulnerability, most husbands will want to fix whatever is bothering them.

□ ○ △ □ ○ △

When my mother comes to me for advice on how to handle my younger brother, how do I explain that she's making the same mistakes with him that she made with me?

MARY JO: I've had a real struggle this week with a lot of family things, but my main concern is my mom and dad. I have children thirteen and eleven, but my parents are having a lot of trouble with my younger brother, Phil, who is also thirteen. Phil is a real hard kid to handle and, because I've got a child thirteen myself, my mother keeps asking me a lot of questions on how she should discipline, when she should do this, or when she should stop that. I'm not sure I have a lot of answers about Phil, and I'm also not sure of what I can say to help her. There was so much that went on in the home where I grew up that I didn't agree with, that I would have changed. But how can I tell her?

RANDY: What did your parents do that you didn't like as you grew up?

MARY JO: For one thing, there was no communication. If any of us did anything wrong, we got spanked for it, but we didn't get to talk about it. We never got to explain or defend ourselves, and now they're doing the same thing with my younger brother.

RANDY: This sounds like a very negative pattern.

MARY JO: Our home was always filled with a lot of negative attitudes, and it resulted in all of us growing up with low self-esteem. I'd love to say something to my mother, but I'm afraid to because it would hurt her. My mom's always been the most negative of all, especially with labeling and name-calling.

KEVIN: Do you think your parents might be open to going to a counselor to learn how to handle Phil?

MARY JO: They might. They've been talking with one of the teachers at school about Phil's problems. He's supposed to have a high IQ but he has a learning disability.

RANDY: A lot of kids with learning disabilities have a high IQ. Has Phil been a constant problem while growing up?

MARY JO: He's always been very strong-willed. The rest of us were more obedient, I guess. We didn't like it, but we took it.

KEVIN: Do you think that your parents have any idea that consistent love and discipline go hand in hand—that it isn't one or the other but both?

MARY JO: I would have to say I doubt it.

KEVIN: You could really be a help if you could reflect back to them some of your own feelings, but I understand that it's very sensitive and you don't want to hurt them. Remember that your mother has asked you for input, so take the initiative. I suggest going to your mom and sitting down with her over lunch or a cup of coffee and just telling her that you see her and your dad parenting Phil much as they parented you and your other brothers and sisters, and that it wasn't always that positive. Tell her that you think a counselor would give her some practical answers, that you'd be happy to come in and talk with the counselor, too, if that would help.

RANDY: Another good idea would be to get her a practical Christmas gift—it's a book called *Making Children Mind Without Losing Yours* by Kevin Leman. It's full of help that your folks could really profit from, particularly the ideas on encouraging kids in Chapter Three.

□ ○ △ □ ○ △

How can I get my perfectionistic husband to back off and not be so picky with our kids?

JUNE: My husband, John, is a good guy, but he's very demanding with our kids—our son is nine and our daughter is six.

KEVIN: What do you mean by demanding? Is he very strict and authoritarian?

JUNE: No, he doesn't demand anything with "Do it or else!" or anything like that. Maybe the better word would be *picky* or *critical.* You see, I home school and my husband is in charge of our Bible memorization program. He tells the kids, "You have to memorize these verses the way they are written. They have to be letter perfect."

KEVIN: I see—your kids have their little King James Versions, because what was good enough for the Apostle Paul is good enough for him! Would you call your husband legalistic?

JUNE: No, not really, it's just that when things are done, he believes they're supposed to be done right. We've come a long way in nine years of marriage and we've worked on a lot of things. For example, he's a neatnik and I'm a slob. His desk at work is always clean with hardly anything on it. His fellow workers razz him and tell him he isn't getting anything done, but he's one of the most productive people in the office.

KEVIN: You mention that you feel you've come together with your husband over the last nine years, but apparently you don't feel together with him about his being picky with the kids. Where have you learned to agree?

JUNE: Well, we've come together as far as the house, you know. I try to clean up more and keep it neat for him, and he lives with my clutter with a lot more patience than he used to. But I want to find the balance with the way he's dealing with the kids—his pickiness. I see my daughter becoming very much like him. The other day she put a verse she had printed out up on the refrigerator and there was one minor word misspelled. I said, "Oh, that's great, Honey," but Daddy said, "Oh, oh, I have a problem here. This isn't *right.*"

KEVIN: Are you sure John's middle name isn't Nicodemus? It sounds as if he might have made a great Pharisee. I'd try to get John aside and point out to him that it might be okay to let an error go by here and there because he's teaching the kids to be perfectionists, and perfectionism is slow suicide. Tell him you have some real fears about how your kids are going to grow up and see life. Explain that when you put up the verse on the refrigerator and allow it to be not quite perfect, you are encouraging your child, not teaching her bad habits. She'll see the misspelled word and change it herself the next time. But what we want to do is encourage our kids and tell them they're okay. They need that message every day as they grow up.

RANDY: If your husband likes to have some fun now and then, maybe you could tease him a little and say things like, "Oh, John, you're so right. You know, I've really been worried about this. I want to make sure the kids get those Scripture verses letter perfect every time! If they miss even one, we're probably all doomed." You know the kind of things you could say to your husband. But a little laughter might soften the situation and get him to back off a bit on his perfectionism. Do you think you have good enough communication to do that?

JUNE: Yes, I do—that wouldn't be a problem. He's not really touchy—he just gets very serious about "doing things right."

RANDY: Humor is a key ingredient in communicating. I know in our own family, we get pretty uptight at times, but when we're willing to laugh at ourselves it really reduces the tension. Try to get your husband to lighten up and that will help your daughter to lighten up on herself too. Be aware, however, that changing a perfectionistic husband is a slow process—two steps forward, one step back. Stay positive, and when he does get perfectionistic with the kids, do all you can to balance things out and let them know that they are loved even when they make a mistake or don't do everything perfectly.

□ ○ △ □ ○ △

How do I deal with a grandmother who not only spoils her grandchildren but interferes when I'm trying to discipline them?

NANETTE: My husband and I basically agree on discipline, but when my mom watches the kids, they get away with murder. And she interferes or criticizes when I try to discipline them.

RANDY: Could you give us an example of how she might interfere?

NANETTE: The other day all the kids were out in the yard with Mom and me. I had just stacked up about six garbage bags of leaves and the kids started jumping on the bags. I told the kids to get off and stop jumping on them, and they did—until I turned my back. When I looked again, my youngest son, who is five, had the whole bag of leaves undone and was standing in the pile kicking leaves all over the yard! I walked over and gave him a couple of good swats because I had told him not to play in the leaves. Mom said, "What are you spanking him for?" And I told her it was obvious—he had untied a bag of leaves and kicked them all over, something I expressly told him not to do. "Well, he's just a little boy—he doesn't know what he's doing," my mother said. I told her he knew *exactly* what he was doing and that I didn't want him to grow up like so many kids you see nowadays. I want him to know that when I tell him to do something, I expect him to obey me.

KEVIN: That's good. My only suggestion is that you should have spanked your mother too!

NANETTE: Sometimes I'd like to. I just got a job and the other night when I went to work I left the kids with Mom for a few hours. When I came back to pick them up, I asked her how they had behaved, and she said they had been fine but at dinner they had been "just too polite." I asked her what she meant by "too polite," and she explained that she had asked them if they wanted something else to eat and Rachel, our oldest daughter, had said, "Yes, Ma'am." She told me, "These kids are too good. Why don't they ever throw a fit? I want them to have a tantrum or something." I suppose she's kidding me, but I'm not sure it's all kidding. Comments like that get to me, but I don't know how to get through to her to tell her I don't appreciate them.

RANDY: What kind of discipline did you get when you were growing up?

NANETTE: I don't recall my mom being very strict at all. I don't remember many spankings, but I know I deserved a spanking now and then. Since I've had my own kids I've tried hard to be consistent, but it's like she doesn't want me to be consistent—especially when she's around.

KEVIN: Right. She doesn't want you parenting differently than she did and maybe she doesn't want to allow you to grow up and be the mother for a change.

NANETTE: Sometimes I wonder if she must think that I can't spank my kids and love them at the same time.

KEVIN: Well, it's typical for grandparents to latch on to the notion of love, love, love. If we just love little Harlan enough, everything will be fine. Nothing could be further from the truth. You instinctively know that as a mom, and you are able to stand up to your own mother and tell her you aren't going to tolerate disobedience from your kids. Keep it up because I think you are right on. I think that as you stand up to your mother, without getting angry, of course, she will learn to back off and respect the way you want to parent the kids.

RANDY: Where is your husband in all of this?

NANETTE: Well, during the leaf episode, he was at work. He's gone a lot because he's a high school coach, but he is at the point where he doesn't want Mom to watch the kids, either.

RANDY: Nanette, we both want to encourage you to keep doing what you're doing and don't let anybody intimidate you on this issue: Grandma, other parents, neighbors, whoever.

KEVIN: Let me share something that will encourage you. The other night we went out to eat and a couple of booths away I could hear a little ankle-biter beginning to crank up the volume. I glanced over and saw the look on Mom's face. I said, "Here it comes." And in the next ten seconds, she grabbed her little two year old, put her under her arm, and out the front door of the restaurant they went.

Three or four minutes later, back they came and Little Miss Temper Tantrum was willing to sit in her high chair, nice as you please, and that was the end of the problem. But you could have heard a pin drop when that woman picked up her child and left, because everybody was looking at her, and a lot of them were thinking, *Oh, my goodness, what is she going to do to that poor little child?*

I'm not sure what she did. I hope she gave her a good swat or two, then a big love as she waited for her to get over her tantrum. But that's what I call parenting. That's called guiding and taking time to discipline and to train. The last thing you need to do as a parent is to just sit there and take it while your child acts up, screams, has a tantrum, or disobeys in a thousand ways, and you don't do anything because you don't want to look like "a monster." Well, if you don't discipline your kids, you and I both know who'll become the monsters, and they'll devour you and everybody around them.

□ ○ △ □ ○ △

Do grandparents who criticize the way you parent ever change? Does it really pay off to stand up to them?

MITCH: I attended one of your seminars and you gave some advice that my wife and I took to heart. My mother-in-law was with us when the whole family went out to eat the other night. Our son—who is eight—got a dish of fruit with his meal and he was picking through it, eating some of the fruit, but not the rest. In fact, he did that with the whole meal, and barely ate half of it. All we said was, "Eat what you want. If you don't want to eat it, fine, but when we get home, that's it."

We finished the meal and went back home and we barely got in the door when he said, "I'm still hungry." We told him, "Well, could it be because you didn't eat your whole dinner? We'll see you at breakfast. You'll be able to eat then." My mother-in-law instantly got upset. She went in the kitchen, opened up the freezer, and pulled out three little chocolate covered ice cream balls. When we saw what she was doing, I took our son out for a walk on the patio, and my wife took her mother aside and told her then and there that we weren't going to have that tonight. If she felt she had to extend the rules when the children were at her house, that was one thing, because we wouldn't be around. But when our children are at our home, we will discipline them the way we see fit.

RANDY: It makes me feel good, Mitch, to hear you say you were willing to stand up to your mother-in-law. Parents must remember that they are in healthy authority over their children, and they alone are ultimately responsible for how their children are parented. Sometimes communicating that—particularly to a grandparent—can be difficult. Whatever you say, however, it helps not to be overly harsh on grandparents and to cut them some slack if at all possible.

KEVIN: I agree on not being harsh with grandparents. They usually mean well and they're the best support system most moms and dads have. I hope there will be a day when Mitch and his wife can convince Grandma not to spoil her grandson whether he's in his own home or at her house. But until that happens, Grandma has to know that she doesn't rule the roost when it's his home and his set of rules.

RANDY: From the different questions we've dealt with, it is obvious that the more united parents are on the discipline front, the more successful they will be. When grandparents disagree with parents' disciplining of their kids, it can get confusing. When parents themselves disagree, then it can really get crazy. Kids smell that in a minute and just start playing one parent against the other. Moms and dads should do all they can to set down some principles and rules they both agree on. And they should continue to communicate—check with each other every now and then to see if there is anything that one is doing that bothers the other. Parenting works best as a team operation. When Mom and Dad work as a team, they'll win a lot more than they'll lose.

CHAPTER 17

■●▲■●▲

DO I DARE USE REALITY DISCIPLINE WITH TEENAGERS?

RANDY: Teenagers are what Kevin Leman likes to call "the hormone group." This nice little kid is going along just fine, thank you, and all of a sudden he hits puberty and life is never the same for anyone in the family. Kevin, can parents use Reality Discipline successfully when dealing with their teenagers? After all, they aren't little kids anymore.

KEVIN: Randy, it's the only way that makes any sense. For a lot of parents, it's the only way they can survive.

RANDY: It wasn't long ago that you were the father of at least three teenagers, but now that Holly's in her twenties, you're down to two—Krissy and Kevey. What have you found to be your greatest challenge as a dad of teenagers?

KEVIN: To listen. So many times we parents want to be instant problem solvers or instant judges. Teenage kids come up with an idea or a plan and immediately we torpedo them with brilliant comments like, "That is the stupidest thing I ever heard!" "You can't be serious!" "If you don't start studying, you're going to end up like your Uncle Milton!" We are always on their case. I think the toughest thing for many parents to learn is to back off and to have fun with their teenagers. Lots of people write to us who say, "How am I ever going to get through these teenage years with these kids of mine? They are driving me up the wall." I am here to say that this has not been the case in the Leman family. We have had fun with the kids, and we encourage them to bring their friends to our home. We think that is important.

RANDY: We are heading into the teenage years at our house, too, and I think I'm acquiring new sympathy for the parents who write in and say, "How am I going to make it with my teenagers? They are so unpredictable!" How can a parent be consistent with teenagers when all those hormones are flowing through their systems? One day they seem to be communicating and in touch with reality, and the next day you wonder if they just landed from Mars.

KEVIN: One of the biggest challenges in parenting teenagers is that you may have only one teenager in your family, but you have two adolescents running around your house. One of them is the "ideal" adolescent—the adolescent that your son or daughter wants you to see. And then there is the real adolescent—the one with all the doubts and fears and questions.

RANDY: And a certain amount of rebelling is to find out who he is. And yet, Kevin, we like to maintain that kids want rules. They want limits. Do you think this is true even for teenagers?

KEVIN: I carry evidence of that in my briefcase. When Holly and Krissy hit sixteen and began driving, they both wrote out their own sets of rules that spelled out how they intended to use the family car. They did a better job than I could have done. So I maintain that this Reality Discipline that you and I have been talking about is tailor-made not only for the young kids but also for the hormone group. So bring on the questions. Reality Discipline will give us the answers.

How can I get my college-age son to help me around the house?

MAE: I have a problem on how to approach my nineteen year old, who is not doing as much around the house as I think he could do to help me. He is a fine young man and I love him very much. His dad and I are going through a divorce, and he has left both of us, so to speak. I work full-time, and Lance is in college and has a part-time job. I know he needs time for his studies, but I need some help around the house too.

KEVIN: Could you be a little more specific? What kind of help do you need from Lance?

MAE: For one thing, yard work. I just got through vacuuming the pool, which I asked him to do yesterday. He didn't get it done, so I did it, and here I am, resenting having to do something that I assigned to a big, strong kid. I know you're going to say that if I asked him to do it, I should have left it for him to do, but we are trying to get the house sold and everything is changing very quickly—faster than I would like.

KEVIN: Do you give him an allowance of sorts?

MAE: No, he earns all of his own money with his part-time job. I do help him with his tuition and books for school—he's a full-time student.

KEVIN: Obviously, he's a pretty busy young man. Tell us, what do you do for Lance? Are you the one who cooks his meals?

MAE: I cook the meals. I do his laundry. I clean the house.

KEVIN: Then you need to go eyeball to eyeball with Lance and say, "Look, I love you and I'm proud of the way you're going to school and working, too, but we have a problem and I need your help. We have to negotiate some kind of an agreement for who does what around here because I am not going to do it all."

RANDY: It's always helpful to list your expectations. For example, why not make out a list of chores entitled "Things I Need Done This Week," and put it on the refrigerator door with a magnet or Scotch tape. Give Lance a chance to circle things he will do and things he thinks he doesn't have time to do. And then you can negotiate some kind of agreement.

KEVIN: Coming back to your having to vacuum the pool, if this is something Lance agrees to do from your list and he doesn't do it, then you might consider hiring a neighbor to do it and tell Lance that he's the one who will have to pay the expense. It's time for Lance to wake up and live in the real world. He needs to realize that he has it made living with you while he's going to college and that he'd better start doing some regular work around the house. Reality Discipline is a perfect way to help him come to.

□ ○ △ □ ○ △

How tight a rein should I keep on my teenagers' social lives?

MARTHA: I am a single parent of four children. The older two are teenagers—a girl, fifteen, and a boy, fourteen. I am trying to raise them in a Christian atmosphere, but they keep wanting to go to the dances held at their school. Many times I have put my foot down and refused to let them go. They are very good kids, and I trust them, but I worry about the atmosphere at a dance. I don't know where to draw the line between being too lenient or too strict.

RANDY: Martha, you have asked the proverbial question that all parents struggle with at one time or another. We love our kids, but we want to set the right limits too. It all comes down to the kind of relationship we have with our children.

KEVIN: If you say you trust them, I think you've got to start to let them go. You have to give them that freedom because they are out there living in the real world. Temptation is everywhere, and part of growing up for all teenagers is learning how to deal with temptations and challenges with confidence and personal convictions that are really theirs and not their parents'. So I understand your concern, but there are two real dangers in drawing the line too tight: One, you don't give your teenagers a chance to grow and mature; and two, you risk having them become resentful and rebellious.

MARTHA: That's what I'm afraid of. You've just mentioned that kids ought to have their own strong personal convictions. Well, I have this strong conviction that I shouldn't let them go to dances.

KEVIN: Where does that conviction come from?

MARTHA: I was brought up to believe that Christians don't go to dances. But my kids don't see anything wrong with dancing. I don't want to push them so hard that they're going to rebel and not want to go to church, and that kind of thing. But I also don't want them to think that they can go to anything they want any time they feel like it.

KEVIN: That's a judgment call that parents always have to make, but I think you have to go back to basics, Martha. You are trying to raise adults, not children, and your goal is to have open communication and a solid relationship with your kids. I think there are points where you have to draw the line, and one family will find the line here, and another will find it there. I think kids respect drawing lines as long as they know the line will be drawn consistently.

RANDY: One approach you could take, Martha, would be to sit down with your teenagers and have an open discussion about dancing. Maybe, then, they could share with you their convictions and you could share your convictions with them. You may be able to work something out, but no matter what happens, you'll keep the lines of communication open.

There are a few things you can remember, Martha, that may help. First, always pick your battles carefully because you can win the battle but you may lose the war. And the other thing is something our friend Josh McDowell said that we like to pass along to parents: "Rules without relationships lead to rebellion." When you sit down with your kids, don't just try to show them that you are right and they are wrong. Make it your first goal to preserve and build your relationship with them.

□ ○ △ □ ○ △

Is it possible to let younger teenagers start dating in controlled situations?

BRENDA: I'm calling to say I identify with Martha because my husband and I have gone through what she's going through with her teenagers wanting to go to dances. Our daughter is fourteen and we are very fearful of these situations. One thing we've come up with is that at fourteen and fifteen, whatever she goes to, there must be adult chaperons and we drive her there and back home again. Wherever she wants to go, we try to meet the parents who will be there or call and make sure that one or more adults will be present. It makes us feel better and it also allows her to go out and have a good time with her friends.

KEVIN: That's an excellent approach, because it tells your teenager that you want her to go out and have fun, but as Mom and Dad you also want to know where she is, who is there, and when she'll be back. And what you said brings up something else. Brenda, do you ever let your daughter invite her friends over to your house?

BRENDA: My husband isn't as good as I am about tolerating kids, but I like to make sure she knows that she can have friends stay the night or come over to just "hang out," as the kids put it.

KEVIN: Please tell that good-looking husband of yours that I said he had better wake up, okay? Until he loosens up a little, your daughter probably won't feel too free to invite many friends over.

At what age should teenagers be allowed to single-date?

RANDY: Tell me, Brenda, at what age will you let your daughter single-date?

BRENDA: I guess I'm playing it by ear right now. I know people say sixteen is the "magic number." The way I feel about it, if I think she's capable of single-dating when she turns sixteen, I will allow her to do it. But for now, I want her to be with her friends, in groups.

RANDY: How have you dealt with this dating question, Kevin, with your two daughters?

KEVIN: When Holly and Krissy were in high school, I think we knew just about everyone in their school. We have a very open door policy at our house, and we have had lots of boys around for quite a while now. I keep stumbling over them. I had one knock at our door the other night at about a quarter after twelve. You see, kids have a different time clock, but that doesn't say they shouldn't respect Mom and Dad.

When Krissy, our second born daughter, was sixteen she had gone out for the evening with her boyfriend to a basketball game. It was a Friday night and she called me around 10:00 P.M. and said, "Dad, what time do I need to be home?" I said, "Honey, you know what time to be home." She said, "Dad, what time do I have to be home?" I said, "Honey, you know the right time to be home, so be home." To shorten the story, I didn't give in on setting a time. She called me again at 11:25 P.M. and said, "Dad, we're at the pizza house and the team hasn't even gotten here yet. We're waiting for them so we can all have pizza together. Do I have to come home now?"

I said, "No, you don't have to come home now." So she said, "Well, when do I have to come home then?" All I said was, "Honey, you come home at the right time. You know what time to be home."

About an hour later, I was in my semiconscious state, sort of sleeping with one ear open, when I heard her come in, and in my opinion, that was fine because she had called me twice during the evening to explain the circumstances. I knew exactly where she was, but I had left it up to her when to finally come home. I don't like to be very prescriptive with my kids. I prefer to have them learn to be accountable and responsible, and the best way to do that is to give them responsibility, trust them, and stay close to them.

RANDY: You will notice, Brenda, that we haven't put the stamp of approval on sixteen as the "magic number" for dating. A lot depends on the teenager's maturity and readiness, and a lot depends on what kind of date it's going to be. Who are they going out with, and where are they going? There's a big difference between going bowling and having a sundae afterward with someone the family knows and spending all day at an amusement park with a virtual stranger and coming home after the park closes. Teenagers should be allowed to go on dates where they can learn and mature, and not get into situations where they are in over their heads.

□ ○ △ □ ○ △

How can I keep my teenagers' phone bill somewhat less than the national debt?

RANDY: I'm surprised, Kevin, that we haven't gotten a call about controlling teenagers and their use of the telephone. There have been days when I start at 2:00 in the afternoon, trying to call home to talk to Donna for a minute, and I can never get through. I know you've said the best solution is to just put in another line, but that seems like the coward's way out and, besides, it's an extra expense that a lot of people don't want to pay for.

KEVIN: So at age fourteen, Evan is on the phone a lot?

RANDY: Constantly. The girls call *him.* You are a veteran of the phone wars, Kevin. You've had two teenage girls in your home. Are they worse than boys?

KEVIN: In our case, I don't think so. Kevey gets lots of calls, too, and, by the way, the kids have codes. Have you gotten to the code stage yet? One ring, two rings—everything means something.

RANDY: No, but there's been a lot of the phone ringing and when we answer, nobody is there.

KEVIN: When I was in junior high, we used to call up this woman in town whose name was Lord. She would answer and we would say, "Is this the Lord's residence?" And she would say, "Yes, it is." Then we would say, "Let us pray!" Then we would laugh hilariously and hang up. Aren't you glad I didn't live in your neighborhood?

RANDY: For numerous reasons, Doctor, numerous reasons, but I see a call coming in. Is it from a teenager or from a parent with a question about phones, or maybe even an answer . . . ?

CHERIE: The way we handle our teenagers and the phone is with specific rules. We just re-outlined the rules the other day. My daughter is sixteen, and she was at the kitchen table, doing geometry, with the radio blasting, and talking to her boyfriend on the phone, all at the same time. I said, "There is something wrong with this picture. I don't know how you can listen to the radio, talk on the phone, and do your geometry too."

So we went over the rules again. She is to get her homework done first, then she can make her calls. She gets forty-five minutes on the phone every day, and she can divide that up among as many friends as she wishes. There are no calls during dinner and no making calls or receiving calls after 9:00. After 9:00 we turn on the answering machine to take care of incoming calls.

RANDY: What about long distance calls or 900 calls?

CHERIE: We had a little rash of those 900 calls about a year ago. My daughter's younger brother—he was thirteen then—called Santa Claus to see what he sounded like. At least it wasn't the Playboy Club.

KEVIN: My son called Santa Claus once. It was $2.00 for the first minute and $1.00 each minute thereafter. He paid the bill.

CHERIE: As for long distance calls, my sixteen year old hasn't gotten into those yet, and neither has her little brother, but their older brother, who's in college, more than made up for it. His girlfriend lived out of town and when they broke up I suddenly found a phone bill of $445 for the month.

KEVIN: And most of that was getting through the break-up?

CHERIE: It took him a little while to say what he had to say, I guess. He's still working off the bill.

RANDY: I can see why you finally made some rules. Stay on the line while we have Carmen join us. Maybe she has a question or some other ideas on controlling teenagers and the phone.

CARMEN: Our daughter is also sixteen, but when she was fifteen she started receiving a lot of calls from friends. At the very start I told her, "I am sorry, you only have three minutes for any one call. After three minutes, I will pick up the extension phone." She didn't believe me at first, but she changed her mind after I'd start listening on the line and then I'd finally say, "I'm sorry your three minutes are up. You have to hang up the phone now." This happened about three times, and she finally got the idea that I wasn't joking.

KEVIN: What I hear Cherie and Carmen saying is that they have to have fairly strict rules governing the use of the phone in their families.

CHERIE: We have four kids from eleven to nineteen, plus two adults and a grandmother, all living in the house. We have to have phone rules for survival. People just can't stay on the line for as long as they would like. Three minutes per call would be a little short at our house because that's a lot less than most of their friends get to talk. But I can see negotiating somewhere between three and ten—maybe six or seven minutes a call would be a good rule for us.

CARMEN: I admit three minutes is pretty short, but my husband was complaining that he was trying to call home and could never get through.

KEVIN: I think we all agree that every home needs telephone rules—especially when teenagers live there. At our house, we have very few rules about the phones. One big one is, no making or taking calls during dinner time. We never have had to limit calls to so many minutes, but I guess if someone stayed on *all night,* that would be different. I think, however, the more free flowing it can be in a family and the less you have certain rules for things, the more the family blends together.

RANDY: I think you've been lucky, Kevin, or maybe very patient. Betsy's on the line with a very obvious solution to the interminable phone call.

What are the pros and cons for putting in Call Waiting for teenagers?

BETSY: A device that we have found invaluable is Call Waiting. At nominal cost, it's like having the benefits of having a second line. While you're talking on the phone, you hear this signal, and you can put that call on hold while you take the incoming call. That way, whenever your phone is busy, you still have the capacity for other people—like your frantic husband—to get through.

KEVIN: Betsy, when someone puts me on Call Waiting, I am gone. I hate Call Waiting.

RANDY: There are definitely two sides to Call Waiting. When someone is calling you and is right in the middle of telling you something important, and you say, "Wait a minute, I have to get another call," you definitely run the risk of irritating your first caller. I can remember we had a lady call "Parent Talk" not long ago who has Call Waiting. Right in the middle of her conversation with us, she could hear the click and she said, "Wait just a minute, I have to see who's calling me."

KEVIN: And I said, "All right, lady, we'll see you."

BETSY: How ludicrous. That sounds like a poor decision.

KEVIN: That is why America is so great, Betsy. People like you who want Call Waiting can have it, and people like me who wouldn't have it can hang up.

RANDY: And now the nation knows there is at least one person they don't want to put on Call Waiting. We can take only one or two more calls about phone battles, and here comes one now. . . .

□ ○ △ □ ○ △

When does it make sense to let your teenage daughter spend a lot of time on the phone?

ROSIE: This is a little different approach. A very wise friend of mine once told me that she actually encourages her older teenage girls to spend a lot of time talking on the phone with boys that they are dating.

KEVIN: I know where you are headed, Rosie, and I think I like it.

ROSIE: The reason she encourages them is that it's so important to get to know each other, especially the other person's values. By talking on the phone, her daughters can often decide if they want to continue a relationship or not. This mom would rather have her kids spend three hours on the phone late at night than three hours talking in the backseat of a car.

RANDY: The idea has merit, but I'm not sure I'd go for three-hour calls.

ROSIE: Well, my friend's idea has really helped me with my girls. We also have Call Waiting, which we try to use discreetly. I have a couple of sensitive friends who hate Call Waiting too. When they're on the line, I just ignore the click and keep talking. But when our girls are talking and Call Waiting comes in, they answer it. The boys calling them don't seem to mind and we can still get any important calls we need to get. I think we've got the best of all worlds.

How do you discipline a teenager for breaking the telephone rules?

RANDY: We've talked a lot about telephone rules, but I'm wondering what happens if the rules are broken. How do you apply Reality Discipline to somebody who breaks the telephone rules at your house?

CARMEN: At our house it's simple. Go past three minutes and you don't get to use the phone for the rest of the evening.

CHERIE: If our kids go over now and then, there are no repercussions. But if they'd really abuse it, there would be a family meeting and possible curtailment of their phone privileges for the week.

RANDY: Those sound like reasonable consequences to me, but we have one more call—from Stephanie who is seventeen years old. She has the other side of the story. . . .

STEPHANIE: While I am talking on the phone, the one thing I can't stand is having my mother say, "Get off the phone—I need to use it." And then she'll talk for forty-five minutes or an hour, and I don't get to call my friends back because I have to go to work, or whatever. I think limiting a teenager's calls to three minutes or six minutes or whatever is ridiculous, particularly when the mom just wants to sit on the phone forever herself.

KEVIN: Stephanie, suppose you were my daughter, and I would say to you, "Honey, rather than have strict rules about using the phone, I'm going to let you use your good judgment." How would you handle that? How much time would you spend on the phone in a given evening if that were the "rule" in the family?

STEPHANIE: The longest I have ever talked on the phone is about half an hour, which is really not that long. Most of my calls are much shorter.

KEVIN: So you're saying you wouldn't abuse your telephone privileges? It would be possible for your parents to put the responsibility on your shoulders?

STEPHANIE: Hey, I'd be willing to try that. Maybe you can call my mother sometime and talk her into it.

RANDY: Well, there you have it—different ideas you can use to control the use of the phone at your house. You can put the responsibility on your teenagers' shoulders, and if they can handle it, that's great. But if they need rules, you may have to set them and then hold your kids accountable.

□ ○ △ □ ○ △

How do you handle a teenager who is blackmailing you by not working hard enough to graduate?

CARRIE: My son is seventeen, and he and I have always butted heads. I've tried to be patient with him, but now that he's a senior he seems to be taking it out on me especially. He's failing two of his classes, and he needs the credits to graduate. I'm not sure how to handle this.

RANDY: Let's back up a little. What kind of a relationship does your son have with his dad?

CARRIE: He and his dad are buddy-buddy. He really likes his dad.

KEVIN: So he takes it out more on you than on anyone? Are there other children in the family?

CARRIE: Yes, we have two other sons—thirteen and eight.

KEVIN: I need a little more on your seventeen year old—describe his personality in a few words.

CARRIE: Everyone says Tommy is really likable. And unlike many firstborns, he isn't that conscientious or achieving—actually, he's more laid back. He brings home a "D–" and he says, "Well, at least I didn't fail."

KEVIN: Carrie, it's my guess you are an only child or a firstborn daughter.

CARRIE: Firstborn out of five, how did you guess?

KEVIN: It really wasn't too hard. It sounds as if you are the key parent in this situation and very concerned about your son and his schoolwork. Chances are you have a very good idea of what your son ought to be like, how he ought to measure up, and how he should improve. You are probably guilty of "shoulding" on your seventeen year old; that is, you're always saying that he should do this and he should do that. But that way he can drag his heels and not live up to that famous word called *potential.*

CARRIE: You know, you've hit it on the nose. It's always been like this, since he was in second or third grade.

RANDY: Our message to you, Carrie, is that it's time to back off and give your son a little more space to maneuver. Let him make mistakes, but still hold him accountable.*

* For additional ideas on getting children to do their schoolwork, see Chapter Twelve.

CARRIE: But this is his senior year! I don't want him to fail.

KEVIN: But don't you see? When he comes home and laments the fact that he is failing two classes, it is his way of pushing your buttons. Then you get in a stew and around and around you continue to go with him.

CARRIE: Actually, I haven't said a whole lot to him. About all I've said was, "I can't believe that you can't pass two classes." I really didn't yell or scream or anything.

KEVIN: That is commendable, but I think that if you back off and make him totally responsible on this one, chances are he will surprise himself and you in the process.

RANDY: You will be giving him space, the opportunity to succeed or to fail. If he chooses to fail twelfth grade, that is his choice. You are not going to force a twelfth grader to graduate. Tell me, is your son thinking past high school?

CARRIE: My son is not thinking past tomorrow.

RANDY: It is easy to focus on the weaknesses of our kids. How are you and your son alike, Carrie?

CARRIE: I guess you could say we both have a strong will.

RANDY: Carrie, let's try to bring this into focus. There are parents all over the country in your situation. As a strong willed, firstborn mother, you are knocking heads with your firstborn son and you need to back off. And, Kevin, don't you think Carrie should be shifting more of the responsibility to Tommy's dad—to her husband?

KEVIN: It would be nice if she could do that, but chances are Carrie will end up being the fall person.

CARRIE: That's right, my husband just won't say anything to him. He always just says, "Well, you were talking to him and I didn't see any point in my saying anything."

KEVIN: Which is always a good out and allows your husband to be critical of you and say later, "I told you so."

CARRIE: Well, getting back to my son's problem, is it all right to ground him until the four weeks are up in the hope that he will study harder?

KEVIN: It's all right to ground him if that's what you want to do, but it is always more fun to take away the car. Does he drive a car?

CARRIE: Yes, but he needs it to go to work.

KEVIN: I say, hit him with the car—not at forty miles an hour, of course—but just take away the keys and let him hoof it to work, or get a friend to drive him. Or maybe you can drive him to work. But don't give him the privilege of driving the car himself until he shows a little more improvement in school. You see, we want you to have a balance here. Back off and don't be involved with badgering him, nagging him, but at the same time hold him accountable.

RANDY: Kevin, though we've barely scratched the surface on teenagers, I hope we have illustrated how and why Reality Discipline can work with adolescents as well as younger kids. Do you have any final thoughts about the hormone group and how to deal with them?

KEVIN: One thing I'd like to leave with parents is a word of caution about being too zealous when holding teenagers accountable. Reality Discipline will work beautifully, as long as you don't come on like the gestapo. When children hit adolescence, many parents make the mistake of thinking, *Now I really have to crack down or they'll get into drugs or promiscuous sex.* Actually, this isn't the time to tighten the reins, but to loosen them. If you've been using Reality Discipline for the first twelve years or so, you should be able to trust your teenagers and start cutting them a little slack.

RANDY: Can you give an example of how to "cut a teenager a little slack"?

KEVIN: One thing I always recommend is that we lighten up on the teenager's responsibilities around the house and assign more chores to the younger kids in the family. Why? Because when a kid hits the freshman year of high school, he usually gets very busy and involved. He doesn't need more to do at home, but less. I'm not saying that you cut out all chores and home responsibilities, but I am saying that you keep in mind that a teenager's schedule is usually somewhere west of whoopee, and instead of resenting the fact that your son or daughter is always busy and never has time for the family, work with that busy schedule and you may be surprised. Your teenager may have more time for you than you would have hoped.

RANDY: What about spiritual issues? We recently had a speaker at our church who is a youth specialist, and he claimed that 70 per cent of the youth from evangelical Christian families walk away from their parents' faith after they leave home. He said we teach our kids what to believe, but we don't teach them to think for themselves and make good decisions on their own.

KEVIN: I'm not surprised at those statistics because they only emphasize my point. You have to turn your teenagers loose and give them the opportunity to think for themselves and make their own decisions. You don't withdraw guidance, but you loosen up on the controls. One of the biggest mistakes parents make is that they think that because they have a relationship with Jesus Christ that their kids will automatically tailgate. That isn't the way it goes. Kids have to make real choices and then be held accountable for those choices.

RANDY: But what do parents do, Kevin, when their teenagers just won't cooperate? They won't go to church, they won't study, they won't do their chores. . . .

KEVIN: Up to around fifteen or so, maybe parents can gently but firmly insist that their kids come to church with them. After that, I think you have to leave it up to the teenager. This is what making choices is all about. As for schoolwork, we've touched on that in several places already. The bottom line, however, is that you leave the teenager with a choice: study or fail. It's his responsibility.

Concerning chores, one of the best approaches I can think of is to hit them in the pocketbook. One of my favorite stories concerns our son, Kevey, when he was thirteen. Every Sunday night, his job was to take several big bags of garbage down a long driveway out to the road for trash pickup early Monday morning. Somehow he never seemed to get all the bags out there. He kept telling me that he "just didn't see" the ones that he would leave behind. I told him that he had six days, and he wondered, "Six days for what?"

"Six days to take on your responsibility and do it right," I said, "or I'll get another family member to do it for you and that family member will be paid out of your allowance." Kevey knew I was thinking of his older sister, Krissy, who has always had an insatiable desire for a little more cash. That was the end of the problem. As if by magic, his eyesight improved and all the garbage bags were always at the curb on Sunday night, waiting for the trash man to come by Monday morning.

RANDY: And don't forget the car keys. When teenagers need discipline, taking away their wheels is a powerful lever.

KEVIN: Revoking driving privileges often does the trick, but I repeat, we need to caution parents that Reality Discipline is always a combination of limits mixed with love. No matter what you do to make teenagers accountable, they need to know that you love them and that you're trying to understand.

One mom told us on the phone the other day she was pacing the floor one night when her daughter was out late on a date. She finally went on to bed but lay there awake, waiting for her daughter to get home. When the daughter finally came in to tell her she was home, the mom broke down and started to cry. "What's wrong, Mom?" the girl asked. And Mom replied, "You are going to have to be patient with me, Honey, this being a parent of a teenager is new to me, but as long as we are up front and honest and open with each other, we're going to make it."

I think that story has a lot to tell us about living with teenagers. Yes, we need to guide them; yes, we need to set some rules for them to work with as they try their wings; and, yes, we need to confront them when they fly a little too far and a little too fast. But along with all that, we need to love them and understand them and trust them. If we do that, I guarantee we'll make it.

For "Parent Talk," this is Kevin Leman and Randy Carlson . . .

UNTIL NEXT TIME, KEEP USING REALITY DISCIPLINE

RANDY: It's too bad, Kevin, we were just getting warmed up and now it appears we are "out of time." Our inside look at the principles that are the heart and soul of "Parent Talk" has to come to an end, and there are so many other questions that I'm sure parents have.

KEVIN: There is a lot of other good stuff we could have covered, Randy, but I still think we have given parents the "secret" to raising kids, by doing what we said at the beginning—explaining and demonstrating the principles of Reality Discipline. No matter what the problem, Reality Discipline works, because it is based on common sense and logical consequences.

When you use Reality Discipline you are in healthy authority over your children, but your goal is to be loving, patient, and kind, never harsh or punitive. At the same time, the child knows there are limits. You are firm, even tough, when necessary. When children cross the line, you have to "pull the rug out" and hold them accountable for their behavior, which means action and not a lot of words. You do what it takes to teach accountability, and then you stick to your guns. You never back down.

RANDY: I think the greatest strength of Reality Discipline is that it is based squarely on a biblical value system that teaches children what is expected of them. When they are just toddlers, the kids learn that you expect them to obey your authority. As they grow older, they learn that you expect them to be at home when it's time to eat. You expect them to do their chores, practice the piano, and do their homework. As they move into the teens, they learn that you expect them to stay away from drugs and promiscuous sex.

Children who grow up under Reality Discipline aren't simply asked to be obedient; they are asked to make reasonable choices and decisions based on right thinking. This is what sets Reality Discipline apart from systems that focus on modifying behavior but don't have the ultimate goal of changing the mind and the will.

KEVIN: I always like to say the major difference between behavior modification and Reality Discipline is that "behavior mod" works well with white rats while Reality Discipline is for human beings. You can train a white rat to do almost anything you want, and the "behavior mod" school of thought has the same opinion of humans. Behavior mod says to toilet train a kid, you give him three M&M's every time he goes potty. It is based on treating people with rewards and punishment. You extinguish this, you reward that. This may work, but only as long as you fork out the rewards or hand out the punishments. It's not a great way to bring up children.

RANDY: But Reality Discipline *is* a great way to bring up kids because it is ultimately concerned with changing their hearts, and if you don't change their hearts you haven't done the whole job. Reality Discipline leaves room for those wonderful teachable moments when you can help your child connect his behavior with what the Scriptures teach about accountability: whatever we sow is what we will reap. In other words, you get back from life exactly what you put into it. That's what being accountable is all about.

KEVIN: Another thing about Reality Discipline that we sometimes neglect to mention, Randy, is that it's for parents too. One of the most humbling things about being a parent is that you never arrive: you always have something more you can learn. There's another Scripture verse that I especially like, the one about forgiving seventy times seven. When Reality Discipline guides the family, everybody learns to balance responsibility with forgiveness and love.

RANDY: I think every parent has memories of times he needed his child's forgiveness. One that I still vividly recall, is when I was sitting at dinner one evening trying to act like the interested husband and father, but in reality my mind was still back at the office wrestling with projects, problems, and radio programs. Andrea was about eight years old at the time, and she was chattering happily about a party she planned to attend on Friday night at the home of a new friend she had made at school. The party also included an invitation to sleep over, and could she go? When all Andrea got from me was an absentminded grunt, she became all the more determined to get through, and finally she practically shouted, "DADDY, ARE YOU LISTENING?"

The rising decibels penetrated my fog enough to irritate me and I said, "Andrea, that's enough of being such a chatterbox. Can't you just be quiet for a few minutes?"

"But, Daddy, you *never* listen to me," Andrea shot back. "You don't care. . . . You *never* listen!"

By now Andrea had my full attention and I rose to defend my position of authority in the family. "That's *enough*, Andrea!

You're being disrespectful, and you can go to your room *right now*!"

Andrea stormed away, crying bitterly, and we could hear the door slam to her room down the hall. We finished dinner in silence, but I was very aware of Donna's steady and unapproving gaze. I finally had the nerve to meet her eye and she said quietly, "Randy, you *don't* listen to her a lot of the time." I didn't argue because in my heart I knew she was right.

After dinner dishes were cleared away, I went down the hall to Andrea's room and found her lying across the bed where she had cried herself to sleep. I gently woke her and I said, "Andrea, Daddy wants to apologize to you, first for not listening when you were trying to tell him something that was very important. You're right, I wasn't listening to you, I was thinking about all the things I have to do down at work, and I'm sorry. But, also, I want to apologize for raising my voice to you and sending you away from the table because I thought you were disrespectful. I'm the one who was disrespectful, and I hope you will forgive me."

Her little arms went around my neck and she said, "I forgive you, Daddy." Then I prayed with her and told God that I was sorry I hadn't listened and that I wanted Him to help me listen more carefully in the future. I think that maybe the prayer meant more to Andrea than my apology. It was like the cherry topping on an ice cream sundae for her.

KEVIN: I've never heard you tell that story before, but what it says to me is that parents and children should have mutual respect for one another—another key principle of Reality Discipline. I also have some "foot in my mouth" scenes with my kids that are burned into my memory bank. Probably the one I share the most is the time I was arguing with Holly at the breakfast table. She was about twelve and I don't know what we were arguing about, but I do know that it got pretty heated and I finally chopped her really low. I was congratulating myself on leaving her without a comeback when she glared at me and said, "Well, you know what you ought to do?"

"No," I said, walking right into her trap. "What?"

"You ought to read some of your own books, that's what!"

She got me good with that one, Randy. I have never forgotten it. My little buzzard pulled out the rug and sent *me* tumbling. Talk about provoking your child to wrath! When Holly was leaving for school a little later, I stopped her and said, "You're right—I should read my own books. I was wrong and I'm sorry. I apologize."

"Oh, that's okay, Dad, I gotta' get to school. See ya' later," was all Holly said as she ran down the walk. I stood there and watched her go, the so-called expert in child psychology who had needed forgiveness from his own daughter. I'm glad it happened though, because that's the side of parenting we all tend to forget. We may be in healthy authority over our kids, but we aren't perfect. As long as we are willing to be open and vulnerable with our kids, there is hope.

Today, Holly is a lovely young lady of twenty-one, and Sande and I wonder where all those years went so fast. Ask anyone who has a senior graduating from high school or a son or daughter who has gone away to college and they will tell you the same thing. My advice, Mom and Dad, is to make the best of every moment. With all your faults, with all your blemishes, you are still the best teacher your children will ever have. Balance love with limits as you trust God, trust yourself, and, above all, trust your kids to grow into responsible adults. Then, when they have children of their own, remember Leman's rule of thumb: *Never agree to baby-sit more than once a week!*

Notes

Chapter 3. How to Make God a Real Friend to your Kids
1. Sally Leman Chall, *Making God Real to Your Children* (Grand Rapids: Fleming H. Revell, 1991).
2. Sally Leman Chall, *Mommy Appleseed: Planting Seeds of Faith in the Heart of your Children* (Eugene, OR: Harvest House Publishers, 1993).
3. Debbie Anderson, *Here and There and Everywhere: Jesus Is with Me* (Elgin, IL: David D. Cook, 1988).

Chapter 7. Courage! Bed wetting almost always stops before they leave for college
1. *Diagnostic and Statistical Manual of Mental Disorders* (Third Edition—Revised), Washington, D.C., the American Psychiatric Association, 1987, p. 85.
2. See *Diagnostic and Statistical Manual of Mental Disorders* (Third Edition—Revised), Washington, D.C., The American Psychiatric Association, 1986, p. 84.
3. Jeffrey R. M. Kunz, M.D., and Asher J. Finkel, M.D., eds., *The American Medical Association Family Medical Guide* (New York: Random House, 1987), p. 705.
4. Jeffrey R. M. Kunz, M.D., and Asher J. Finkel, M.D., eds., *The American Medical Association Family Medical Guide* (New York: Random House, 1987), p. 705.

Chapter 11. Mommy, Where Do Babies Come From?
1. Sidonie Gruenberg, *The Wonderful Story of How You Were Born*, Revised Edition (Garden City, NY: Doubleday, 1970).

Chapter 13. "Dennis the Menace," or A.D.H.D.?
1. A.D.H.D.—"Attention Deficit Hyperactivity Disorder and Learning Disabilities," a booklet published by Larry B. Silver, M.D.
2. *Diagnostic and Statistical Manual of Mental Disorders*, 3rd ed., Rev. (Washington, D.C: American Psychiatric Association, 1987), 52–53.
3. Ibid., 50.

Conclusion
1. Galatians 6:7.
2 Matthew 18:22.

INDEX

■●▲■●▲

For more information regarding counseling, speaking, and seminars with Dr. Kevin Leman or Randy Carlson, write or call:

Dr. Kevin Leman
7355 N. Oracle Road, Suite 205
Tucson, AZ 85704
(602) 797-3830

Randy Carlson
Parent Talk
Tucson, AZ 85704
(602) 742-6976

If you are interested in learning more about "Parent Talk" and would like a list of radio stations which carry the program, or are interested in information on sponsoring a Parent Talk seminar featuring both Kevin and Randy, contact Randy Carlson.